From the workplace to the war zone, the Bush administration has wrapped female-friendly rhetoric around some of the most hard-core policy since Ronald Reagan. Some well-placed women have helped to pull off that con job. Invaluable to the president, underscrutinized in the press, the Bushwomen—the women appointed to the inner circle of the president's cabinet and sub-cabinet—are cast in the public mind as moderate, malleable, maverick, irrelevant or benign. Their carefully crafted images tap into stereotypes, while the reality of their records has remained out of sight . . . until now.

This is the first book to investigate Bush's women, and to report on how they rose to power and what they've done. Find out why Chevron named a tanker after National Security Advisor Condoleezza Rice; how financial ties to big tobacco corporations got Secretary of the Interior Gale Ann Norton dubbed "The Woman from Marlboro Country"; how Labor Secretary Elaine Chao bullied union longshoreworkers to benefit her trading-with-China family and friends; read excerpts of Lynne Cheney's lesbian novel; and discover how Karen Hughes got her first job thanks to the National Organization for Women.

Women swing voters can decide elections now, and the Bush team will do whatever it takes to win their support. The cynical crusade to put a female face on anti-feminist policy is revealed in this scathing and entertaining investigation of the sinister politicians we call the Bushwomen.

BUSHWOMEN

By the same author

Real Majority, Media Minority: the Cost of Sidelining Women in Reporting

BUSHWOMEN

Tales of a Cynical Species

◆

LAURA FLANDERS

VERSO

London · New York

First published by Verso 2004
© Laura Flanders 2004
All rights reserved

1 3 5 7 9 10 8 6 4 2

Verso
UK: 6 Meard Street, London W1F OEG
USA: 180 Varick Street, New York, NY 10014–4606
www.versobooks.com

Verso is the imprint of New Left Books

ISBN 1–85984–587–8

British Library Cataloguing in Publication Data
Flanders, Laura
  Bushwomen : tales of a cynical species
  1. Women cabinet officers–United States 2. United States–
  Politics and government–2001-
  I. Title
  973.9′31′0922

  ISBN 1859845878

Library of Congress Cataloging-in-Publication Data
Flanders, Laura.
  Bushwomen : tales of a cynical species / Laura Flanders.
      p. cm.
Includes bibliographical references and index.
  ISBN 1-85984-587-8 (hardback : alk. paper)
  1. Women cabinet officers–United States–Biography. 2. Women
politicians–United States–Biography. 3. Bush, George W. (George
Walker), 1946–Friends and associates. 4. United States–Politics and
government–2001- 5. Conservatism–United States. 6. Women in
politics–United States. 7. Anti-feminism–United States. I. Title.
    E840.6.F58 2004
    973.931′092′2–dc22

                                                              2003023743

Typeset in Perpetua by YHT Ltd, London
Printed in the USA by R.R. Donnelley

To Claudia Flanders (1933–98),
who taught us to say nothing at all if we couldn't
say something positive.
You'd understand; you always did.
And to sister Stephanie—go get 'em, girl!

CONTENTS

ACKNOWLEDGEMENTS

First thanks are due to Eileen Clancy, researcher extra-ordinaire, information-hunter and gatherer, the good guys' Director of Intelligence. I couldn't have written this book without you, my colleague and friend. What's next? At KALW in San Francisco, Matt Martin, Nicole Sawaya, and Rose Aguilar put the "team" into production team, which made this undertaking possible. Michael Kieschnick, Laura Scher and Christina Allen of Working Assets put their company's money where their mouths are in order to model new ways of sup-porting media. Thanks to Niels Hooper, for his enthusiasm, Gloria Loomis, for her early eagle eye on the contract, and to Jane Elizabeth Hill, for cool, clear editing at the end; to Laura Ross for research assistance and solidarity, and PA Skantze for a distance-shrinking friendship. Amy Scholder is Pushwoman number one. Thank you for applying just the right pressure, and for watching my back throughout. Finally, Elizabeth Streb, who inspires and excites me always, you are my dream partner and co-conspirator. Thank you.

Private Servants: it should also be noted that the Bushwomen themselves contributed to this book. If even one had been willing to agree to a request for an interview, it might have turned out different.

WINNING WOMEN

George W. Bush might never have snagged the White House if one woman had been laughed at less: Katherine Harris, Secretary of State of Florida. No one did more, more carefully, to use the power of her public office to steal the presidency for her candidate; no one was made more fun of in the media.

By the time Harris came to public attention as the arbiter of the Florida vote count in 2000, she had already been slip-sliding around election rules for years. The ambitious child of one of Florida's most powerful families, there were corporate campaign-contribution violations in her very first run for office in 1994; financial-disclosure problems when she served the state senate. Harris's record smelled so bad that when she sought to become secretary of state (Florida's top election-cop), the vice-president of Common Cause Florida wondered if anyone could credibly expect her to enforce the law: "How can you come down on somebody else for violating something when you have a reputation for violating the law yourself?" he asked.[1]

In Florida, Harris was well known as one of the most cut-throat ambitious politicians to hit the state, but in November

2000, when she came under the national spotlight, what did Democrats, the media, and the vast majority of the public focus on? Not her record, but her mascara, her eyeshadow, her hair. Joe Klock, her attorney, characterized Harris as "a very busy, occupied person" who was suddenly "thrown into the center of this maelstrom,"[2] and for the most part, the spin-effort worked.[3] Aides to Democratic contender Al Gore called Harris a "lackey" and a "flack," and Harris became known not as a crook (when lawyer Alan Dershowitz called her that, he was roundly slapped down) but as "Cruella De Vil"—a cartoon character. *The Washington Post* devoted an entire article to her make-up. Harris is easy to mock, wrote staff writer Robin Givhan, "because, to be honest, she seems to have applied her make-up with a trowel."[4] Harris's make-up was hardly the point.

Invaluable to the President, under-scrutinized in the press: it's that that qualifies Harris as an honorary Bushwoman. The Bushwomen—the women appointed to the inner circle of the President's cabinet and sub-cabinet—are an extremist administration's female front. Cast in the public mind as maverick, or moderate, or irrelevant, laughable or benign, their well-spun image taps into convenient stereotypes, while the reality remains out of sight. If women were taken more seriously, the Bushwomen con job wouldn't stand a chance, but in the contemporary United States, it just might. Bushwomen: they're the one thing Bush has that Ronald Reagan didn't, and they ease his way to accomplish things that Reagan never could.

*

From the post-September 11 perspective, it is hard to remember just how tenuously Bush held power before multiple terror attacks conferred on him the macho mantle of homeland protector and man at war. George Walker Bush, eldest son of Barbara and George Herbert Walker Bush, sneaked into office with a minority of the popular vote, the slimmest Electoral College margin in 124 years, and the worst showing among African-American voters of any Republican president in a third of a century. That he made it at all is largely thanks to Katherine Harris.

By rights, Harris should have sat out the whole election dispute. Her dual role in Florida took "conflict of interest" to a new extreme. Elected in 1998, the same year as Governor Jeb Bush, the candidate's brother, she became a co-chair of Bush's Florida campaign the next year. She didn't just show Bush around when he came to town, she campaigned for him—in Florida, and in New Hampshire, during the tight primary campaign against Arizona Senator John McCain. During the recount, Harris allowed Republican Party operatives to use her state computers and offices. Among the files found on her computers later were partisan speeches written during the campaign. (Many other files used by her employees during the election wrangle were illegally erased.)[5] As campaign co-chair, she enlisted retired General H. Norman Schwarzkopf to speak at pro-Bush rallies; as secretary of state, she hired him to make supposedly non-partisan, public-service announcements. (Stormin' Norman was so well associated with Bush that it hardly mattered that in the TV ads he didn't actually name whom to vote for.)

In June 2000, Harris's office sent county election supervisors a list of more than 700,000 Floridians said to be disqualified from voting. She claimed she was enforcing a state law that banned felons and ex-felons from voting for life. Passed by white legislators in 1868, the law was a deliberate effort to diminish the power of newly-enfranchised former slaves. It worked to serve the post Civil War backlash; and it worked the same way in election 2000. With African Americans still over-represented in the prison population, and nine out of ten of them voting Democratic, the state's felon disenfranchisement law handily diminished the Democratic electorate. But Harris's list did more than follow the letter of the Jim Crow law. As reported by journalist Greg Palast and others, on her instruction, the corporation hired to draw up the purge list deliberately cast its net wide, and thousands of people—who'd gone through the process of getting their rights restored, or had never committed any crime—were caught up.

In a state where Bush beat Gore by only 537 votes, according to the official election count, the wrongly-disqualified voters—who numbered in the thousands—might easily have flipped the result. And then there were Floridians who had other problems for which the secretary of state was responsible. In certain areas, but not others, voting machines malfunctioned; poorer (disproportionately black and Hispanic) districts lacked the up-to-date computers that enabled other districts to check the voter rolls; others had voting machines which could have alerted voters who made mistakes, but didn't. Some people with disabilities found machines that were inaccessible—in violation of the federal Americans with Disabilities

Act. Other voters arrived too late to vote—the roads to their polling stations having been mysteriously dotted with highway patrolmen conducting "routine" traffic stops. Some found that their polling station, unbeknown to them, had been moved.[6]

It's possible that Harris (and her handlers in the GOP) knowingly steered public attention away from her actions[7] and towards her looks. (She gleefully repeated jokes about her own appearance.) Planned or not, the decoy effort worked. While the facts about the voter-purge languished in the US media, Harris catapulted to Republican Party stardom. Her celebrity helped elect her to Congress in 2002, where she was made assistant majority whip in the House of Representatives, a select spot.[8] In January 2001, Harris was the belle of the GOP's Florida state Inaugural Ball—the second-biggest celebrity there, after the incoming President. Country singer Larry Gatlin brought her up onto the stage: "In France it was Joan of Arc; in the Crimea it was Florence Nightingale; in the Deep South there was Rosa Parks; in India there was Mother Teresa; and in Florida there was Katherine Harris."[9]

"What a time for America," said Harris to the grateful crowd. "It's going to be a great four years . . . eight years! God bless America."[10]

George W. Bush was in, but he was in trouble. Chief Justice William Rehnquist administered the presidential oath of office in Washington that inclement January 20, while thousands of angry citizens marched in protest at the 43rd President's "selection" by Rehnquist's court. With a closely-divided Congress and questions abounding about George W.'s legitimacy, the Bush team's challenges were as clear as the picket signs: "Hail to the Thief." They had to win over some very disgruntled Americans. Before the Bush clan even made it to their sleet-smattered huddle, someone pelted the official motorcade with eggs.

"I will work to build a single nation of justice and opportunity," George W. declared through the drizzle. The words stuck, as if frozen, to his lips.

If the incoming President was as petrified as he appeared, he had plenty of cause. After all, Al Gore, who stood just feet behind him on the soggy platform, received 539,898 more votes on election day. The Democratic and Green votes combined added up to the largest center-left turnout since 1964. Over 154 million adult Americans had not voted for W.—either they'd preferred one of his opponents or, most likely of all, they'd simply opted out—and 51 percent of those voters who had managed to push, pull, or otherwise mark a ballot in Bush's support told pollsters they did so with doubts.[11] Of those who had voted for W. for President, some knew just what he stood for, but, as George was perfectly aware that chilly January morning, a heck of a lot did not.

When he was on the campaign trail, George W. repeated one phrase: "compassionate conservative." He said it so often that it acquired a familiar ring, but its meaning was anyone's guess. Did most people understand "compassionate conservative" to encompass a commitment to eliminate the Endangered Species Act, to withdraw from the Anti-Ballistic Missile Treaty, to reject the Kyoto Treaty on global warming, and to eliminate the Occupational Safety and Health Administration's latest workplace safety standards? Probably not, but

Bush's agenda included all that and more.

Standing there, on that frigid inauguration platform, George W. knew just what kind of a program he'd signed on to, and he knew something else as well. Had his team done less to obscure their party's agenda, no amount of vote-counting shenanigans could have tipped the balance their way. Centrist Democrats like to say that there aren't enough liberals in America to elect a liberal president. The jury's out on that, but one thing's for sure: there certainly aren't enough voters who believe in government-sponsored religion, life at conception, an end to family planning, and the death of the Endangered Species Act to elect George W. Bush, without his image-makers. Instead, Bush dressed himself up in ''W. Stands for Women'' clothing and, in place of policy details, candidate Bush gave the public fluff. The Republican National Convention's millennium stage was packed with women and children, and gospel singers, and Chaka Khan. The ultra Right were kept out of sight. Now, packing their bags to take a seat in the new administration was a cohort of outspoken extremists who were eager for payback, and chomping at the party bit to pick up where Ronald Reagan had left off.

Among those who would ride into town with Bush was John Ashcroft, the son of an Assemblies of God (Pentecostal) minister who, as Governor of Missouri, spent millions of taxpayer dollars to sue the National Organization for Women (NOW) for trying to pass the Equal Rights Amendment. In 1999, Ashcroft received an honorary degree from Bob Jones University, a Southern college famous for its ban on interracial dating, and its homophobia (a BJU dean once told a gay alumnus that he'd be arrested for trespassing if he returned to campus, as long as he was "living as a homosexual").[12] He announced in his acceptance speech that America "has no king but Jesus."[13] Quite a record for the nation's first enforcer of the law.

Also coming to town with Bush was Kay Coles James, a former dean of the Pat Robertson School of Government, who was put in charge of the White House Office of Personnel Management. Responsible for hiring staff for the nation's largest employer (the federal government), James, who is African American, opposes affirmative action—except for men. In 1998, she and her husband Charles signed a Southern Baptist Convention declaration stating that wives should submit to the authority of their husbands.[14] (Charles James found a position at the Department of Labor in the area of civil rights.)

To the Food and Drug Administration was headed David Hager, a physician who refused to discuss contraception with unwed female patients and preaches prayer to relieve premenstrual stress. Hager joined the FDA's reproductive health drugs advisory committee. (Only a public outcry forced the President to withdraw his nomination to serve as its chair.) Patricia Ware, the administration's choice to head the presidential advisory council on HIV and AIDS, selected Jerry Thacker, a man who had called AIDS the "gay plague," to join her on the panel. (Thacker withdrew, and Ware quit, when his description of homosexuality as a "deathstyle" rather than a lifestyle hit the press.)[15]

Tommy Thompson, who, as Governor of Wisconsin, had led the nation in setting tough work requirements and strict time limits on poor mothers receiving welfare benefits, was about to become Bush's secretary for Health and Human Services. His second in command was to be Wade Horn, a founder of the National Fatherhood Initiative, a man who had spent a decade fighting alleged anti-male bias in domestic violence and child-custody laws. Horn came to Washington as an advocate of using welfare to push women into marriages—even denying benefits to unmarried couples who insist on living together—and withholding money from single mothers until married couples have received their benefits first. During his confirmation, Horn claimed he'd abandoned those ideas, but hey presto—the department was soon requesting taxpayer dollars for "promoting marriage" and pushing legislation that granted health benefits to "the care of the unborn" but not their moms.

That was what you might call the administration's "back-story." George W. knew all about it, but the American public did not. The "compassionate conservative" charade continued. It had to, because, after twenty years of pandering to anti-tax libertarians and religious reactionaries, the very same policies that attracted the GOP base turn the majority of Americans off. Election/selection 2000 showed that it was still possible to slip into office in 21st-century America with a minority of the vote—and a minority that was disproportionately white, male, and Southern at that—but it wasn't easy, and governing was going to be harder still.[16] Looking ahead, the electoral map showed a country split almost perfectly in half. In 2004, the spoils would go to the campaign team that most successfully wooed "unattached" voters. At the top of the Bush team's target list were independents, moderates, and above all, suburban, married women. From day one, the Bush White House practiced what any one of their Madison Avenue advertising consultants would have told them: if not enough of your target customers are likely to buy what you're selling, pretend to be selling something else.

Bush's White House hawked "unity," "diversity," "inclusion," and women. While more controversial players were quietly slotted into powerful positions that didn't require public confirmation by the Senate, the spin machine went into overdrive as the President-select named his cabinet. Seven of Bush's nominees were approved within hours of his swearing-in. Ann Veneman of California as secretary of agriculture was one. Bush's other choices included a handful of highly-placed firsts: the first African-American secretary of state, Colin Powell, and national security advisor, Condoleezza Rice, and Karen P. Hughes, the first female White House counsel.

The selection of five women, two African Americans, one Hispanic, one Arab American, one Asian American, and a Democrat provoked *The New York Times* to offer congratulations: "With the completion of his cabinet selections today, President-elect George W. Bush has put forward a governing team every bit as ethnically and racially diverse as President Clinton's."[17]

Other media were equally effusive: "Not his father's cabinet," wrote David Broder of *The Washington Post*.[18] "A rainbow," a guest on CNN called it.[19] "A symphony of diversity," quipped *Time*.[20] "Dozens of women—more than any other president," gushed the *Boston Globe*.[21]

It quickly became the conventional wisdom that while Bill

Clinton, in 1992, had promised "a cabinet that looked like America," George W., in 2001, had appointed one. In fact, George W. Bush appointed exactly the same number of female cabinet secretaries as did Bill Clinton: three out of thirteen (Environmental Protection Agency director was not a cabinet post, until Bush elevated it.) More broadly, his executive branch could boast dramatically fewer women and people of color than his predecessor's.[22] That didn't stop Republican women from bragging, "More women are presidential advisors than ever before," in a get-out-the-vote videotape. Democrat Robert Torricelli commended Bush for his "inclusiveness." Even NOW's president, Patricia Ireland, who protested that Bush's nominee for Attorney General (Ashcroft) was an "extremist," called it "a significant breakthrough" for Bush to elevate Hughes and Rice.[23]

Before W. took office, *Time* magazine dubbed him "2000 Person of the Year" for having "remade and united the Republican Party." It was bunk. The GOP electoral base remained what it had been for a generation, and his political agenda was the same contradictory mix cobbled together by his forebears: economic liberty (tax cuts, deregulation, limited government) and social control (anti-reproductive choice, mandatory work for the poor, expanded government intervention, pro-church). With respect to scaling back federal mandates and extending religious ones, the Bush agenda was the same as Ronald Reagan's, only more so. The only thing "remade" was the GOP's public image, and the Bushwomen were a big part of that new look.

Their mission is to solve the GOP's female problem. For

twenty years, a smaller percentage of women than men have cast their votes for Republicans than Democrats. The "problem" shows up most clearly as a "gender gap," but there's a whole lot more wrapped up in it than that. The fact is, after thirty years of gender-baiting, the party has hit a bump.

An update on red-baiting, the Republican Party demonized Democrats in the years after Democratic President Lyndon B. Johnson signed the 1964 Civil Rights Act. The then-emerging New Right successfully pursued disgruntled Southern voters by linking up together desegregation, crime, and taxes, and tying them all to the Democrats. The Republicans' response was a vigorous defense, not of segregation or racism or inequality, but of healthy-sounding values like "privacy," "small government," and "states' rights." Over the next decade, the GOP pursued disaffected Democrats and independents in every state, by tapping into anxieties about a whole range of issues that could be broadly defined as the feminist agenda—not just desegregation and civil rights, but also equal rights for women, abortion, equal opportunity in the workplace; affirmative action, sexual liberation for gays and lesbians; environmental protection; income supports for poor mothers, and new laws that made it possible to sue in court over harassment and domestic violence.

The GOP targeted white men because they assumed their wives would do as they did in the voting booth, but they were wrong. The anti-backlash backlash was immediate. In 1980, 54 percent of men gave Reagan their vote, but only 46 percent of women. The disparity remained throughout the 1980s. In 1996, 54 percent of women cast their vote for Democrat Bill

Clinton, compared with 43 percent of men: an eleven-point gender gap, or what the people at Emily's List (a political action committee that raises funds for pro-choice women candidates) called a "gender canyon." It was the same in 2000: George W. won an eleven-point margin over Gore among men. He lost women by the same amount.

Ronald Reagan came to office in 1980 with an Electoral College landslide—but he won with a campaign that was geared to appeal to a shrinking fragment of the US population: white males. What he didn't have were people of color or women—not in his voter base, and not in his inner circle. Reagan scouted about for women to solve his "woman problem." Trouble was, there were scant few women in the New Right in those days. There were no women of any note in the 1980 Reagan campaign. "I haven't figured out yet why there were no women," wrote insider Lyn Nofziger later, "Except there never had been, and Reagan probably figured, if he bothered to figure at all, that that's the way it was supposed to be."[24] There was one woman in the first Reagan cabinet, Jeane Kirkpatrick, whom Reagan appointed ambassador to the United Nations (generally regarded as a low-prestige spot). Kirkpatrick supported the Equal Rights Amendment and was thought to be "unsure" about abortion, but, like Whitman, she was placed where women's rights were not part of her portfolio. There it stopped. As Susan Faludi put it, "The few women who did slip past the no-girls allowed sign on the White House lawn didn't exactly feel at home."[25] The numbers of women appointed to the federal bench, on the White House staff, or in positions requiring Senate confirmation fell for the first time in a decade.

In the twenty years since, while the Democratic Party has relished its advantage among women voters, Republicans have made a concentrated effort to cultivate their own female fighting force. Right-wing foundations (the same set that funded the Heritage Foundation, the New Right's assault on affirmative action, welfare and the Clintons) invested millions in custom-made women's organizations: the Independent Women's Forum, to name but one. On Women's Equality Day, August 26 2001, Ashcroft named Nancy M. Pfotenhauer, the president of the Independent Women's Forum, and Margot Hill, another IWF board member, to sit on the national advisory committee on violence against women. A small, self-selected group established in the wake of the confirmation of Clarence Thomas to the Supreme Court (despite allegations that he had sexually harassed women co-workers including Anita Hill), the IWF serves as the Republican Right's Women's Auxiliary. The group prides itself on its long and vigorous opposition to Title IX, the Equity Pay Act, the Women's Educational Equity Act, and the Violence Against Women Act (VAWA). The only thing the IWF opposes as vigorously as that last piece of legislation is the notion that women still suffer discrimination in the workplace, so it was entirely fitting that IWF president Pfotenhauer also secured a spot at the Department of Labor under Bush, on the committee on workplace issues.[26] Abigail Thernstrom, a founding IWF board member, and affirmative action foe, was appointed to the US Commission on Civil Rights, where she did her best to sabotage the investigation of the Florida election process. (Sexism colored coverage of the commission's report on voting irregularities, too. Unsurprisingly, Thernstrom clashed with commission chair Mary Frances Berry, but rather than investigating the substance, the media focused on the "catfight."[27] *The Washington Post* called it the "Great Florida election flapdoodle." Readers might have felt differently, if they'd actually learnt what went wrong.)[28]

Do high-level female appointees like the Bushwomen make a difference to voters? Halfway through the President's first term, democratic pollster Anna Greenberg doubted that the "average Jane" voter had even heard of Labor Secretary Elaine Chao, Secretary of the Interior Gale Ann Norton, or Agriculture Secretary Ann Veneman. Female appointees don't guarantee female support come election time, says Greenberg; but even if highly-placed females don't necessarily translate into votes, it's clear that the Republican Party thinks the Bushwomen can help. Just seven months into the Bush presidency, a Republican pollster looked at a survey and winced. "This is not happy data," he told the press. The veneer on Bush's White House was eroding, and the GOP's sweeping tax cut as well as the administration's moves on the environment seemed to be alienating a disproportionate number of women. (Bush tried to roll back reductions on the amount of arsenic permitted in drinking water and summarily pulled the US out of the Kyoto Protocol.) According to a July 2001 poll, while men said they were more likely to vote for a Republican than a Democrat by 43 percent to 37 percent, women were more likely to do the opposite, by 47 to 32 percent. The President's approval rating stood at a historic low for a leader so early in his first term (51 percent), and the same poll revealed a "precipitous drop" in

Republican support among married women with children, the subset with whom GOP candidates traditionally do best.[29]

The Republican answer was to pump up the profiles of the highest-ranking women in the Bush administration. In July, the White House invited female magazine editors and publishers to meet female office-holders. The RNC (Republican National Convention) announced that it would drive millions of dollars a year into a new campaign, "Winning Women," that would feature profiles of figures such as Karen P. Hughes, Christine Todd Whitman and Condoleezza Rice. The effort was to be led by the RNC's new co-chairwoman, Ann Wagner, whose name appeared nowhere without the emphatic self-description, "38-year-old suburban mom." Her ID exactly fit the demographic niche that held the party's strategists in thrall.

After the deadly attacks of September 11 2001, American voters swung heavily towards supporting their commander in chief. The President claimed, "I really don't think about politics right now," the following January,[30] but his political team were still at work. As the 2002 midterm elections approached, female "swing voters" were still dancing like sugar-plum fairies in their heads. Late that spring, someone on the President's staff lost a computer disk that made its way to the media. On it was senior advisor Karl Rove's election advice, laid out in Power Point. President Bush, he said, needs to "grow" his outreach to Latinos, suburban women, Roman Catholics, and union members.[31] The mix presents its challenges, but Rove knows the numbers. (It's not for nothing that he's called "Bush's Brain.") Fifty-two percent of those who vote in the US are female. With suburb-dwellers making up 51 percent of the population, suburban women constitute about 25 to 30 percent of the electorate. As pollster Greenberg explains, women, especially white, married, suburban women, are "the least solidly attached voters out there," the biggest swingers. "Enormously important," she says; everything else remaining as it is, in 2004 they could win or lose the election. They are certainly the largest "unattached" block within the Republicans' grasp.[32]

In 2003, another GOP memo turned up. From the dizzy heights of Bush's post-9/11 popularity, mounting job losses and dying soldiers in Iraq were sending Bush's numbers tumbling below their pre-9/11 low mark. In California, the GOP was hoping to benefit from an unusual, "voter-initiated" election on whether to recall and replace Governor Gray Davis. (The "voter" who initiated the recall was a single Republican millionaire who hired workers from out of state to gather signatures from Californians.) The memo, by California GOP organizer Julie Leitzell, declared that the recall election presented a unique opportunity to target disaffected voters, *especially women*, before the 2004 presidential race. "It's important that we use this opportunity (and hot news hook) to present an image of diverse Republican women (moms, educators, business owners, students, working women)," wrote Leitzell. "We want to make sure the media are steered toward the 'common-sense women against Davis' angle ... We are working on getting a big-name female draw for each local event."[33]

The Republicans' lead candidate at the time was Arnold Schwarzenegger, who combined the odd qualities of *opposing* the GOP's party line on abortion (he's for choice), gun control, and gay and lesbian equality, and having a reputation that infuriated the religious Right. In London, the papers were calling him the "groper governor" on account of the number of women who had gone on the record that he'd felt them up in public. In one recent instance, a woman told *Premiere* magazine that he had walked up to her and pulled her breast out of her blouse. "That's sexual harassment, which is illegal," said Karen Pomer, a women's rights activist in Los Angeles.[34]

The GOP's cynical Bushwomen plan shouldn't work, but then again, in US politics there are a lot of "shoulds." Democratic Party leaders, for example "should" call a Bushwoman a Bushwoman. All too often, what "should" be obvious goes unsaid. When it came to confirming the White House's nominations to the cabinet, Democrats opposed Bush's nominees on a very limited, quota basis. They chose two to hoot and holler about—Linda Chavez (Bush's first selection for labor secretary), and John Ashcroft. Chavez, who had a long history of opposing affirmative action and multilingual education, withdrew after it emerged that she herself had broken labor laws, and Democratic senators said lots of damning things about Ashcroft's record of opposition to desegregation and the right to choose. Then all but one member of Ashcroft's confirmation committee voted to confirm him. The rest of Bush's nominees passed into office with minimal scrutiny.

Looking at the bigger picture, the problem's not just Congressional and Senate chumminess, it's a more serious matter of convergence between the parties. While the Republicans, to win over women and moderates, have been pulling out every hypocritical stop, the Democratic leadership has been running *away* from their core supporters. In his 1992 book, *Who Will Tell the People*, political analyst William Greider noted that the Democratic Leadership Council, co-founded by Bill Clinton in the mid-1980s, emphasized catering to "middle-class" Americans, a euphemism for not feminists, not civil rights advocates, not labor union activists; in fact, jettisoning anyone who might cause trouble with the DLC's wealthy donors among America's corporate elite. "The DLC's main objective," wrote Greider, "was an attack on the Democratic Party's core constituencies—labor, schoolteachers, women's rights groups, peace and disarmament activists, the racial minorities and supporters of affirmative action. Its stated goal was to restore the party's appeal to disaffected white males, especially in the South."[35]

By 1988, as Susan Faludi puts it, "the party for Democratic women was over."[36] The Democratic leadership not only refused to take its own side in a fight, but did its best to ditch the home team. Paul Kirk, chairman of the Democratic National Committee announced that such "narrow" issues as the Equal Rights Amendment and the right to abortion had no place on the party platform, depite the fact that large majorities of Democratic voters clearly disagreed. He tried to disband the party's women's caucuses and, quietly, the DLC omitted abortion rights from its agenda.

The Clinton years that followed saw the Democratic leadership talk up a storm about shrinking government and, in the President's famous phrase, "ending welfare as we know it." Clinton said it with the same fervor that Bush said "compassionate conservative;'' unfortunately for poor families, Clinton followed through. Under his administration, investment in public education and affordable housing and childcare took a back seat to budget balancing and fiscal conservatism. The President pushed for NAFTA (the North American Free Trade Agreement) against the will of hundreds of thousands of union members, environmentalists, and consumers' rights groups. The boondoggle drug war blundered on, boosting the US prison population during the Clinton years from 1.4 million to more than 2 million.[37] A draconian 1996 Anti-Terrorism and Effective Death Penalty Act not only added scores of new crimes to the list for which a criminal could be executed, but made it tougher for death row inmates to prove their innocence, and made it possible to deny bail to foreign nationals accused of minor immigration violations on the basis of secret evidence.[38] (It was a short leap from Clinton's law to Ashcroft's USA PATRIOT Act—the acronym for the Uniting and Strengthening America by Providing Appropriate Tools Required to Intercept and Obstruct Terrorism Act of 2001.)

Clinton remained in favor of Roe (the Supreme Court decision, in Roe v. Wade, that legalized abortion), for which pro-choice groups lauded him to the end. But on his watch, hundreds of restrictions on abortion access, such as ''parental consent'' laws, went into effect. He sacrificed his support of homosexuals—which is to say, non-discrimination—in the military, as soon as right-wingers raised a fuss. He signed a so-called welfare ''reform'' law that not only looked a whole lot like Tommy Thompson's, but also opened up federal coffers for the first time to explicitly religious groups. The provision, which permitted religious service-providers to apply for federal welfare dollars, was called "charitable choice."

On the international front, it was under Clinton and Gore, in May 2000, that the Joint Chiefs of Staff released their blueprint for the coming decade. The Defense Department was charged to pursue what was called "full spectrum dominance," meaning the ability to defeat any adversary anywhere, using a "full range" of military techniques, including nuclear weapons. Paul Wolfowitz and Donald Rumsfeld couldn't have come up with a more chilling term.[39]

By 1999, many Democratic core supporters were none too sorry to see Clinton go. By way of parting gift, the President saddled his party with his personal problems. Bill Clinton's stupid affair with White House intern Monica Lewinsky played right into the GOP's hands. When it comes to women's rights, the Republican leaders who took Clinton to task had more than Oval Office mischief and lying in mind (many of them had sketchy marital records themselves to boot), but they successfully gussied themselves up in their best Moral Guardians' outfits. Bush–Cheney hit the campaign trail as the answer upstanding women had been waiting for after eight long sleazy years of Clinton and Gore.

Political conservatives, profit-driven all, have figured out how to rearrange themselves around the phenomena called "feminism" and "civil rights." Forty years after Dr Martin Luther King Jr's "March on Washington for Jobs and Freedom," politics in the United States has become all about "personality," or what the George W. campaign called (without a shred of irony) "character." On Capitol Hill, as in the establishment media, there's been an embrace of identity politics, except it's all identity—and no politics.

It works because the largest women's organizations tend to keep their criticisms of powerful women to themselves (operations like the Ms. Foundation's White House Project continue to advocate gender-parity no matter what, as a worthy goal in itself). Left media—no haven from sexism—mostly dismissed Bush's female cabinet secretaries as pawns, or tools, or lackeys. Establishment media (by which is meant the TV, radio and newspapers owned by powerful corporations, which depend on multinational advertisers and friendly licensers in Congress) can generally be relied upon either to disregard a female face, or to report mostly on its femaleness. With respect to the Bushwomen, they did both.

When George W. announced his earliest appointments, reporters emphasized demographics above any question pertaining to his nominees' policy backgrounds, corporate ties or politics. Journalists at one White House briefing even prodded the incoming President to make his point. They asked whether he intended to send a message with his choice of women and minorities: "You bet," he answered. The message? That "people who work hard and make the right decisions in life can achieve anything they want in America."[40]

In fact, Bush was sending many messages, first and foremost about himself. If news accounts revealed little of substance about his female cabinet members, the fact of their selection was handled as if it said everything about George. The women and people of color he chose to populate his inner circle became to the President as a reflective surface is to a fashion model—excellent for casting him in a flattering light. It was as if, at the dawn of the 21st century, it is still a mark of good character for a man to hire capable women to do his work. Whereas Clinton, who appointed what at the time was the most diverse cabinet in US history, was crucified in the press and by advocacy groups for taking weeks to announce his nominations, and later, because his cabinet choices were not diverse "enough," George W. scored points simply for not naming a team of Neanderthal men in white sheets.

While Bush's administration, even in its earliest days, pursued policies that took a disproportionate toll on the lives of women and people of color, the women and people of color on Bush's staff acted as his cover from those who charged him with racism or sexism. The Bushwomen do for the Republican Party's image what "pro-life" language did for its rhetoric. They provide a shield that makes the party's anti-civil rights, anti-feminist agenda acceptable to those who don't like to think of themselves as backward or, heaven forbid, racist. For example, in a debate on MSNBC in 2003, when a white, Anglo-American panelist criticized the Bush administration's position against affirmative action, an on-air caller complained: "How dare that white woman think she knows better than Condoleezza Rice?"[41]

In the hot seat after the resignation of Trent Lott over comments he had made on Strom Thurmond's hundredth birthday, Bush was forced to defend his own record on racism. (At Thurmond's birthday bash, Senate majority leader Lott had praised the retiring South Carolina senator's 1948 campaign, in which Thurmond had run as a segregationist.) Asked about his own civil rights record and his consistent refusal to meet with NAACP (National Association for the Advancement of Colored People) leaders, Bush told the press that his secretary of state and national security advisor were black, as if that in itself was a sufficient substitute for policy.

"Let's see," said Bush. "There I was, sitting around the leader with—the table with foreign leaders, looking at Colin Powell and Condi Rice."[42]

When it came to waging war on the people of Afghanistan and then Iraq, the White House deployed its female faces to cast a glowing light, not just on the commander in chief, but on the nation as a whole. In mid-November 2001, word was filtering out of Afghanistan that US forces had dropped two "daisy-cutter" bombs on alleged Taliban positions. The BLU-82, called a "daisy-cutter" because of the blast pattern it leaves, is a 15,000-pound bomb so large that it can only be delivered by dropping it out of the doors of a cargo plane. The bomb disperses a slurry of ammonium nitrate, aluminum powder, and polystyrene, which it then ignites, causing enough pressure at the blast to deflate the lungs—and kill—every living thing within a 300 to 900 feet radius.[43] It was just then that the First Lady, who'd come to the comfort of bereaved American families after 9/11, went on the radio to reassure Americans that the war on Afghanistan was not about revenge, but rather about liberation. In case the public were beginning to think that the most powerful state in the world was blowing an impoverished feudal society to bits, Laura Bush emphasized that the Taliban's power was great. Running down the long-ignored record of Taliban brutality towards women, she claimed that

the US wasn't alone: "civilized people through the world are speaking out in horror, not only because our hearts break for the women and children in Afghanistan, but also because in Afghanistan, we see the world the terrorists would like to impose on the rest of us."[44]

Bush likes to cast his wars as "defensive." Who better, then, to sell them to the people than women, who are well known, as a group, to oppose unnecessary violence. On October 7 2002, the President told the nation, "Our smoking gun could come in the form of a mushroom cloud." National Security Advisor Condoleezza Rice said exactly the same thing the next day. Pentagon spokeswoman Victoria Clarke said the same thing again on October 9. Congress voted to go ahead on October 11. A woman for whom a grateful Chevron Corporation had named a tanker, Rice wasn't an oilman of Dick Cheney's stature, but she'd served on the Chevron board for a decade, and had been involved for just as long in negotiations to gain US access to new, Central Asian and Middle Eastern oil routes. Still she had the advantage of not *looking* like an oilman. If the public were in doubt, she constantly redirected their attention to her "story," growing up in segregated Alabama. In fact, although African Americans disproportionately opposed the US first-strike invasion of Iraq, and thanks to what amounts to a poverty draft, are over-represented among the footsoldiers who are daily under fatal attack, Rice claimed that the occupation was really about civil rights. In August 2003, she addressed the National Association of Black Journalists:

Like many of you, I grew up around the home-grown terrorism of the 1960s. The bombing of the church in
Birmingham in 1963 is one that will forever be in my
memory because one of the girls who died was a friend of
mine ... [Forty years later] We should not let our voice
waver in speaking out on the side of people who are seeking
freedom. [Denying people freedom] was wrong in 1963 in
Birmingham, and it is wrong in 2003 in Baghdad.[45]

US soldiers writing home in anguish, and Iraqis, paint quite a
different picture. The US invasion has made Iraq safe for ethnic
warfare, they say, and the repression of women: "Females can
no longer leave their homes alone ... It feels like we've gone
back fifty years," wrote a US-educated, Iraqi Muslim woman.
"Before the war, around 50 percent of the college students
were females and over 50 percent of the workforce was
composed of women," the anonymous woman wrote, in a
web-log. "Not so any more." The writer, "Riverbend,"
described being chased out of her job as a computer pro-
grammer by her former co-workers, men who told her that
"females weren't welcome any more." "I cried bitterly all the
way home—cried for my job, cried for my future, and cried for
the torn streets, damaged buildings and crumbling people."[46]

George W. Bush likes to pit singular stories against the
argument of anyone who would point to the bigger picture.
Speaking of his cabinet, he says, "Each person has got their
own story that is so unique, stories that really explain what
America should be about."[47] Condoleezza Rice has internalized
the whole notion of herself-as-narrative: "In many ways, I'm a

typical American story,'' she wrote in an article for the journal *Foreign Affairs.*[48]

But the Bushwomen are anything but typical. According to Census 2000, poverty among women and children grew in the 1980s and '90s, even as the country's economy enjoyed a boom. Seventy percent of American women under the age of sixty either work or are looking for work, and yet almost half of all children who live in poverty live in households headed by someone female. Of male-headed households, 11.7 percent live below the poverty line. Over twice that number—27.8 percent—of families headed by a woman live in poverty. As politicians debate shifting Social Security into private investment accounts ruled by Wall Street, their decisions will disproportionately affect women: 6.9 percent of men over sixty-five spend the last part of their life in poverty, whereas 11.8 percent of older women live that way.

Economic disparities like these, according to Bush's women, are not the result of discrimination or institutionalized bias, but rather women's personal choices. It is choosing to have a child that causes women to earn less than men, they claim. Women as a group face no barriers, their argument goes: behold how some women succeed. It is in this context that the Bushwomen are invaluable. By their individual accomplishments, they are supposed to prove that opportunity exists for all. But Bush's women are a very special case. The Bushwomen have had the advantage of generous corporate support and foundation grants, and premium jobs in think-tanks with their allies. They've received good educations, many of them in publicly-funded schools, and they've had the legal right and necessary access to family planning at the very least. Of the five female cabinet secretaries profiled here, only one has any children at all; two are successful, unmarried professionals, the remaining two are in childless marriages they entered late in life. To a greater or lesser extent, they've benefited directly from feminism—the movement they now cast as women's enemy—and from the hard-won gains of the civil rights struggle, in the destruction of whose victories they actively collaborate.

The Bushwomen are the media-friendly face of an extremist administration, one that's lawyered by anti-civil rights, anti-government fanatics, and fuelled by the theocratic Right. As women, they play a particularly insidious role: fiercely ambitious, power-hungry, they preach freedom for corporations and liberty for Americans like themselves, while they act as cover for both a presidency that seeks to dominate the world, and religious autocrats who would like to rewrite the nation's laws according to their interpretation of the will of some god.

Theirs is the politics of masquerade—part of a long-term project to save the GOP by gaining it new support. Their mission: to overhaul the party's image without changing the policies that have set it and mainstream America on a collision course. It only works for as long as no one takes too deep a look; for as long as no one takes these women, or the rights of all women, seriously enough to give the whole 21st-century Republican Party makeover plan too much scrutiny. Consider this an exercise in taking women seriously: seriously enough, actually, to tell their stories.

October 2003

SWEETNESS AND LIGHT*

Condoleezza Rice

Condoleezza Rice became George W. Bush's national security advisor having directed an oil company, managed a multi-million-dollar university, and served as a Sovietologist in Washington during the collapse of the Soviet Union. She was assuming a post in her second Bush administration, the top national security position in the cabinet. Nonetheless when *The New York Times* ran a story on the forty-six-year-old professor, it didn't discuss her views on national security until the twenty-seventh paragraph. The subject cropped up near the end of the *Times*'s long feature, which was dominated by talk of her dress-size, her hair, her hemline, and her place of birth.[1]

"She eats either a bagel or cereal every day for breakfast," wrote the *Times*. "She is always impeccably dressed, usually in a classic suit with a modest hemline, comfortable pumps and conservative jewelry." The paper-of-record reported that Rice, then Provost of Stanford University, "keeps two mirrors on

---

* Rice's mother, Angelina, is said to have created the name Condoleezza from the Italian *Con Dolcezza*, a musical annotation meaning sweetly.

her desk, apparently to check the back as well as the front."
And oh, yes, "She has an oil supertanker named after her, a
result of being on the Chevron Corporation Board."[2] That was
it for discussion of Rice and Chevron.

Los Angeles attorney Connie Rice, a second cousin of Rice's,
says such coverage is simply sexist: "You don't hear the press
asking where Dick Cheney likes to shop."[3]

No *Times* story so far has dwelt on Vice-President Dick
Cheney's youth as a white man in pre-civil rights Nebraska, but
the *Times* dedicated fully half its feature on Rice to her childhood. In that, the paper was hardly alone. Read a dozen
features on Condoleezza Rice, and you're likely to read twelve
almost identical stories about her family and her childhood, and
almost nothing about just what's she done on the way from
there to here.

Kiron Skinner, a former dissertation student and friend of
Rice's, thinks the fascination with Rice's personal narrative
smacks of racism. It's no wonder that the US media are
interested in Rice's background—American "trailblazers" are
inherently newsworthy, and Rice is certainly one of a kind.
But, "I think there's a kind of racism going on to keep puzzling
about why she's doing what she's doing at this point," says
Skinner. "I think she's exactly where she should be, given her
background, her education and her experience."[4]

But the public mostly doesn't *know* about Rice's experience
in politics and business. And that's because it seems to have
been decided that the national security advisor's professional
career makes for less heart-warming spin than her firecracker
rise out of "Bombingham."

The daughter of two African-American teachers in the South, Rice was born in 1954, in Birmingham, a city Dr Martin Luther King Jr was to call "by far the worst big city in race relations in the United States."[5] Children in 1950s Birmingham learnt to recognize the sign "colored" even before they could read. Their lives depended on it. The town featured whites-only schools and whites-only cinemas and whites-only libraries. The local police commissioner, "Bull" Connor, had a habit of driving through black families' neighborhoods in a freaky white-metal tank and announcing on the radio when a "nigger family" moved into a "white" part of town. So common were bombings of black homes in one area that it earned the name "Dynamite Hill."[6] (A third of Connor's police force was said to be in the Ku Klux Klan.)[7]

Rice's childhood coincided exactly with the make-or-break years for multiracial America. In the year she was born, the Supreme Court, in *Brown v. Board of Education*, ruled public-school segregation unconstitutional. A year later, the Mont-gomery bus boycott led the court to ban bus segregation, too. By the time Rice turned eight, the Birmingham city govern-ment had yet to implement either ruling. That spring, in 1963, Dr Martin Luther King Jr and his colleagues came to town and subjected themselves to multiple arrests to protest, but local papers studiously kept them off the front page. To up the ante, thousands of students and high-school children organized and took to the streets themselves.

Forty years later, still the most famous—and horrifying—pictures of the civil rights struggle tend to be pictures of what happened next. When Connor's men loosed dogs and water cannon on the nonviolent demonstrators, the images of children beaten, bitten and washed down Birmingham's streets were seen around the world.

Repulsion at the events in Birmingham helped to draw a quarter of a million people to Washington that August. People who'd never before heard or seen the Rev. Martin Luther King Jr watched his "I have a dream" speech live on all three TV networks. ("He's damn good," President John F. Kennedy is said to have told an aide.)[8] But the defenders of white supremacy weren't about to concede. In the months after the youth marches, bomb attacks had increased. A gas bomb was thrown into the house of the Rices' across-the-street neighbor, civil rights attorney Arthur Shores, and just two weeks after the March on Washington, bombers targeted Birmingham's 16th St. Baptist Church, the hub of the local civil rights movement.

The device in the church was planted precisely to target the city's rebellious youth. The explosion took place just as Sunday school began. The four murdered children were all downstairs, fixing their clothes before joining the service. Eleven-year-old Denise McNair, and fourteen-year-olds Cynthia Wesley, Carole Robertson and Adie Mae Collins were high achievers, popular in town. One attended Rice's school, a second lived on her street.

Rice wrote about the event for *Time* magazine in 2000:

I remember being at a church which was a few blocks away from the 16th St Baptist Church, and just being completely shocked by the sound. It was almost like a train coming . . . I don't remember being frightened at that moment although it was a terrifying time. I just felt sad.[9]

One reason that personal biography has come to dominate the media coverage of Condoleezza Rice is that she herself appears happy to place her family's history center stage. At the Republican National Convention in 2000, speaking in prime time, George W.'s foreign policy guru dedicated fully half her precious slot to talk about her father and her grandfather.

"My father was the first Republican I knew," said Rice. "My father joined our party because the Democrats in Jim Crow Alabama of 1952 would not register him to vote. The Republicans did. I want you to know that my father has never forgotten that day, and neither have I. [Cheers, applause.]" She also told a story about her father's father, John Wesley Rice Sr, a sharecropper who converted from Baptist to Presbyterian to get a free education. "The Rices," she said, "have been Presbyterian—and college-educated—ever since."

In September 2001, just before the attacks on Washington and New York, *The Washington Post* magazine ran a long Sunday feature in which Rice talked in depth about family beliefs. "My father was not a march-in-the-street preacher," she said. Rather than agitate, Rice's parents stressed self-improvement. Her mother, Angelina, and her mother before her were music teachers; her father, John Wesley Rice Jr, preached at the weekends in the local Presbyterian Church, and worked as a guidance counselor at Ullman High School.

"My parents were very strategic," Rice told the *Post*'s Dale Russakoff. "I was going to be so well prepared, and I was going to do all of these things that were revered in white society so well, that I would be armored somehow from racism. I would be able to confront white society on its own terms."

Rice says it didn't take a movement or the government to open doors for her. "Black Americans of my grandparents' ilk had liberated themselves," she told the *Post*. The family strategy was to ignore racism, she said: racism in Birmingham was so routine, "you ceased to notice its existence." She was conditioned to succeed: "My family is third-generation college-educated . . . I should've gotten to where I am."[10]

To a party-political spinmeister this is spine-tingling stuff. Used to justify extremely conservative, anti-government beliefs, personal biography is gold in the political economy. Usually uncontested, often uncontestable, any carefully selected detail can be deployed for broad political effect. Ronald Reagan, the son of an alcoholic shoe salesman, had his story. Bill Clinton, fatherless child of a single mom—the "man from Hope"—had his. Verisimilitude matters less than the power to melt hearts, make good media, and cast a negative light on those who talk about structural discrimination and want the government to act to change it. The up-from-oppression narratives of powerful people of color pack a particular punch: they can cast liberal complainers as bigots. Those who bemoan discrimination against groups—so goes the argument—underestimate the power of one.

The Yale men of the Bush dynasty are hard up for hard-luck stories, but the first and second Bush presidents have kept people around them who aren't. Linda Chavez, Reagan's anti-civil-rights civil rights commissioner, points to her own success as a Hispanic in America. She wasn't held back by bias, she says. Bush's Labor Secretary Elaine Chao has no end of stories to illustrate how she overcame the obstacles faced by Chinese immigrants. The most famous and contentious African-American narrative belongs to Clarence Thomas. Judge Thomas would never have been confirmed to the Supreme Court if it hadn't been for his supposedly "inspirational" life story. Born to a destitute teenage mother in segregated Georgia, Thomas edited out that part of his history that involved getting help from government programs such as welfare and affirmative action, and claimed he'd graduated by dint of determination alone, "from the outhouse to the courthouse." It wasn't entirely true, but it worked.[11]

With Condoleezza Rice's story, the Republicans hit the rhetorical jackpot. Here was an African American who grew up in the middle of the most brutal period of anti-equality backlash, and yet her parents kept her out of the movement for government intervention—and her father registered with the GOP, the party that opposed the 1964 Civil Rights Act.

Call it "up-by-the-bootstraps version eight," Rice articulates a new model of an old program. Years after Thomas, her story depicts not a single miraculous individual who fights against racist odds, but an entire group of middle-class African Americans—the children and even grandchildren of industrious souls who were never beaten down by the legacy of slavery. From a Republican strategist's point of view, Rice's story contains the potential to challenge the whole notion that African Americans as a group are the "natural" constituents of the Democrats (the party that passed the Civil Rights Act). The Act was a historic advance, Rice has said, but she bristles at any suggestion that she was ever held back on account of her skin color. To hear her tell it, her success was assured, virtually

predetermined—not by federal laws or the civil rights movement, but by her family heritage. Her love for the Bushes is a
family thing, and it goes both ways. "George W. Bush would
have liked Granddaddy Rice," she gushed to the GOP.

Romanticize US race history and this is the cozy picture you
can end up with. It works because people want it to, and
because the nation's memory tends to be fuzzy and short. By
way of reality-check, George W. never met Granddaddy Rice,
but while John Wesley Sr was trading his church for an education, Bush's grandfather, Prescott Bush, was running a Wall
Street bank.[12] Prescott's son, the first President Bush, opposed
the Civil Rights Act of 1964 when he ran for the US Senate
from Texas that year. George W. grew up in Midland, Texas, a
de facto segregated place, where the Bushes' black maid recalls
being banned from wearing anything but work clothes downtown.[13]

George W.'s arrival in the White House was based directly
on the systematic racial profiling of Florida's electorate and the
illegal disenfranchisement of thousands of legitimate African-
American voters through the manipulation of that state's felon
disenfranchisement laws. George W. Bush would certainly not
have liked Granddaddy Rice—not if he was trying to vote
Democratic in Florida in November 2000.

Rice's rosy picture conveniently glosses over the past.
Generations of smart young African Americans "should" have
risen to the highest places in US society as she has, but the fact
is that legal discrimination shut them out. In the case of Rice, a
child born in the wake of a slew of measures outlawing discrimination, we will never know where she "would" have

ended up if there had been no Rosa Parks, no Dr King, no Southern Christian Leadership Council, no March on Washington and no congressional and presidential support for the end of American apartheid.

Rice's father, John Wesley Rice Jr, spoke frankly about such things. For racial minorities, ''The great American Dream has been the great American lie,'' he once told the *Denver Clarion*, the campus newspaper at the University of Denver, where he was hired as assistant dean in 1969.[14]

The Rices left Birmingham not long after the church bombing. The next year, Congress passed the Civil Rights Act, making it illegal to deny a person a job on account of race. The second of two presidential Executive Orders requiring affirmative action from federal contractors followed. In 1964, John Rice got a job at his family's alma mater, Stillman College in Tuscaloosa, and a few years after that, he was hired at the University of Denver (DU) and the family moved to Colorado. At the age of fourteen, Condoleezza entered St Mary's Academy, a Catholic school, the first integrated school of her life. In no small part, the Civil Rights Act and affirmative action were responsible.

To quote the campus newspaper the *Denver Clarion*: ''About the time [John] Rice was brought to Denver, the cry for Black studies departments, for Black faculty and Black administrators was very loud. There can be no doubt that in this hue and cry lay some of the reasons for Rice's appointment.''[15]

The university was an expensive, overwhelmingly white, private college in a town with a sizable black population, and Dean Rice took the challenge of addressing bias on campus seriously. He opposed the tactics of more nationalistic black students in the country who were just then taking over buildings and even taking up arms, but he was adamant that integration had to be real.

Dean Rice's approach to integrating the campus was quite specific. He worked to increase the amount of scholarship money made available to poor students, and initiated an exchange program with historically black colleges. He advocated active recruitment of black teaching staff. ("Blacks and browns," as he called them, would not be likely to apply as long as the university's white reputation endured, he pointed out.)[16] And he initiated an open seminar series "to bring the real story of the American Negro to the Denver community."

Hosted by Rice, "The Black Experience in America" series brought speakers to campus. Among others, Rice brought Dennis Brutus, the exiled South African poet, Fannie Lou Hamer, leader of the Freedom Democratic Party of Mississippi, the Rev. Andrew Young, then executive vice-president of the SCLC, Muslim leader Louis Farrakhan, and Margaret Burnham, legal counsel for Angela Davis, then incarcerated on trumped-up charges in California.

Chip Berlet, now a director of Political Research Associates, the American Left's premier opposition-research group, took Dean Rice's seminar. He also edited the *Clarion*, which reported on its sessions. "If I was to characterize it as a reporter, I'd say it was a course on radical social change and civil rights and race in America," says Berlet.

"Dean Rice played a major role in making me a radical political activist," he adds. "A very religious man, Rice taught

that white supremacy and race in America were not just things
to be aware of—there was an absolute moral imperative to
act."[17]

The Dean's daughter, Condoleezza, would drop by when
Rice invited his seminar students home to continue their
political discussions. Already a student at DU at the age of
fifteen, she was "scary smart" even then, recalls Berlet. He
remembers her playing piano to welcome the Rev. Young to
campus.

Rice's family story, it turns out, is more complicated than
the version performed for the public at the RNC. Second
cousin Connie Rice says that she and Condoleezza were "cut
from the same cloth . . . In deeply segregated America, where
African-American humanity is openly in question at all times,
you have a few ways to bring up a child. One is to program
them to achieve, no matter what, and that's what our family
did."[18] It's a recipe for what she calls a "tungsten and Teflon
personality," but what you do with that personality is up to
you. While "Condi," as she's known, went on to embrace
market capitalism and the Republican Party, Connie went on to
study law, join the NAACP Legal Defense Fund and become a
fast-talking, affirmative-action-defending lawyer who describes
the workings of the market this way: "It's not an invisible
hand, it's an invisible penis, and my clients always get
screwed."

Although Connie only came to know Condoleezza in
adulthood, she says the Rices weren't as beaten down as other
Alabama blacks because they enjoyed advantages stemming
from history. Not only are the Rices "third-generation college-

educated," as Condoleezza told *The Washington Post*, they're also descended on both sides from white slave-owners and favored slaves.[19] They were protected from Birmingham's brutal daily worst by what Connie calls the "color caste system," and by economic class. For one thing, the Rices had a car, so they didn't have to ride in sit-in-the-back buses to get to work. "We weren't going to upset the apple cart," says Connie.

Rice talks about "self-improvement" as if it is a substitute for activism. Another Birmingham child, Angela Davis, disagrees. Ten years older than Condoleezza Rice, Angela Davis was also raised in Birmingham. She took piano and ballet lessons too. "The black middle class in those days," she says, "meant anyone whose female relative didn't work as a domestic." The Davises owned their own house and packed Angela and her sister off to classes. But unlike Rice, Davis recalls being bothered even at an early age by what she calls the "Booker T. Washington syndrome" of "work hard and rise above all obstacles." In her autobiography she writes that it irked her because "it was as if these obstacles would always be there, part of the natural way of things, rather than the product of a system of racism which we could eventually overturn."[20] Davis left Alabama and eventually joined the Communist Party.

Lost in the slur of political speech is the fact that affiliation with the GOP didn't mean the same thing in 1952 as it did half a century later. Davis's parents, who had a history of radical activism, also inclined towards the GOP, "not so much to affiliate themselves with conservative views as to connect to the party that emancipated the slaves," says Davis.[21]

As for the GOP registering African Americans when Democrats wouldn't, the *Post*'s Dale Russakoff investigated and found that, while it's true that Democrats of the day used every trick to deny black people the vote, the GOP didn't register black voters either. An individual Republican worker in the county registrar's office would do it—only in secret—and only if the voter agreed to register as a Republican. The party didn't contest the disenfranchisement of blacks, in other words, it only handed out favors. It's not quite the outstanding moral image Condoleezza Rice's story conjured. Neither was John Rice quite the sort of Republican that party faithful might imagine on hearing his daughter's words.

John Rice was a close friend of Ralph Abernathy, a key player in the civil rights mobilization in Birmingham. In later years, Rice raised money for Dr King. He opposed the tactics of the demonstrations, but not their goals. Like many black parents, he saw no reason to put children at extra risk, but he recognized the significance of what was going on. Rice did not release his students from class to protest, but he didn't punish them for skipping out, either. And when marchers filled the city's streets and jails, he took his daughter down to see. Condoleezza says she remembers riding on her father's shoulders at the age of eight, to watch history being made.[22]

That the Rices remained safe had much to do with privilege, but there was something else as well. After a bomb devastated the home of the Rices' friend Arthur Shores (one of the leading lawyers in the state) and another was thrown nearby where they lived, John Rice took up a shotgun and patrolled the neighborhood with local men. Clearly he didn't believe in intellectual armor alone. Condoleezza left that part out when she spoke to the GOP.

After all, self-improvement is a fine idea, but it can't save a life. The families of the four girls murdered in the 16th St Baptist Church found that out. The murdered girls were dance-class, flute-class, know-where-they're-going girls just like Rice until they were buried in the church bomb's blast.

Rice entered college with the intention of becoming a concert pianist. She had been studying with her grandmother since the age of three. Her mother denied her request to give up the piano at ten, because, she said, "You're not old enough or good enough to make that decision."[23] She carried on, practicing, playing, studying, day in and day out, until junior year in college when she says she realized at a music camp that she would never make it to Carnegie Hall. "I lacked virtuoso talent and I hated to practice," she told CNN. "And I realized that if I continued with music, I was destined for a career not at Carnegie Hall, but in a piano bar, or perhaps teaching thirteen-year-olds to murder Beethoven."

At seventeen, after dedicating years of her life to the instrument, she looked around at the talent she was up against, did some calculations and quit. Her friend Kiron Skinner says Rice tends to make tough decisions clinically this way. "She doesn't believe in wasting time," Skinner says. "Especially on things and people you have no power to change."[24]

How Rice felt about failing at her mother's dream is unclear. One gets the impression Rice doesn't pause too long over feelings. "Instead of studying Russian composers, I decided to study Russian generals," she says.[25]

At Denver University, Rice cast about for a new major and took a class from Josef Korbel, a Czech refugee who taught international affairs. Korbel happened to be familiar with the ambitious girl phenomenon. His own daughter, Madeleine Albright, became secretary of state under President Clinton. Maybe it was Korbel's mentoring style that suited Rice, or his "outsider" perspective on US power that resonated with her own. DU Professor Alan Gilbert co-taught classes on communism with Korbel. According to Gilbert, in Nazi-occupied Czechoslovakia Korbel was a left-wing social democrat, all of whose friends were communists. "He was afraid of the workers in the streets but they were the ones fighting fascism,"[26] says Gilbert. In Korbel's on-the-sidelines relationship to the anti-Nazi resistance of his youth, Rice may have found a parallel to her own distance from Birmingham's history-making children. Korbel came to the United States and shifted from being a left-leaning social democrat to an anti-communist centrist, tilting right. He was searching for a niche for himself in the US and found one. Rice was searching too. Whatever the cause, her passion switched, from piano to international politics.

Studying with Korbel, Rice became interested in Russian language and politics. She wrote a year-long paper on the politics and music of the Soviet Union, says Gilbert.

It was at Notre Dame University, Indiana, where she studied for her Master's, however, that Rice became fascinated with Soviet military might. Her father, John, had researched possible graduate schools for his daughter. Notre Dame had one of the country's leading Soviet studies centers at the time and, in 1974, Rice began to study the Russian military. The balance of

forces between the Cold War superpowers was the issue of the
day. In 1972, Richard Nixon had signed the historic Anti-
Ballistic Missile Treaty and SALT I (the Strategic Arms Lim-
itation Treaty). In 1975, the Soviet Union, the United States
and thirty-three other nations signed the Helsinki Accords, a
pledge to uphold human rights. Helsinki also recognized Soviet
dominion over the Baltic states of Estonia, Latvia, and
Lithuania. At Notre Dame, a conservative Catholic institution
concerned for the Catholics of Eastern Europe, the pact must
have been seen as mixed news at best.

In 1975, Rice toyed with the idea of following her cousin
Connie to law school (Connie was then studying law at Harvard), but Korbel persuaded her to return to the Graduate
School of International Studies at DU, of which he was one of
the founders. There, Rice began learning Czech and continued
her study of the influence of the Soviet military. Most research
of the period relied almost exclusively on Soviet documents,
but under the influence of Korbel, Rice studied Czech sources
and made a dramatic impression.[27]

As part of her dissertation research Rice took a seven-week
trip to the USSR, where she got to visit the concert halls where
Tchaikovsky worked. She became fluent in Russian. Upon her
return, she traveled to the other superpower capital,
Washington, where she took up an internship at the Department of State.

It's not clear what Rice made of what she saw of the Carter
administration. She says that she voted for Carter in 1976 but
by 1980 she had lost her faith in the Democrat. After the
USSR's invasion of Afghanistan Carter said he was shocked and

saddened and that his opinion of the Russians had "changed most drastically." He embargoed grain sales to the USSR, called for a boycott of the 1980 Moscow Olympics, and postponed ratification of SALT II. Rice says that she thought Carter's response was feeble. "I remember thinking, 'What did you think you were dealing with? This is a horrible government—of course they invaded some foreign country!' " she told *Vogue*.[28]

In 1981, fresh out of graduate school, Rice received a fellowship at Stanford University's Center for International Security and Arms Control. It was a first. The center had never before awarded such a fellowship to a graduate from a non-elite university, let alone a woman, let alone an African-American woman. Almost immediately she was appointed assistant professor—unquestionably an affirmative-action appointment. Rice's telling of her history has become increasingly vague on a few points over the years. One is when she first voted for Ronald Reagan. The other is the degree to which she has benefited from affirmative action, but even she accepts that in '81, the program worked for her. "They didn't need another Soviet specialist," she told *Vogue*. "But they asked themselves, 'How often does a black female who could diversify our ranks come along?' "[29] (Actually, she first benefited from affirmative action when her father was brought to Denver and helped her to secure a place at his university.)

The Reagan question is trickier. Rice likes to say now that she first voted Republican in 1980. In her current political home, Gipper-love is pretty much the entry-price. American Enterprise fellow and Soviet specialist Anders Aslund remembers Rice making much of the fact that she was a Republican in a Democrat-dominated faculty when he met her for the first time in 1984. "She made a big thing . . . that she was the only black, female Republican on the Stanford faculty," says Aslund. "I mean she really advertised that she was a Republican in circles where it was not popular."[30]

But in that very same year, Rice also worked as a foreign-policy advisor to Democratic Senator Gary Hart's disastrous primary campaign. Perhaps Rice was still considering her options. Professor Alan Gilbert, with whom Rice took five seminars at DU (including one on "Just and Unjust Wars"), got the impression that Rice was very enthusiastic about Hart's agenda.

"Rice was a thoughtful and bold student whom it was a privilege to teach," he says. A longtime activist who teaches Marxism and radical politics, Professor Gilbert stayed in touch with his former student during her first few years at Stanford, and remembers that when she was hired they joked about the university counting her six times in their affirmative-action statistics. "She outdid the Holy Trinity. They counted her in three separate departments," Gilbert chuckles.

He remembers Rice talking in disparaging terms about Caspar Weinberger. Then Ronald Reagan's secretary of defense, Weinberger made frequent visits to the Stanford-based Hoover Institution, a place the *Christian Science Monitor* has called "the West Coast's citadel of anti-Communism."[31] Gradually, says Gilbert, Rice changed.

"Caspar clearly had something that I didn't," Rice's former professor reflects. Rice stopped being in touch with Gilbert before the end of the decade. (He sent her his latest book, *Must Global Politics Constrain Democracy?*, halfway through the George W. for President campaign.[32] Three years later, he was still waiting for a response.)

By the late 1980s Rice was not only a high-performance professor, earning teaching awards and campus honors, but she had become amazingly knowledgeable about Soviet troop arrangements in Eastern Europe. Brent Scowcroft ran into her at Stanford in 1984 and invited her to attend foreign-policy meetings at the Aspen Institute, and then in Washington.

These were big years for a young Sovietologist with an interest in military matters. Ronald Reagan and Mikhail Gorbachev were holding "summits," the first in Geneva in 1985, the next in Reykjavik the following year. The rhetoric of the day was all about cooperation and détente, but the two leaders were actually at loggerheads. Gorbachev wanted to extend the Anti-Ballistic Missile Treaty in order to delay development and deployment of a costly new generation of missiles; Reagan (and "Cap" Weinberger, and Richard Perle, his assistant) wanted to escape the treaty altogether and forge ahead with, among other things, weapons in space, or "Star Wars."

To a close observer it must have been clear that Reagan was using "arms control" as means of superpower control and, ultimately, defeat. Reagan believed that the Soviet Union's inefficient economy could not survive real competition with the United States over armaments. His long-term plan (articulated in a speech to the Chicago Council on Foreign Relations in 1980) was not cooperation, but domination—the same goal embraced by the administration of George W. Bush today.

US policy towards the Soviet Union needed to change from "balance" to overwhelm, declared Ronald Reagan:

> First it must be based on firm convictions, inspired by a clear vision of and belief in America's future. Second, it calls for a strong economy based on the free market system which gave us unchallenged leadership in creative technology. Third, and very simply, we must have the unquestioned [military] ability to preserve world peace and our national security.[33]

The National Security Strategy that Rice released in September 2002 contains virtually the same language. "In pursuit of our goals, our first imperative is to clarify what we stand for," begins the NSS of 2002, and it sets out as its goals: "We must build and maintain our defenses beyond challenge," actively "pre-empt" proliferation by other powers . . . US power must be "unparalleled," wrote Rice.

The trends that define the present—reconfiguring nations, toppling governments, and challenging arms control—were already emerging years ago when Rice was a full-time professor as well as student. The European map was being redrawn, the US saw to it that the governments of Nicaragua, Grenada and later Panama were overturned—the terror attacks of September 11 may have accelerated the timetable, but the momentum had been building since Reagan. And Condoleezza Rice has occupied a ringside seat—either in government or very close by—for every moment of it.

By the end of its first term, Reagan's administration had hiked the US military budget to historic highs. Ignoring a million people who massed for disarmament in New York's Central Park, the Democratic-controlled House of Representatives went right along. What strengthened Reagan's hand on national defense was terrorism. A 1983 truck attack on the US marine barracks in Beirut killed 241 Americans; in '85, Shiite extremists hijacked a commercial TWA flight on its way from Athens to Beirut. In October that same year, four US F-14 Tomcats intercepted a plane carrying the hijackers of the Italian cruise ship the *Achille Lauro*. Reagan addressed himself in fine Hollywood style to terrorists: "You can run," he said, "but you can't hide."

The run and hide dictum was selective, mind you. When a Berlin discotheque favored by Americans in Germany was bombed, killing two US servicemen and a Turkish woman and injuring sixty Americans, Reagan ordered the US Air Force to strike the Libyan capital, Tripoli. When the news broke that US bombs had hit the home of the Libyan leader Qaddafi, killing his young daughter, the President told the nation that conclusive evidence had been found tying Libya to the Berlin bombing. It turned out there was no such evidence.

Just thirteen months after the bombing of Tripoli, the US took no reprisals against Iraq when Iraqi planes, engaged in the war with Iran, fired a missile that killed thirty-seven US sailors aboard the USS *Stark* in the Persian Gulf. Iraq's President Saddam Hussein apologized for the deaths, and Reagan accepted the apology. Iraq was a close US ally at the time.

Beginning early in 1982, when Iraq was still on the State Department list of terrorist-supporting nations, Secretary of State George P. Shultz lobbied for delivery of crop-duster

helicopters to Baghdad. Shultz, who had joined the administration after an eight-year stint heading up the San Francisco-
based Bechtel Group, dispatched his Middle East envoy Donald
Rumsfeld to meet Saddam Hussein to advance a joint US–Iraq
oil pipeline project to be built by Bechtel.[34]

Right through the Reagan and into the first Bush administration, the CIA supported arming Iraq against Iran. Reagan
official Howard Teicher, who was a National Security Council
staffer from 1982 to '87, testified in court that "I personally
attended meetings in which CIA Director Casey or CIA Deputy
Director [Robert] Gates noted the need for Iraq to have certain
weapons such as cluster bombs and anti-armor penetrators in
order to stave off Iranian attacks."[35] In part, some believe, the
administration was still hoping to secure Saddam Hussein's
agreement on the plan for a Bechtel-built oil pipeline. The Bush
administration pushed Congress to continue supplying Iraq,
even after the gassing of Iraqi Kurds and Iranians in 1988.
(Shultz's helicopters are believed to have been used in the
attack. The chemical weapons may well have come from the
petrochemical plant Hussein ordered, built by Bechtel, in the
early 1980s.)[36]

Condoleezza Rice did not just watch these affairs as the decade
progressed, she played her role in them. Rice published two
books during the 1980s: *Uncertain Allegiance: the Soviet Union and
the Czechoslovak Army 1948–83*, and *The Gorbachev Era*, a collection of essays she co-edited during her first fellowship at the
Hoover Institution. In 1986, she spent a year at the Pentagon, on
a rare fellowship from the Council on Foreign Relations working
as a special assistant to the director of the joint chiefs of staff. If

she hadn't met him before, Rice would have met Colin Powell at this time. Powell was a military assistant to the secretary of defense, and very involved in arms policy and the Moscow summit of 1988. Powell and Rice have family connections, too. Powell's wife, Alma, was also born and raised in Birmingham. In fact, Colin Powell's father-in-law had been principal at Ullman High School, where Rice's father had worked.

Brent Scowcroft brought Rice back to Washington, in 1989, to join his staff at the National Security Council. By this time, Powell was chairman of the joint chiefs of staff. Robert Gates, a Sovietologist, was Scowcroft's deputy. Rice received several promotions on the job, becoming director of Soviet and Eastern European affairs.

There was a lot going on. Rice traveled with President Bush Sr to Poland to celebrate Polish independence, and to Germany to mark the fall of the Berlin wall. She attended the Malta summit in December 1989, where Bush first met Gorbachev. Bush introduced Rice as the woman who "tells me everything I know about the Soviet Union," and Gorbachev famously turned to Rice saying, "I hope you know a lot.")[37]

In public, Rice was a big success, appearing on television, speaking to the press, getting written up in *Cosmopolitan* magazine as one of the "new women of Washington."[38] Inside the White House, it was a different story. Indeed, in the memory of most of the men who worked with her then and went on to work with her again under George W., the big thing about Rice is that she was doggedly, disastrously wrong on the most important development to take place on her watch, in her policy area.

To put it briefly, the Bush cabinet was split over the US relationship with Mikhail Gorbachev. The President, Scowcroft, James Baker, (secretary of state) Powell, Gates, and Rice were on one side; Dick Cheney (then secretary of defense), Paul Wolfowitz (his deputy), and Lewis Libbey (now Cheney's chief of staff) were on the other. The Bush faction was what you'd have to call the ''conservatives,'' to Cheney's radicals. They wanted to cling to what they knew and roughly supported the Soviet leader's vision of a reformed but still coherent Soviet Union. The Cheney crew anticipated the break-up of the USSR and wanted to encourage it. ''Regime change'' writ large in Europe and Asia was what they were after, with resulting opportunities for American interests if the US got in on the action early.

Bush and his team were slow to grasp the scope of the changes that were seizing Europe, slow to encourage the unification of Germany, slow to support the break-up of the Soviet Union. A speech Bush gave with Rice's assistance in Kiev became notorious as the ''Chicken Kiev'' speech because in it, the President urged the people of the Ukraine to remain part of the USSR. At the same time,[39] the President balked at giving Gorbachev back-up that was worth anything—either at arms talks, or in terms of foreign aid—and the Soviet leader's domestic currency took a nose-dive.

In what remains her most famous move from that period, in 1989, Rice physically blocked Boris Yeltsin from storming into the Oval Office. Yeltsin, then a rising Russian politician, was to meet with Scowcroft, not the President (Bush was going to ''drop by'' unofficially, according to the plan). The idea was not to rock Mikhail Gorbachev's standing as the head of the Soviet Union. Rice stood her ground, explaining that the meeting would be with the national security advisor or no one and finally she persuaded a very furious Yeltsin to back down.

The incident is reported as "cute" by the media, but to Cheney-ites it's very symbolic. Two years later, the Soviet Union broke up, Yeltsin became the region's most powerful leader, Gorbachev floundered and resigned, and instead of driving the action in a transforming eastern Europe and central Asia, the US was left to play catch-up. Cheney and Wolfowitz left the Bush administration with a silent victory—their radical world view had been right—and Rice, who claimed expertise in just this area, had been wrong. They were the loyal losers, but they aren't forgetters. Neither is George W. Bush, who was involved in his father's re-election campaign by then. When it came to foreign policy, father Bush sidelined the extremists; son Bush was not going to. Fast forward to 2000 and one can only assume that the more the candidate and party talked publicly about Rice's brilliance, the more it must have smarted. The public didn't know the back-story, but Cheney, Wolfowitz, Rumsfeld and W. did. Like Powell, Rice entered the second Bush presidency weakened and vulnerable.

"Rice? She was wrong, but she was loyal, and her views didn't seem to be too rigid," says Anders Aslund, who spent much time on Capitol Hill in those years. After she left Washington to resume her position at Stanford in March 1991, Rice continued her service to the administration in the media, appearing on ABC's *Nightline* and elsewhere. NSC director Robert Gates was facing stiff grilling during his confirmation to become director of central intelligence (DCI). Gates was accused of having prepared false testimony for former CIA director Bill Casey on the Iran–Contra Scandal, the illegal campaign to foment a coup in Nicaragua. He had completely missed the boat on the collapse of the Soviet Union. Most damaging of all, it appeared he had skewed intelligence to mislead Congress into permitting arms sales and loans to Saddam Hussein's Iraq for two years after the gassing of the Iranians and the Kurds. Iraq's access to US agricultural products and biological agents including anthrax and botulinium toxins was first cut off on August 2 1990, the day of the Iraqi invasion of Kuwait.[40]

Gates's confirmation went ahead nonetheless, boosted by Condoleezza Rice, his close colleague. "Gates is the best man for the job in all its dimensions and ought to be confirmed without delay . . . We could not ask for a better CIA director," wrote Rice in September 1991.[41]

By that time, Rice was settling down in civilian life. The revolving door between government and business had spun her out into a cushy spot. One of her last big jobs before leaving the first Bush administration had been to lead Gorbachev's first visit across the United States. The story that gets told is that at the airport in San Francisco, a Secret-Service agent who had no idea who Rice was tried to prevent her from stepping onto the tarmac with the rest of the group. "He was right in my face in a confrontational way," Rice told the press (but there was supposedly nothing racial about it—President Bush later said that he was satisfied "it was a big, big mistake and nothing egregious, or singling her out of any kind").[42] What is not mentioned is one of the outcomes of that visit.

In 1979, Soviet geologists had made the world's biggest oil discovery in three decades—the Tengiz oilfield—in what was then the Soviet republic of Kazakhstan on the Caspian Sea. The Tengiz field had an estimated six to nine billion barrels of oil reserves (more than the North Sea) and the San Francisco-based Chevron Corporation wanted a piece of it. The company had been negotiating for years. In June 1990, Chevron's vice-president finally signed a contract with a top Soviet energy official *during* Gorbachev's trip.[43]

Almost immediately upon returning to California, Rice joined the board of directors of Chevron. The company expanded their board by one to include Rice (from twelve board members to thirteen). The Chevron directorship guaranteed her $35,000 a year in addition to her Stanford salary, plus $1,500 per meeting (plus expenses—there were at least six meetings a year). She assumed a spot on the directors' public policy committee, one of six, alongside Carla Hills (former US trade representative) and Kenneth Derr, a Chevron executive. The committee held additional meetings to address Chevron's public policy questions. By her tenth year with Chevron, Rice owned stocks worth $255,000.[44] She also had a tanker named after her, just like Shultz: the *Condoleezza Rice*. (It's part of a long-standing practice to name tankers after board members, according to a Chevron company spokesperson. It's supposedly an honor, but it's also a commitment. It requires accepting the risk that the boat bearing one's name might be an *Exxon Valdez* waiting to spill.)

After Kazakh independence, a whole new deal needed to be

drawn up. According to Rice's biographer, Antonia Felix, Condoleezza worked on the Tengiz oilfield contract for Chevron. "Her expertise on the states that made up the former Soviet Union made her a valuable asset for Chevron's oil interests in Kazakhstan. She worked extensively on those deals, including their plan to help build a pipeline from the Tengiz oilfield across southern Russia to a Russian port on the Black Sea," writes Felix in an effusive volume published in 2002.[45]

As it happened, Dick Cheney could help with the brokering—he joined the twelve-member Oil Advisory Board of Kazakhstan after leaving the Bush administration (the independent board advised the government on plans to develop the oilfields).[46] Cheney advised on the deals, then joined one of the companies with the most to gain by them—the Halliburton Corporation, of which he became CEO in 1995. Halliburton, the world's largest oil-industry supply company, works hand in glove with the drillers. In Africa, Asia and the former Soviet Republics, where Chevron went, Halliburton was sure to follow. Halliburton built the refineries on the Tengiz field. Whatever their differences may have been in the Bush administration, Rice and Cheney were on the same team in the oil world.[47]

A key person in Rice's segue into the business world was George P. Shultz. After he left the Reagan administration, Rice and Shultz became acquainted. The former secretary of state returned to San Francisco's Bay Area, where he rejoined Bechtel, this time as a board member. He also took up a seat on the board of advisors of Stanford's Institute for International Studies, where Rice was on the staff. (Stephen Bechtel, a former CEO of the company, also sits on the SIS board.) Shultz

took up a fellowship at the Hoover Institution, where he was
working with Rice's student and friend, Kiron Skinner on his
memoir.

''Shultz helped her move into the corporate world,'' says
Skinner. Shultz served on the Chevron board before Rice joined
it. In quick succession she followed him to the Transamerica
board, where she served for eight years, and later the Charles
Schwab board, where she and Shultz served concurrently. At
J.P. Morgan Chase she became a member of the International
Advisory Council, which Shultz directed.[48] ''Shultz is a critical
person in Rice's life,'' says Skinner. A four-time cabinet
member, he's been a critical person in the lives of four
Republican presidents, too.

In 1979, it was Shultz who pulled together Ronald Reagan's
foreign-policy team. Nineteen years later, it was Shultz who
invited Rice to George W. Bush's ranch, where she became a
regular advisor, eventually joining Bush's presidential campaign, and then his cabinet.[49]

A second Bush administration seemed an unlikely prospect in
1993. George the first was out of office. Clinton had been
elected. Rice told *The New York Times* that she had to put aside
plans for a book on the Kazakhstan oilfields when she was
approached by the President of Stanford to take the post of
provost.[50] In April 1993, Chevron concluded a $20 billion
agreement with the Kazakh government to form the Tengiz-
chevronoil joint venture.[51] In May, Rice was given tenure at
Stanford. In June, she was offered the provostship.

At Stanford, Rice was the first African American, the first
woman and the youngest person ever to hold the position. Not

only was she responsible for a $1.5 billion annual budget, she was also the chief academic officer, making policy on hiring, tenure and pay that affected the entire 1,400-strong campus teaching staff. The university faced a $20 million deficit. In the first year alone, Rice cut $6 million from the budget, and caused an uproar by firing Cecilia Burciaga, the first Chicana who had managed to make it up the administrative ladder. An assistant dean of students and one of the most popular resident fellows on campus, Burciaga was considered by many the "soul of Stanford," but that was of no consequence to Rice. Citing budget concerns, she refused to back down even after students went on hunger strike for Burciaga's reinstatement.

There were more demonstrations to come. Stanford distinguished itself at the time as one of the least diverse among the elite universities. The percentage of African Americans in the student body was actually declining.[52] Of the seven schools that make up the university, all were headed by men. Women constituted just 11 percent of the tenured faculty, way below the national average. In 1993, a special committee of women staff members put the administration on notice. Five years later, the female teaching staff issued a follow-up report showing that there had been barely any improvement. Morale, they declared, was low, verging on "crisis."

"Nobody was saying we needed to lower standards. What we were saying was there were many ways to turn things around,"[53] Professor Estelle Freedman, a member of the women's caucus, explains. Scrutinizing hiring and tenure procedures was one way; investigating charges of bias was another. The university could develop innovative courses (an update on

John Rice's "Black Experience . . ." seminar perhaps?) Above all, to turn around the university's reputation, "we needed to improve the climate," the women declared. The caucus's report called on Stanford to "show moral leadership." It's an argument Rice's father would have appreciated.

Rice's response was to debate the data angrily. "It's hard to imagine a male administrator behaving as she did," says Freedman. "It was probably easier for a black woman to be that antagonistic."[54]

Sharon Holland has a different perspective on the matter. Holland was one of very few African Americans in the group of incoming teaching staff when she joined Stanford's English department in the mid-1990s. An out lesbian with progressive politics, Holland remembers being very suspicious when Rice invited her to drop by the Provost's office for a meeting. "The first thing I said to her was, 'Why? Where I come from you are the devil.' Condi just smiled." They met every few months for several years. "There was a pernicious old-boy network on campus . . . and I felt that Condi really wanted to look out for me," says Holland, now at the University of Illinois.

Holland quit in frustration and grief after a female friend at Stanford committed suicide, having been denied tenure under new, even more rigorous, rules. The so-called "diversity" situation was intolerable, says Holland. But she doesn't put all the blame on Rice. The problems went far beyond the Provost, she says. As for Rice's policy decisions, her take on Rice is simple: "She's a conservative, what do you want? If she had done the same things in another body, would there have been the same outrage?"[55]

Holland has a point. The staff at Stanford should have known well what to expect when they learnt of Rice's appointment. She'd been connected to the Hoover Institution for a decade already, and her relationship with the Bush administration was clear. In 1992, Rice shared a platform with Patrick Buchanan at the Republican National Convention in Houston. She may not share the far Right's views on homosexuality, affirmative action or reproductive rights (Rice is "mildly pro-choice" or "a pro-choice evangelist," depending on whom she's talking to), but she's proved very willing to accommodate herself to right-wing masters.

As for race-politics, Rice belongs to the "solidarity" school. She has helped advance individual African Americans, especially women. Kiron Skinner and Jendayi Frazier—both Rice's students—are two of a tiny number of well-placed African-American women working in international affairs. (Frazier, who specializes in African affairs, was hired, with Rice's help, by Denver University, then by the Kennedy School at Harvard, and brought by Rice to George W.'s NSC.) Rice also helped to create the Center for New Generation in East Palo Alto. With her father's help, she founded the project to provide after-school and summer-enrichment programs for underserved local public-school students. John Rice, who moved to live close to his daughter when his wife died (after a long struggle with breast cancer in 1985), fought for playing fields, formed a speakers' club and advocated more money for area schools.[56]

In 1992, the GOP showed Rice off at the RNC in an effort, if not to win black voters, then at least to alienate fewer of them. (The 1988 Bush campaign played directly to race-panic when it blamed Michael Dukakis for the abuse of a Massachusetts prisoner-furlough program that led to the release of murderer Willie Horton, an African American who went on to commit a rape and an assault.)[57] Republican leaders also made it known that Rice had been considered to fill California Governor Pete Wilson's seat in the Senate (even though the Governor actually chose someone else). Then and since, the party consciously used Rice's presence to send a message about "diversity."

But racial solidarity like Rice's is not necessarily a sign of progressive politics. To the contrary, there is a long historical tradition going back to Booker T. Washington of black racial solidarity wedded to black political conservatism. Moreover, as the party knows, Rice's role is not to formulate a civil rights agenda but to bolster Bush's foreign policy. She's been very much inside that particular fold—and making no trouble—for years.

Kiron Skinner, the editor of several volumes of Ronald Reagan's letters and a member of Donald Rumsfeld's Defense Policy Board, confirms that Rice can be very tough and reluctant to show vulnerability, especially when she is in a position of power. The royal treatment Rice received in the corporate world did nothing to boost her humility, and she brought to Stanford an almost superhuman confidence from her time in government.

"There was this feeling, 'If I can unify Germany within NATO without a major war, then I can do anything,' " Skinner claims. The same attitude, she says, remains with Rice still: "She does not believe that there is anything she cannot do, and

I don't believe she thinks there is anything the United States cannot achieve.''

Rice didn't resolve the campus bias dispute. By the time she stepped down as Provost to return to Hoover and to advise George W. Bush, the university was facing 400 pages of complaints alleging sex discrimination and affirmative-action lapses. A Labor Department investigation was underway.[58] Ironic as it seemed to many of the female teaching staff she left behind, Rice departed Stanford only to emerge within months as a leading figure in George W. Bush's ''W is for Women'' campaign.

Bush's run for the presidency featured some glaring gaffes on the foreign-policy front. He wanted to ''keep good relations with the Grecians,'' he told *The Economist* magazine in June 1999. Andy Hiller of WHDH in Boston flummoxed the candidate by asking Bush to name several foreign leaders. ''Can you name the President of Chechnya?'' asked Hiller. ''No. Can You?'' snapped Bush. He went on to misname the President of Taiwan, and call Pakistan's leader (Pervez Musharraf) ''the General'' and ''this guy.'' Bush couldn't name the Prime Minister of India. The campaign hit another bump when, in reply to a question about the Taliban, Bush shook his head and stood mute until a reporter hinted: ''repression of women in Afghanistan . .?'' ''Oh, I thought you said, 'some band.' The Taliban in Afghanistan! Absolutely. Repressive,'' said Bush. ''A key to foreign policy is to rely on reliance,'' Bush told *The Washington Post* just six days before the election.[59]

Someone else might have run screaming from any suggestion that they take responsibility for the candidate's foreign-policy training. Not Rice. She basked in the glory, most notably on the GOP stage in Philadelphia. On a night dedicated to "diversity," Rice took her turn in the spotlight for the second time at a Republican nominating convention.

She talked about her father (her "first Republican") and Granddaddy Rice (whom George W. "would have loved"), and the United States. "In America, with education and hard work, it really does not matter where you come from; it matters only where you are going," she said.

Rice wants to have it both ways; for it to matter not a jot where some Americans come from, and for it to matter 100 percent in her case. The truth is, it matters a lot where Rice came from—not just the Birmingham part, but all the rest as well. GOP spin notwithstanding, there is nothing about Rice's success that was predetermined. Her trajectory wasn't decided by place or bloodline or paternal preconditioning; it was the product of a set of choices. Angela Davis and Connie Rice and Chip Berlet made theirs; Rice chose world politics and the exercise of power. That doesn't mean her history hasn't shaped her, but forty years after she left Birmingham, the traces of her childhood influences are more than matched by the mark of military men and oil magnates and two Republican presidents.

Rice employs her own specific story to suggest something is generally true about race, but her success represents her race's advance about as accurately as George W. Bush's presidency represents the wealth and power of most white Americans. As Rice spoke to the GOP in Philadelphia in 2000, the American neighborhoods and schools beyond remained racially divided. According to the census of that year, although white men make up only 48 percent of the college-educated workforce, they hold over 90 percent of the top jobs in the news media, 96 percent of CEO positions, and 85 percent of the tenured places on college faculties. African Americans are more than twice as likely as whites to live in poverty, but half as likely to have a job; almost twice as many blacks as whites were medically uninsured. And long after the Civil Rights Act, there still remains one legal way to deny a man a job and the right to vote. Three out of every ten African-American males will serve time in prison, a status that renders it legal for employers to deny them work, and for states (like Florida) to disenfranchise them.[60]

As for the US role in the world, Rice came to her second Bush administration as a director of Chevron, a corporation which stands accused of human violations in Africa. It is the US company with the largest operation in Nigeria. Oil revenues provide 90 percent of the Nigerian government's foreign earnings, more than enough to pay for its military, which, in exchange for the government's share of the oil profits, does whatever is required to keep corporate operations running smoothly. In the mid-1990s, large parts of the Delta, notably Ogoniland, a small area where demonstrations had led to the closure of oil production, were occupied by military forces for five full years. Suppression led to the killing of leading Ogoni activists, including writer Ken Saro-Wiwa.

Throughout the period in which Rice was a director of Chevron, shareholders brought resolutions before the board seeking reform of the company's dealings with the corrupt Nigerian government. One such resolution (in 1996) called for

the company to press that government "to cease the perse-
cution of Nigerian political activists." Two more called on
Chevron to develop and report to stockholders general
guidelines for company investment "in all countries experi-
encing political unrest and human rights violations."[61] The
committee that reviews such resolutions and then advises
shareholders is the public policy committee, of which Rice was
a dutiful member. In each and every case, Chevron's board of
directors turned such proposals down.

In 1999, plaintiffs in Nigeria sued Chevron in state court in
San Francisco. They charge the company with complicity in the
killings of non-violent protestors on two separate occasions in
1998 and '99. Chevron denies responsibility for the killings,
but when Chevron executive Kenneth Derr was asked point-
blank in a radio interview if Chevron would officially demand
that the Nigerian military not shoot protestors at Chevron sites,
Derr's response was, "No."[62]

According to the complaint, some of the plaintiffs were
summarily executed, others were burned in a fire set during the
attack, or tortured by police thereafter. One plaintiff, Ebiere
Eferasua, describes being shot from a helicoptor as she stood on
the ground below, waving. Her grandmother, Bripale Oroupa,
who was also shot, fell to the ground at her side and later died.
Eferasua was seven years old, about the same age Rice was
when she was brought by her father to the street-corner's edge
and watched "Bull" Connor's police set dogs on her school-
mates.

Ask Rice about the affair, as I did in July 2000, and the same
woman who will wax eloquent about the industrious ambitions

of her family will quickly change the subject. Chevron does business on six continents and in twenty-five countries. A corporation like ours can't pick and choose the governments they deal with, said Rice. Besides, she added, corporations have a responsibility to defend the interests of their shareholders.[63]

In 2002, more than 600 women from the villages around the Niger Delta took over a Chevron terminal, demanding jobs for their men, investment in their communities and an end to the killing of local residents by soldiers claiming to be acting in defense of the oil company. Floating on what Paul Wolfowitz might call "a sea of oil,"[64] the land on which the Delta people live is some of the wealthiest in the world, but its people are some of the poorest. After decades of oil development, the land is racked by environmental damage: oil spills dot the coastline, corporate-built canals permit sea water to leach salt into the drinking supply, eroding local farmland. "It is the women who fish and who farm," says Annie Brisibe, co-founder of Niger Delta Women for Justice. "When the water is spoiled, it is our babies who have to drink it. When the soil is poisoned, it's the girls who are pulled out of school to go to prostitution." The Niger people don't want wealth, she says. "We just want the basics: electricity, water, jobs, healthcare, peace, and some say in the use of our own resources."

Yet even after the transition to supposedly "democratic" rule in Nigeria, the government regularly uses its national military, not in defense of its people or the country's natural environment, but to "protect" supposedly imperiled foreign corporations.

Brisibe says Rice should come to the Niger Delta. "She is a

black woman like me. She should come see. She has the power to do something.''[65]

In June 2003, Rice did go to Nigeria (although not to the Delta) on a five-day visit to five African states with President George W. Bush and Secretary of State Colin Powell. The trip came at a tense moment for the United States, when the White House was eager to improve the country's image in the eyes of the world. US troops, without a United Nations mandate, were occupying Iraq, and the arguments the administration had given for that invasion were unraveling.

Rice, the nation's top national security advisor, was in a particularly awkward spot. After September 11 2001, she had claimed that the White House had had no prior knowledge that al-Qaeda was planning to hijack planes in a terrorist attack. That assertion was proving wrong. According to a bipartisan 9/11 commission report, ''Intelligence reports from December 1998 until the attacks said followers of bin Laden were planning to strike US targets, hijack US planes, and two individuals had successfully evaded checkpoints in a dry run at a New York airport.''[66]

Throughout 2002 and into 2003, Rice insisted that war with Iraq was only a last resort. In October 2002, she said on CBS, ''We're going to seek a peaceful solution to this. We think that one is possible.''[67] In March 2003, she claimed on ABC, ''We are still in a diplomatic phase here.''[68] But Richard Haass, Bush's director of policy planning at the State Department, who is very close to Rice, had told the press the decision had already been made by July 2002. When asked exactly when he learnt war in Iraq was definite, Haass said:

The moment was the first week of July [2002], when I had a meeting with Condi. I raised this issue about were we really sure that we wanted to put Iraq front and centre at this point, given the war on terrorism and other issues. And she said, essentially, that that decision's been made, don't waste your breath. And that was early July. So then when Powell had his famous dinner with the President, in early August 2002 [in which Powell persuaded Bush to take the question to the UN], the agenda was not whether Iraq, but how.[69]

In the run-up to the invasion of Iraq, Rice appeared almost daily on television. She can say things in a way that Donald Rumsfeld can't, and her public image is not so corporate. Besides, she's popular. In April 2003, a poll by a Sacramento Republican consultant found that Rice would "crush" Arnold Schwarzenegger in a GOP primary and defeat both the likely Democrats in the 2006 Governor's race in California.[70] Asked to run, at a Los Angeles Town Hall meeting in June 2003, she said, "I've got my hands full right now." It was an understatement.

Two days before the first anniversary of the 9/11 attacks, Rice told CNN's *Late Edition* that delaying action against Iraq would be dangerous. "We don't want the smoking gun to be a mushroom cloud," she said. "How long are we going to wait to deal with what is clearly a gathering threat against the United States, against our own allies and against his own region?"[71] Months after the invasion and occupation of Iraq in 2003, no such threat had been found when the Bush and Rice and Powell left for Africa.

On the eve of the trip, the President himself was forced to

admit that "evidence" on which he'd based the nuclear case against Saddam Hussein was false. Quizzed about Iraq's alleged attempt to procure uranium from the African state of Niger, National Security Advisor Condoleezza Rice talked to the press from Air Force One in the skies between South Africa and Uganda. The precise wording of the uranium allegation, which appeared in the President's State of the Union address in the immediate run-up to the assault on Iraq, had been approved by the CIA, she said. "The CIA cleared the speech in its entirety." But she wasn't blaming CIA director George Tenet, she added, saying he had served "very well." "I'm really not blaming anybody," Rice told reporters.[72]

She probably had too much on her mind just then to hear a garbled echo, but a decade earlier Rice had extolled the service of another CIA director. Then, Robert Gates, the agency's deputy director, stood accused of skewing intelligence to mislead Congress into arming Saddam Hussein. Now, ten years later, Rice was holding the CIA responsible for flawed intelligence which goaded Congress into destroying him. From a marginal player in a big-time corporate interest and congressional lying scandal, Rice has moved to the hot seat at the heart of another one.

US policy towards the Iraqi President may have changed, but US corporate interests in the region remain consistent. Shortly after he helped to secure the White House for George W. Bush, James Baker, at Dick Cheney's request, authored a report that called for weakening Saddam Hussein's regime through weapons inspections, followed by "military intervention" to take control of Iraqi oil, because "Iraq remains a destabilizing influence to the flow of oil to international markets from the Middle East. Unless the United States assumes a leadership role in the formation of new rules of the game,'' the report goes on, ''US firms, US consumers and the US government will be left in a weaker position.''[73]

In the absence of a Cold War adversary, US national interests have become increasingly synonymous with corporate interests. Call it the Chevron/Nigeria way of government. Vice-President Dick Cheney's National Energy Group reported in 2001 that the ''national interest'' required the President and the Secretary of State to ''support the [Caspian Sea] oil pipeline'' that will help ''oil companies operating in Kazakhstan'' get their oil to market.[74]

After the successful ousting of the Saddam Hussein regime, Chevron Texaco announced that it would be the first US company to win a contract for ten million barrels of Iraqi crude oil. Bechtel, on whose board George P. Shultz still sits, received one of the first and largest contracts to rebuild Iraq after the US bombardment. The Pentagon granted Halliburton subsidiary Kellogg, Brown and Root a two-year, no bid, $7 billion contract to do everything from putting out oil fires to laundry services.[75]

As Bush, Rice and Powell headed to Africa, some 200,000 US troops were stationed in and around Iraq, 10,000 remained in Afghanistan, and new military bases were settling in nearby Kazakhstan, Uzbekistan and throughout the former Soviet Republics and the Caspian states, all along the imagined route of an oil and gas pipeline to the east, in fact. The US has walked away from the Comprehensive Test Ban Treaty, the Anti-

Ballistic Missile Treaty, and the non-Proliferation Treaty, and signaled to the world that it is determined to launch a nuclear arms race in space. Truly, Ronald Reagan's "Peace through Strength" mission of domination has been realized. At least the strength part.

As Chevron knows, stability comes at a price. Luckily for the captains of industry who lead USA Inc., the bill gets passed to US taxpayers. Thanks to her time at Chevron, Rice is very used to justifying the use of military force in alleged defense of US oil interests. The people of the world, meanwhile, have become close kin to the women of the Niger Delta.

When the President was in Africa, Vice-President Cheney informed Congress that the troop deployment in Iraq would cost twice what the lawmakers had been told before the invasion—some $3.9 billion monthly for the next nine months, with the bills stretching into the indefinite future. The price is being paid in basic services. States in deficit are cutting back on healthcare, jobs, education—and all those after-school programs Condoleezza Rice claims to care so much about. In the week before his Africa trip, the President even supported a bill that gave the states authority to divert funds from Head Start, a federal program for disadvantaged students starting out. The first coordinator of Head Start in Alabama in 1961 was Condoleezza's father, John Wesley Rice Jr.[76]

At the 2000 convention, Rice said her reasons for joining the GOP had been different from her father's. "I found a party that sees me as an individual, not as part of a group," she said. It's not true—the party constantly draws attention to her race and her gender. (Her work with the Republicans' "Winning

Women'' campaign began as soon as that 2004 effort launched.) No matter. The very people who have no time for the
feminist maxim ''the personal is political'' love to deploy
personal homily for maximum political effect. ''I found a party
that believes that peace begins with strength,'' said Rice.

To judge by the printed record at least, her father measured
strength by a different yardstick. ''Young people who gave
their lives for the cause of freedom and for the cause of
eliminating useless war''—that's how John Rice, assistant dean
at the University of Denver, described the students slain at
Kent State and Jackson State in 1970. The occasion of his
speech was a campus rally held to commemorate their killings.
Looking into the crowd, he summoned every student to
embrace the responsibilities that come with privilege.

''As I look out at you, I know that you are the educators of
tomorrow, that you are the capitalists of tomorrow, that you
are the businessmen and the politicians of tomorrow. When
tomorrow comes, will you be the perpetuators of war or of
peace? Are you the generation to bring to America a lasting
peace? Or did your brothers and sisters at Kent and Jackson
State die in vain?''[77]

Dean Rice did not imagine at the time that one person would
become all four: educator, capitalist, business executive, and
politician—his daughter. He died just after she was appointed
to Bush's cabinet. By all accounts he was hugely proud. But has
Rice been a perpetuator of war or of peace? Her father asked
the right question. Look at Birmingham, East Palo Alto, the
Niger Delta, Basra, and Baghdad, and decide.

COVER GIRL

Karen Hughes

The most powerful woman in George W. Bush's presidential campaign got her professional start in large part thanks to the National Organization for Women (NOW).

As Karen Hughes (then Karen Parfitt) tells the story, she was a student at Southern Methodist University in Dallas, on track to a career in law, when she took a course and fell in love with journalism. "I've always been an arguer," she says.[1] In 1977, she landed an internship at Channel 5, the Dallas/Fort Worth NBC affiliate, and as *USA Today* put it, "with typical pluck" she parlayed it into a full-time job. "It was probably the last time anyone got hired straight out of college to do major-market news," says Hughes.[2]

Another way to look at it is that Hughes graduated in one of the all-time best years for American women wanting to make a career in journalism. A new federal law and women willing to use it were rattling open doors in previously white, male-dominated industries, and no profession was more rattled right at that moment than the high-profile worlds of broadcasting and print journalism.

In 1972, Congress passed the Equal Employment Opportunity Act, after vigorous lobbying by NOW. At *The New York Times*, the Associated Press, *The Washington Post*, *Newsday*, *Newsweek*, and NBC, women sued under the federal law and won. NBC (then a unit of RCA Corp.) agreed to pay 2,600 past and present women employees more than $1.75 million in settlement, rather than fight a sex-discrimination suit in federal court. The company also agreed to an affirmative-action program that would hire and train more females at every level.[3] The year was 1977 and, down in Dallas, at a small NBC affiliate, Karen Parfitt came looking for work.

The Equal Employment Opportunity Act required the government to collect data. In the 1970s, the US Commission on Civil Rights conducted an investigation that declared the television industry guilty of job discrimination and of perpetuating racial and sexual stereotypes. The Federal Communications Commission (FCC) took broadcasters to task. Litigation or fear of litigation forced the media's men's clubs open, and a generation of women worked their way inside. It was true when Susan Faludi pointed it out in 1991, and it's still true more than ten years later, that the most successful women in the industry today are women who broke through in those years: Jane Pauley, Lesley Stahl, Judy Woodruff, Diane Sawyer, Connie Chung.[4] In 1976—a first for a woman—ABC paid Barbara Walters $1 million to co-anchor an evening network newscast. And in 1977, NBC Channel 5 hired Parfitt. Smart, strong, blonde, blue-eyed, and free to work late and on weekends, she had just what it takes to make a good news woman and, unlike the legions of similar candidates who came before—and after—

her, Parfitt had the women's rights revolution and the federal government at her back.

In her first year on the job, Texas played host to some makers of feminist history. Thirty thousand people—mostly women—came to Houston that November to attend a federally-funded national women's conference, part of the United Nations' International Women's Year. The IWY was a broad, bipartisan affair where First Ladies (Rosalyn Carter, Betty Ford, Lady Bird Johnson) brushed elbows with activists (Coretta Scott King, Gloria Steinem, Bella Abzug). They talked about federally-funded childcare, equal pay, reproductive and sexual freedom, and the creation of a cabinet-level women's department in Washington.

Phyllis Schlafly came to Houston, too. A right-wing attorney, Schlafly was the leading voice of anti-communist, anti-feminist, pro-religious activism at the time. As IWY delegates piled into the Houston Coliseum to show their support for the Equal Rights Amendment (which was just then nearing its ratification deadline and was stalled three state votes short of becoming law), Schlafly, the director of both the anti-equal rights campaign Stop ERA and the conservative pressure group Eagle Forum, convened her followers at a ''pro-family'' rally at the Astro Arena across town.

''We reject the anti-family goal of the Equal Rights Amendment and the International Women's Year,'' declared Schlafly. People waved their bibles at her from the stalls. *The Washington Post*'s reporters spotted a group of women who held a confederate flag and a banner that read ''LA White Women Oppose IWY Reds, Feds, Dikes and Kikes'' (*sic*) on one side,

and on the other, "Abzug, Friedan, Steinem Are All Anti-
Christian Jews."[5]

The racket out of Houston reverberated across the nation. It
certainly reached Karen Parfitt's home town, Dallas. It was the
sound of US politics hitting a watershed. The forces that had
brought about the Equal Employment Opportunity Act, and
Roe v. Wade (the Supreme Court decision that legalized
abortion), and Title IX of the 1972 Education Amendments Act
(which prohibited sex discrimination in education), had shaken
up the nation, and the pieces were still suspended, waiting to
fall.

In 1977, it wasn't clear who would win: the Steinemites or
the Schlaflyans. It would become clear very soon. After 1977,
no additional state ratified the ERA. In 1980, Ronald Reagan
was elected (with Schlafly's support), and in 1982, the Equal
Rights Amendment failed. By then, the FCC under the Reagan
administration had stopped gathering data on who was
employed in radio and TV. Without statistics, it became nearly
impossible to prove employment discrimination. At the Equal
Employment Opportunities Commission (EEOC), Clarence
Thomas was selected to enforce the rules. A young black
lawyer, fresh from a job with the chemicals corporation
Monsanto, Thomas was a critic of the NAACP and an opponent
of government intervention in the area of affirmative action and
non-discrimination. He was on record opposing the very laws
he was appointed to implement. He was also a novice
bureaucrat. Thomas took over the chairmanship of the EEOC
in 1982 and drove the agency just where he was expected to—
directly into the ground.

At Channel 5, Karen Parfitt's job called on her to pay attention to the way that people navigated the 1970s watershed. For seven years, she covered state and local news and watched no end of people rise and fall on the turbulent political terrain. A friend who knew her then remembers Parfitt rushing to Dallas Airport to interview terrified Iranians returning from Tehran after the fall of the US-installed Shah.[6] The refugees were shattered; Americans were shocked. The sight of blindfolded Americans held hostage by Islamic revolutionaries rocked the public's confidence in US strength abroad. And then there was the 1980 presidential election.

Parfitt was assigned to cover George Bush Sr's bid for the Republican Party nomination. To Republican moderates it was a sad, but instructive episode. As a congressman and an ambassador, the first George Bush had been an outspoken advocate of family planning. So passionate had been his defense of condom-use that in the House of Representatives he earned the nickname ''Rubbers.''[7] Once he left Congress in 1970 he didn't do much on the issue, but his wife Barbara was a well-known backer of Planned Parenthood. As Tanya Melich, a pro-choice Republican, puts it:

[Bush] did nothing to dispel the perception that he was strongly-pro-choice, so it came as a surprise to the pro-choice community when, in announcing his candidacy, Bush opposed Medicaid funding for abortion except in cases of rape or incest or to save the life of the mother. Sometime during his nine-year odyssey for the presidency, he had turned anti-choice.[8]

Bush negotiated the political plate-shifts of his time. The religious Right was gaining power inside his party, and the former Texas congressman was transforming himself to meet their demands. Pro-choice Republicans were outraged, but the newly-minted Bush won Iowa. Then it was on to New Hampshire. There, Hughes got a lesson in the power of performance—and subterfuge.

Just days before the New Hampshire primary, Bush's strongest opponent, the former actor, former General Electric salesman, and former Governor of California—Ronald Reagan—pushed his way to the front of the primary pack. Reagan's team rented a hall for a debate with Bush on the understanding that the debate would be between these two men alone—at least, that's what Bush understood. Ronald Reagan, without telling Bush or the event's moderator (the editor of a local newspaper), had actually invited all the other candidates to participate. While those in the press corps and the rest of the audience looked on, a nerdy-looking Bush and the moderator protested at the violation of the ground rules while Reagan grabbed the microphone, insisted that all participants be allowed to speak, and stole the limelight. Bush looked lost and he was. He never won another primary state.

From the primaries it was on to the general election. Reagan selected Bush to be his running mate. The team faced a challenge: elections that take place during times of foreign strife tend to favor the incumbent. In this case, not only was the American public nervous about what was happening abroad, they were nervous about the Republican candidate. Republican strategists had to convince voters that Ronald Reagan was neither a bigot nor bomb-mad; that he would not resort to a nuclear attack on Tehran, and he wouldn't return the country directly to the 1950s (even though he was against abortion, affirmative action, and integrating schools by busing students, and did want to amend the constitution to permit Christian prayer in schools). To calm one set of fears, they threw up another, they hoped, more frightening prospect: four more years of Carter. To distract from Reagan's vulnerabilities, they went on the attack, and to distract from Reagan's domestic agenda, they focused on foreign policy.

Jimmy Carter was a weakling and a bungler, declared the GOP campaign. Carter had failed to liberate the American hostages held in Tehran—that was one humiliation. The other was the abandonment of the Panama Canal. Against virulent opposition from organized forces of the New Right, Jimmy Carter had negotiated a Canal Zone Treaty that gradually ceded control over the Zone to the Panamanians. Reagan knew that attacking Carter on this issue was a winner. Mary McGrory, writing in the *Washington Star*, claims she was present when Reagan realized just what a political punch it packed. "I saw it born in New Hampshire in the presidential primary of 1976. I watched Ronald Reagan say, 'We built it, we paid for it, it's ours' . . . and I saw the response of the audience . . . and I saw Reagan's reaction to that response. He looked stunned. He smiled. He *knew* he had an issue."[9]

On the question of Panama, Karen Parfitt was hardly an objective on-looker; in the affair that had animated the New Right for over a decade, her own family had played a leading role, and it was hardly the part of hero. From the perspective of the Reagan Right, there was no getting around it: her father was there at the abandonment of the canal. In fact, he was the man who had lowered the flag.

Looking back over her family history, Karen Hughes tends to emphasize that her grandfather was a Pennsylvania coalminer. He was. But her father, Major-General Harold R. Parfitt, was the United States's last military Governor of the Panama Canal. His responsibilities in Panama began in June 1965, when he became Lieutenant Governor of the Zone and Vice-President of the Canal Company. The "Company" was actually a US government agency that administered the ten-mile-wide stretch that housed those who worked on, and protected, the waterway.

Born in Paris in 1956, and living thereafter at various army postings, Karen Hughes spent fourth to fifth grade in the Canal Zone. She likes to say she was an "army brat," but "brat" doesn't quite conjure up the Zone scene.[10] Although it occupies a cherished place at the center of right-wing ideology, the Zone was not exactly standard-issue US. There were no elections, and the constitution did not apply. In fact, for a place so close to Cold Warriors' hearts, the Canal Zone resembled nothing so much as a socialist economy, and Karen Hughes's father was the unelected leader. Healthcare, housing and education were state-run, and the only stores were state-managed, the prices subsidized to ensure an attractive, low cost of living. The Zone was segregated, albeit in a euphemistic kind of way. Instead of a strict racial split, the division was between "silver" and "gold." The terms derive from the years of the canal's construction, when Americans in better-paying jobs were paid in gold-backed US dollars, while unskilled laborers, mostly West Indians, were paid in Panamanian silver currency and lived in malaria-plagued barracks.[11]

The economic divide afforded Americans in the Zone a far more affluent style of life than they might have enjoyed on the same income in the United States. Almost all American households could afford domestic servants, and at the top of the hierarchy, where the Lieutenant Governor and his family lived, entertaining was lavish and relentless. Formal dinners served up to 60 guests, receptions up to 300. Congressmen and senators and business leaders came through by the score (especially as negotiations over the treaty became heated). In her earliest years, therefore, Karen Parfitt spent time around powerful members of the US government.[12]

Zonians were a tightknit lot, recalls Margaret Huber, whose husband Walter was a Lutheran chaplain in the Air Force. Margaret Huber remembers Karen and her family attending services at the chapel: "The Parfitts were fine Christian people,"[13] she says. Her husband, Rev. Huber, was a man of clear convictions. "There is no place for nuance and compromises in the divine," he wrote to a newspaper years later, when Karen's rigidity was criticized. "The will of God allows for no shades of gray," he concluded.[14] Gold and silver; no shades of gray—the Zone was a "very orderly place," recalls Margaret Huber, and it was Harold Parfitt's job to keep it that way.

After all, the business of the Zone wasn't only shipping and entertaining. The narrow strip of land then hosted the Pentagon's "School of the Americas," the military academy for Latin American soldiers. The SOA taught counterinsurgency and psychological warfare techniques, among other skills. So many of its graduates went on to become human rights abusers that the place earned the sobriquet, "School of the Assassins." Among those who graduated while Karen Parfitt lived in the Zone was future Panamanian leader Manuel Noriega. His instructor at a 1967 counterintelligence course said he was "outstanding." A longtime CIA asset, when Noriega ultimately became unreliable, he was indicted by the United States for drug trafficking and racketeering. He was captured by US invading forces in 1989.[15]

In September 1968, the Parfitts left the Zone. Harold Parfitt served a year in Vietnam, but he was reassigned to Panama in 1975, this time to the top spot, as Governor. Daughter Karen stayed in Dallas to finish college at Southern Methodist University, but Panama was not easy to forget in those years. The question of the treaty was about to split the nation. As soon as election season started, the slogan "Keep our canal" popped up, on bumper stickers and anti-Carter campaign buttons. The New Right had found in Panama an issue over which they could get people really excited. Post-Vietnam, post-Watergate, post-civil rights, post-Roe v. Wade, the treaty debate gave disgruntled conservatives a chance to make a big, patriotic racket. The American Conservative Union raised hundreds of thousands of dollars through direct-mail appeals for their efforts to stop the Panama treaty. The group produced a television documentary in which retired General John Singlaub summed up the ACU position by comparing the loss of Panama to the loss of Cuba: the loss of Cuba to communism was a defeat in our hemisphere, he said, but "the American canal which this administration would abandon to Panama is our first retreat from United States soil.''[16]

In the months leading up to the 1976 presidential election, US forces in the Canal Zone came under a series of bomb attacks. Police were stationed at every entrance to the Zone but the bombers were never apprehended. With Carter's election, the bombings stopped. Carter agreed to transfer control over the following twenty years to the Panamanians. On September 7 1977 the treaty was signed, and seven months later it was ratified with a one vote margin in the Senate. In his last official act as Governor, it fell to Karen Parfitt's father to lower the Stars and Stripes in front of the Canal Zone Company head-quarters, which he duly did September 30 1979, with Vice-President Walter Mondale looking on. To Reagan Republicans, the Zone was a paradise lost, and a symbol of American strength shattered by tropical bomb-throwers and sell-out liberals.

Twenty years later, ''Who lost Panama?'' was still a potent enough question to scare a Democrat running for President. Vice-President Al Gore, with his eye on the next election, so feared being tagged ''loser of Panama'' that he pointedly declined to represent the United States at the final handover ceremony in December 2000, lest a photograph of him at a site of such national ignominy was used in an attacking GOP ad in the presidential race. ''It's a very strategic part of the world, and we shouldn't have given it up,'' Karen Hughes, then communications director for George W. Bush, told the press.[17]

There's no mention of the canal debacle in *A Charge to Keep*, the official George W. ''autobiography'' co-authored by Bush and Karen Hughes in 1999. Winning and losing, on the other hand, get mentioned a lot. Reflecting on his father's defeat in 1992, his brother Jeb's loss in the '94 race to be Governor of Florida, and on his own losing bid for Congress back in '78, Bush/Hughes write:

> Defeat humbles you . . . It's hard not to take a political loss personally; after all, it's your own name spelled out there on the ballot. Yet if you believe in the wisdom of voters, as I do, you get over the disappointment, accept the verdict, and move on.[18]

From the man who contested the verdict of the Florida voters all the way to the Supreme Court, this is breathtaking guff, but there's no denying that both Hughes and Bush have indeed been moved by defeat—moved to avoid it. It's personal, all right, a family affair. They have each watched their share of victories and vanquishings, and they're both deeply motivated to do what it takes to come out on top. When Hughes and Bush started working together in Texas, in 1994, one of them had a successful track record, and it wasn't the failed oilman from Midland. For more than a decade by then, Hughes had hitched herself to a winning team or, more accurately, perhaps, a wrecking crew.

In 1984, at the age of twenty-seven, Hughes left television (she was apparently still covering weather) and joined the Reagan–Bush re-election campaign as press coordinator for Texas. Not for the last time, she gave an improbable explanation for a big career shift. "I had gotten married and I had a new stepdaughter," she told *The Washington Post*. "I remember when I was doing the wedding invitations, I got called and sent to a hurricane. I was driving toward the coast and everybody else was driving the other way. I remember thinking, 'Why am I doing this?' "[19]

She wanted a more regular schedule, she said, and more time to spend at home, but Republican Party press work was hardly a free pass to an easy life. The Texan party was running on hopeful, fuelled by the success in 1978 of Bill Clements, the first Republican Governor since Reconstruction. Clements went down to defeat after one term, but that did not discourage ambitious Texas schemers from saying out loud that they could end the Democrats' franchise in the state. "It doesn't take long for the worm to turn," say Texans, and the state GOP was full of serious men with Lone Stars in their eyes who believed that they'd be the ones to turn it.

Karl Rove was one of the most serious. An independent political consultant, Rove was practicing in Texas what direct-mail meister Richard Viguerie had been teaching the GOP since the 1964 Goldwater campaign: build up mailing lists, prospect for donors, fund-raise, fund-raise, fund-raise. In oil-and-technology-rich Texas it was a lucrative proposition.

The more money there was to spend on campaigns, the more cash could be spent on public relations and TV advertising. Karen Hughes bailed out of TV journalism just as that ship was going down. Profit-hungry networks were beginning to cut back on news and politics, especially at the state and local level. The PR industry, on the other hand, was at the birth of a boom.

In 1984, the GOP held its national convention in Karen Hughes's home town. Scores of eager-beaver Reagan Revolutionaries swarmed Dallas, hoping to ride the Gipper's coat-tails somewhere, perhaps into office themselves. It was like a hurricane, and Hughes was heading into it.

The women's rights movement had Republicans worried, and the GOP was trying to lose its Good Old Boy image. Reagan was a hit, but a much bigger one among male voters than female. The GOP majority could be in trouble if Democrats capitalized on the so-called "gender gap" and made theirs the party for the majority of the population. In 1984, Hughes was brought on board just in time to watch the party take its first conscious baby-steps in the dance of bait and switch with women. A decade later, she would be choreographing the moves.

Female personalities spoke from the RNC stage that year even as, behind the scenes, the party toughened its anti-woman policies. The most cynical choice of speaker was three-time Olympic gold medal-winner Nancy Hogshead. Republican feminist Melich fumed because Hogshead had benefited from a Title IX-mandated women's sports program of just the sort that the Reagan administration was right then working to eviscerate.[20]

US Treasurer Katherine Ortega, UN ambassador Jeane Kirkpatrick, and Nancy Reagan spoke to the nation, while the platform committee (chaired by Trent Lott, with Newt Gingrich, Henry Hyde, and Phyllis Schlafly) committed the party for the first time to the notion that "the unborn child has a fundamental individual right to life which cannot be infringed." (By that definition, some kinds of contraception, let alone abortion, were tantamount to murder.)

Enthusiasm, even feigned, for female leadership stopped

right at the GOP gate. On the national scene that year, the party was in league with the anti-reds, "feds, dikes and kikes" people to destroy the one female candidate who had actually dared run for a top office: Geraldine Ferraro. Long before character assassination became the standard stuff of politics, the religious, racist, sexist, and Republican Right teamed up to subject Walter Mondale's running mate to an organized hate-campaign, the like of which was new, and vicious.

Every bit of dirt that could be dislodged was hurled at the country's first female candidate for Vice-President. The Republican Party made sure of it. There were legitimate questions about her husband's finances and her own financial filings to the Federal Elections Commission from previous campaigns, but the anti-Ferraro squad didn't stick to just raising questions. It is barely recalled now in media accounts of the period, but in 1984, pickets followed her campaign around and drowned out her speeches with heckling. They shouted Ferraro down and called her names, and because she was pro-choice, they cast her as a baby-killer. "Ferraro: Vice-President for Death" was one of the kinder slogans. The scene at a Ferraro election-stop looked like what women had seen for years outside abortion clinics. It wasn't unlike what Florida vote-counters would find outside their offices years later in Palm Beach during the vote-count melee of November 2000.

The GOP said that the anti-Ferraro thugs had nothing to do with the Reagan–Bush campaign; the media found out different. Journalists turned up an audiotape of a training session in which the pickets were coached to say "I'm a concerned citizen," not "I'm with Students for Reagan." The troublemakers were tied conclusively to the Reagan–Bush campaign, but the nation's first party-promoted public stoning was effective. Ferraro fell (and no woman has dared run for top office since), Reagan–Bush won re-election by a landslide, and Hughes, well, Karen Hughes, whose Texas candidates fared well in 1984, rose in the ranks of Texas political consultants. She was one of the winners.

For the next seven years Hughes was never short of work, and she was in the thick of a plan for more winning. Her expertise was message-sending. For mayoral races, judges' elections and bond campaigns, she wrote press releases, ran press conferences, and built up her own lists, not unlike Karl Rove. Refining their different skills, they were both independent consultants working in Texas retail politics, and Texas retail had plans to go national.

In 1987, Fred Meyer hired Hughes to do press work for his bid to be Mayor of Dallas. She gave birth to her son Robert between election day and the deciding vote in that race. Five years later, Meyer, then chair of the party in Texas, invited her to become the state's GOP executive director.

The party was not in a great situation in 1992: there were only two Republicans in state office, the Democrats held both houses in the state legislature, both the Lieutenant Governor and the Governor were Democrats, and the Governor, who was hugely popular, was a woman—Ann Richards. She'd ridden into office in 1990 with a hefty share of the Republican female vote.

Even Republican insiders admit that the hiring of Hughes just may have had something to do with knowing it would help for a woman to go head to head with the Governor.[21] Richards's opponent in 1990 had been Clayton Williams, a mad-dog misogynist who scared the wits out of moderates. To quote Molly Ivins, "It's one thing to step on your dick, but Williams just stood there and stomped on his."[22] During the campaign, Williams joked about rape. (It's like bad weather, he said: "If it's inevitable, just relax and enjoy it.") He waxed nostalgic about getting "serviced" in whorehouses (but didn't believe prostitutes or any other woman should have the right to a legal abortion). He refused to shake Richards's hand in public. Women accounted for 53 percent of the 1990 gubernatorial vote in Texas and six out of ten women supported Richards, including 22 percent who said they were Republicans.[23] The GOP wanted that vote back.

For this, Karen Hughes was in every way, "terrific." The word is Mark McKinnon's. McKinnon is a former Democratic political consultant who switched teams in the late 1990s to work on George W. Bush's race for President. "Karen and Karl [Rove] completely overhauled the Republican Party in Texas," says McKinnon.[24] Sure enough, ten years later, Republicans held every state office from Governor through to the Supreme Court, and a Texan Republican was President.

Texas is what reporter Lou Dubose calls "the Wild West of campaign finance."[25] State law permits contributors to give as much as they like, as long as they declare it. Rove raised money, cultivated candidates and built big-bucks mailing lists. Rove labored with the state GOP to bring legal challenges that forced the redrawing of electoral boundaries in ways that favored Republican candidates, and he head-hunted contenders to put in strategic districts. While Rove pulled strings behind the scenes, Karen Hughes performed as the GOP's public face.

"People saw a successful, smart, strong woman, not just a bunch of old white guys," McKinnon says, adding, "She understands the importance of being aggressive." It's a word that comes up a lot when people talk about Hughes. "News is contention," she says herself. "If you're willing to criticize, news people are willing to let you start a fight."[26]

Hughes has a legendary appetite for public-relations combat. She once told Fred Meyer that she would have loved to have done public relations for Exxon after the *Exxon Valdez* Alaskan oil spill.[27] When she arrived in Austin, Texas in 1992, she got right down to fighting. Almost at once, political life for Democrats in that town came to resemble swimming through an oil slick. Bill Cryer, the Governor's press secretary, remembers Hughes's arrival. He'd never heard of her. "She seemed to have parachuted in . . . And suddenly every day there was something in the paper about Republicans attacking Ann Richards."[28]

The Governor was polling high. Whether it was her bold tongue or her hard-living-local-made-good story, Ann Richards was a popular Governor with an alluring national profile. (George W. Bush, she said, was "born with a silver foot in his mouth.") Employment was up, crime was down; Richards had given Texans a tempting statewide lottery and initiated programs to immunize poor kids. She had presided over the most massive prison construction program in state history and supported legislation to keep violent criminals behind bars longer. In 1992, her approval rating stood at 73 percent.

"We thought we were doing pretty well. We *were* doing

well,'' says Cryer. But the newspapers, courtesy of Rove and Hughes, said different. ''Whatever the Governor was doing, Karen made an attack on it.'' She seemed to have a knack for getting air time, says Cryer. He describes her soundbite style as a matter of ''attacking and slashing.''

It didn't help that during this period media diversity in the state of Texas narrowed. In 1990, each of Texas's three biggest cities had competing newspapers. By 1994, Houston, Dallas and San Antonio were all one-paper towns. There was only one place to work for journalists reporting the election, and no incentive for paper-owners to be contentious. Newspapers drive local news coverage; local television follows (when it's inclined). Also during these years, television gradually pulled out of covering the legislature and local politics. At the same time, small, formerly irrelevant, politically-motivated rags gained new influence. Reporters for the *Dallas/Fort Worth Heritage*, a Christian Right publication, and *The Austin Review*, a weekly free paper underwritten by the Republican Right, turned up and asked questions at state government press conferences. ''They'd bring up the wackiest things,'' says Cryer. They'd start whispering campaigns about Ann Richards's association with lesbians and Hollywood celebrities, and soon enough, the power press were running after the ball the Right had paid for.

The work was shared: Rove raked in opposition research, and Karen Hughes spread it to the media. Rove had honed his Machiavellian political skills in the company of a master, the late Lee Atwater. Atwater worked for Rove when they were both college Republicans. He fixed it so that Rove would be elected president of the group. (According to *The New York Times*, "women, even in that election, turned out to be the swing voters.")[29] In 1984, Lee Atwater was deputy manager of the campaign that defeated Mondale–Ferraro.

When Rove and Hughes later arrived in Washington, they voraciously defended official secrecy. If there was a term for the opposite of openness in government, the George W. Bush administration would keep it secret. In Texas, however, when Rove and Hughes were on the outside, they exploited the state's so-called Sunshine laws, right to the last ray of sunlight. Cryer remembers that the GOP requested a list of all employees in government office, all speeches delivered by Richards, all official gubernatorial schedules and appointments, and all correspondence from the office to the state parole board. "It's an insane game of gotcha," he said at the time.[30] In the 1990s, "Gotcha" caught on as a national past-time, but before Whitewater, Paula Jones, and Monica Lewinsky, Texans became familiar with the way it was played.

The Governor in Texas is statutorily the fifth most powerful state office. The power lies chiefly in the authority to appoint. Ann Richards made about 4,000 appointments to local boards and commissions, and she promised at the start that her choices would "look like Texas." So the vast majority were white, middle-class and straight. But six were openly gay or lesbian. Another was a Latina—the first ever—whom the Governor chose to chair the Texas Railroad Commission, the body that regulates the state's oil and gas industry. Lena Guerrero, a young state legislator with all the makings of a fantastic Democratic leader in the Texas of the 21st century, was the daughter of migrant farmers, a Phi Beta Kappa graduate of the University of Texas, and a passionate Richards campaigner. Except she turned out never to have graduated from college, let alone belong to an honors society. Karl Rove found out, released it at the most damaging moment, and Guerrero's climb turned into a spectacular crash, with grim implications for Richards.

"Somehow," says Cryer, "white conservative Texans got the message that Richards was only appointing women, gays, and unqualified racial minorities to high office." They got that message because a sharp-as-a-whip observer of the Reagan years sent it out to every Texan on a daily basis. What Hughes didn't say to the press herself, she ensured that someone else said. In her small office in the state capital, Austin, she set up a "fast fax" system that sent information to county chairmen and party officials daily, keeping them ahead of the news cycle on the major—or minor—stories to which the GOP wanted a response.[31] Rove hooked up the message with likely messengers. "There was a drumbeat that Richards is a liberal big-spending Democrat and a feminist who only wants to protect people who don't look like you," remembers Cryer. It wasn't the same as a traveling mob of sign-waving pickets, but in Cryer's words, "It got pretty rough."

Richards's staff found themselves constantly on the defensive. Even the funny stuff wasn't so funny. From her time in journalism, Hughes knew how to throw a lively line to a worn-out press corps. (Cryer recalls that Ann Richards's staff gave the Governor a parrot for her birthday. Before day's end, the media were quoting Hughes saying, "I hope she's taught it to say "Polly wants a bigger staff."[32] Cryer winces, as much in awe as pain.) She also knew the power of pictures. Just days before election day in 1992, Hughes erected a "Haunted House of Democratic Horrors" at GOP headquarters. The Halloween gimmick featured a "graveyard of Texas jobs," and Richards and Guerrero were portrayed as members of a "good old ghouls network."[33]

By the time 1994 rolled around, Bush's road to the presidency ran right through Ann Richards's State House. Fortunately for George, who wanted to be the next great Republican dragon-slayer, the Democratic dragon was already wounded. Throughout the race, his campaigners declared loftily that he disdained negative campaigning and wouldn't do it. He didn't have to because, thanks to Hughes and Rove, the party had been going negative against Ann Richards every day, sometimes several times a day, for years. (Nonetheless, loyal knights were in place to spur St George's horse on for him, just for good measure. Two months before the '94 vote, for example, a Republican state senator from highly-contested East Texas revived the gays-get-jobs complaint. "I simply don't agree to appointing avowed homosexual activists . . . to positions of leadership," said Senator Bill Ratcliff.[34] To which George W. Bush replied, "This is not an issue to me." That didn't mean it wasn't an issue. "Those things cut," sighs Cryer. Ratcliff happened to be a client of Rove's, and chairman of the local George W. for Governor campaign.)

George W. launched his gubernatorial campaign in November 1993. He brought in Hughes to serve as his communications director. The stage was set, all he had to do was walk on to it. While Rove (who remained a consultant) obsessed about the setting, Hughes focused on the walk.

Six years later, when the same team stepped into the national arena, observers from down home barked and hollered; as one anti-Bush activist put it, "We shouted ourselves hoarse about what had gone on down here with Bush, but nobody would listen." They also cringed. "We made it all happen," exclaims Chuck MacDonald, press secretary for Governor Richards's 1994 re-election campaign. "Without us, there'd be no President George W. Bush."[35]

It's awkward to employ the familiar saw about history repeating itself "the first time as tragedy, the second as farce," when the second time around is a national presidential election in the world's most powerful nation. Suffice to say that to Texans, Bush's presidency and the way he won it looked doggone familiar. The team packaged Bush as a "reformer with results." It was true; he was a reformer. With Hughes's help, beginning in 1994 in Texas, he reformed how the hard Right looked.

History helped. In Texas, Yale Boy Bush had the luck to follow Neanderthal Man. As long as Bush didn't repeat what he'd said to a reporter in 1988, he stood a pretty good chance of seeming more evolved than his predecessor Clayton Williams.[36] (In '88, when David Fink of the *Hartford Courant* asked W. what he talked about with his father, "when you're not talking about politics," George said, "Pussy.")[37] On the campaign trail, Bush kept his frat-boy tongue in his head, and he worked with Hughes to woo women voters back, especially those who'd strayed to Richards in 1990.[38] His very last stop before he officially launched his gubernatorial campaign was with the activists of the Texas Federation of Republican Women. They were going to be the "lifeblood" of his campaign, he assured them.[39]

"[Women voters] were never frightened of George W. Bush," says Cryer. "Bush had a much softer image on issues that those Republican women cared about . . . choice, and schools. And Karen Hughes was a big part of that."[40]

George W. seized on the work of a local professor to give his campaign the calling-card by which he would become known: "compassionate conservative." It sounded soft and kind and moderate. It wasn't. But that didn't emerge in 1994 or 1998 or 2000, because to those two "c"'s the campaign added a third: control. That's where Hughes came in. Blue eyes, upswept hair, 5 feet 10½ inches tall, wearing a size 12 shoe, Hughes was 100 percent the daughter of a major-general, and she was 100 percent on guard.

For a year, George W. Bush spoke about just four things: reforming the state's education, tort, welfare and juvenile justice systems. He didn't just stay on message, he stuck to the same text, which never varied. Hughes later became famous for standing to the side of the crowd, mouthing the candidate's words as he said them.[41] Over at Richards's campaign office, MacDonald did what campaign teams do—he assigned a staffer to tape-record every one of Bush's speeches. "After three months we had to shut it down—the speech never changed." MacDonald reckons the media might have gone easier on the candidate's garbled sentence structure if every once in a while he had said a different sentence.[42]

To say that Hughes was not "cowed" by the press would be an understatement. "I don't know how many times I'll say something and she'll come right at me, hard and strong and loud," Wayne Slater of the *Dallas Morning News* has said.[43] "She wasn't afraid to yell at a member of the press when she wasn't happy," says MacDonald, delicately.

Hughes did more than reflect light on Bush. Perhaps not only metaphorically, she applied the make-up, chose the suit, wrote the script and policed the press conferences. "She started cutting off press conferences in '94, she was still cutting off press conferences six years later," says MacDonald.[44] Trying to pull either one of them off message was like playing tug-of-war with a pitbull.

Bush ran for Governor on being a successful businessman. Richards's crew tried to point out that even with a succession of well-connected family friends to rescue it, Bush's oil business still went bust. Richards talked about Bush's stock trading when he sat on the board of Harken Energy—Bush had unloaded his shares at a profit just before the company crashed. She described the Securities and Exchange Commission (SEC) investigation as "at best incomplete, at worst a cover-up."[45] Hughes fired back that the Richards campaign was "going negative."

Bush also ran on being compassionate. The word means "deep awareness of the suffering of another, coupled with the wish to relieve it."[46] Phyllis Dunham, who headed the Texas Abortion Rights Action League (TARAL) in the early 1990s, remembers her alarms went off when she saw Bush hanging around with Marvin Olasky, an ex-atheist, ex-Marxist, born-again Bible-thumper, then a professor at the University of Texas, the man with whom the "compassionate conservative" idea originated.

Dunham knew Olasky from his work with his wife at the "Austin Crisis Pregnancy Center," which Mrs. Olasky had founded as an adjunct to her anti-abortion activities.[47] Dunham had worked with women who'd gone to the clinic for medical help, only to find themselves bombarded by anti-abortion propaganda and fake promises. "Women who decided against having an abortion were told they'd be taken care of," Dunham remembers. "What they'd get were instructions on how to apply for welfare."[48]

When TARAL tried to raise questions about Bush's "compassionate conservatism," Bush let Hughes do the talking. She'd sound reasonable enough, repeat that the candidate wanted to reduce the number of abortions, and ignore deeper questions, says Dunham. Even in 1998, when Bush was seeking a second term, it was hard to get the media to focus on Bush's record. The Governor had kept the headline-grabbing issue of Roe v. Wade itself on a back-burner, and pursued his ends through strategic appointments. But the politics of his selections remained hidden in the bureaucratic maze, out of the media view.

Quite simply, "When you surround yourself with people of color, you don't look so racist; with women, you don't look so sexist," as Dunham puts it. No matter what was said or done, impressions stuck. Pro-choice Republican friends of Dunham's told her they voted for Bush twice because they thought he wasn't dangerous. They were wrong.

As Governor, Bush increased the pressure on public health clinics even as he loosened the laws on church-run establishments. Over the complaints of family planning professionals (who said the law would scare minors away from seeking care), he supported a law that required workers to call the police when a girl turned up who was under 14 and pregnant or had a sexually transmitted disease. But Bush defended Teen Challenge, a faith-based drug rehabilitation center that the state was threatening to close because it refused to hire licensed counselors. The Governor convened a task force and urged lawmakers to pass a bill that permitted faith-based institutions to "opt-out" of state licensing requirements. The law passed in '97 and immediately reopened was Rebekah House, an evangelical-run center for troubled teens that had been forced shut in 1985 after its rehabilitation routine was revealed to include beatings, isolation, and hours spent kneeling on a hard floor with a Bible in each hand and pencils under each knee.[49]

In January 1998, Bush inaugurated a "month of prayer to end abortion in Texas." His pick for Health Commissioner was William "Ryn" Archer III, a favorite of the American Family Association and Texans United for Life. Archer blamed high rates of teen pregnancy among Hispanics on their culture. Hispanics, he said, "don't want" family planning. He also suggested that African Americans fared better under segregation. In his first month on the job Archer proposed cutting funding for school-based health clinics because he opposed their discussing family planning and abortion. He published a booklet for young women that included incorrect data on breast cancer and its relation to abortion.[50] Archer enjoyed the Governor's full support through many scandals, until in late 2000 he was forced to resign after an African American doctor tape-recorded him telling her that she was "too smart," having used her intellect to get ahead, "because that's what Anglos do, that's what white people do."[51]

It takes some doing to square candidate Bush's rhetoric with Governor Bush's record. On homosexuality (the issue the candidate said was no issue), the governor opposed an effort to repeal an anti-sodomy law that made consensual homosexual acts a crime and supported a bill that would have banned gay parents from adopting. On hate crimes, the candidate claimed credit for a hate crimes law which the Governor had opposed until the last minute before it passed. Candidate Bush claimed credit for extending public health insurance to 2 million uninsured Texas children. On that measure, too, the Governor jumped on board only after support in the Assembly was such that it couldn't be stopped.

Glen Maxey, the state Democrat who sponsored the child health care bill, tells a story about the Governor's agreement, finally, to go along. "As he patted me on the back all smiles in front of the public gallery, Bush whispered in my ear: 'You crammed it down our throats.'" Maxey also says, "Governor Bush wouldn't even give us a public signing ceremony . . . he was afraid that conservative Republicans would get ticked off at him."[52]

And then there was his 1993 comment to the effect that people who do not accept Jesus Christ as a personal savior cannot go to heaven. Even five years later, Bush was still nervously joking with journalists that on his first visit to Israel he'd tell the Jews, "You're all going to hell." Even that, he got away with. George W.'s initial comments came in an interview just before he kicked off his gubernatorial campaign. Communications director Karen Hughes told the media he was "troubled if people misinterpret his comments to indicate anything other than his great respect for people of different faiths." She continued, "As a Christian he believes that Jesus Christ is his personal savior . . . Judgements about heaven and hell do not belong to the realm of politics or of this world. They belong to a higher authority, and he recognizes that."[53]

In the end, Bush's Texas trail looked a whole lot like the one his team traced later, in its presidential race. Patrolled by Hughes, the candidate followed a disciplined, one-note track and dozens of critical news stories shriveled up and died at the side of it.

In a campaign in which questions of "character" figured prominently, Hughes not only projected Bush's public character when he ran for President, but she, with W., created it. Their co-written book, *A Charge to Keep*, let people know the acceptable "official version," just in case they chose to challenge it. (Rumor has it that Mickey Herskowitz, a professional biographer who was initially given the assignment, was dropped after he had the temerity to call one of George W.'s ex-girlfriends.)

Essentially a campaign tool, the book papers over Bush's frat-boy drinking and who-knows-what-else period, his arrests and his mysterious missing year-and-a-half in the early 1970s (when he should have been serving in the National Guard, but wasn't). It describes the killing in 1998 of Karla Faye Tucker, the first woman executed in Texas in more than a hundred years. Bush refused to consider a thirty-day stay of execution for Tucker. In the book, Bush (with Hughes guiding his pen) calls that one of the "hardest things I've ever done."

In reality, George W. is the sort of guy who makes fun of a woman he's about to execute. If he showed that side to Tucker Carlson, on the record for an interview with *Talk* magazine, one can only assume that Hughes has seen Bush's crass side too. *A Charge to Keep* quotes at length from condemned woman Karla Faye Tucker's interview from death row with Larry King. It's the only TV show quoted in the whole book, but the author discusses it at length to demonstrate just how moved he was by her awful predicament. A pretty different picture comes across in Bush's interview in *Talk*, in which he describes having seen Karla Faye in conversation with King:

> "I watched his [King's] interview with [Tucker] though," Bush said. "He asked her real difficult questions. Like, 'What would you say to Governor Bush?' "
>
> "What was her answer?" I wonder.
>
> " 'Please,' " Bush whimpers, his lips pursed in mock desperation, " 'please don't kill me.' "[54]

The *Talk* interview also revealed W.'s ubiquitous use of the expletive "fuck." Hughes spent a good amount of time thereafter denying that the word ever crossed his lips.

To team up with the ultimate winner—George W. Bush—Karen Hughes, who became the director of communications on his presidential campaign in 1998, not only tidied up, she covered up. That she knew just where Bush's political bodies were buried is evident from what happened when he said things she wasn't ready for. Wayne Slater tells a story of what happened when he asked W. whether there had been arrests other than the previously reported one for stealing a Christmas wreath at college. Slater says Bush said no, then wanted to elaborate.

"The clear impression I got ... was he had been arrested and he wanted to explain something," says Slater. "But before he could say it, she cut him off and said, 'Wait a minute, I've not heard this.' She clearly wasn't prepared for whatever it was he was about to say ... To this day, I have no idea what he was going to say. After she got to him, he shut up," Slater told the *New Republic*.[55]

After George W. spoke at Bob Jones University, an anti-Catholic institution that, among other things, barred interracial dating, Hughes pushed the line that he had denounced the institution's anti-Catholic bigotry and racism when he was there.[56] "It's rubbish," says reporter Richard Wolffe, who was present. Bush said one word, afterwards, at a press conference at a hotel. Asked whether he agreed with Bob Jones's policy on interracial dating, Bush answered, "No." "That was it, and he certainly didn't say anything when he was there," says Wolffe.[57]

Wolffe covered both presidential campaigns for the London *Financial Times*. To put it simply, Wolffe says, "I was intimidated." On the Gore bus, the staff would try to mend fences with meddlesome members of the media. On the Bush bus, it was just the opposite. The atmosphere was chummy, but the limits were clearly defined: "You knew there would be repercussions if you stepped out of line." An end to access to the candidate, a refusal to answer any questions? "It wasn't clear exactly what [the repercussions] would be, but everybody just knew," says Wolffe. It wouldn't be pretty.

Hughes's ability literally to herd journalists like sheep has been described as the maneuver of a skilled offensive linesman.[58] She used her height, her voice, her frown, "The way she'd lean over you, the way she'd stick to her guns . . . She used everything," says Wolffe. "You'd feel her presence very heavily."

Perhaps this was because control was harder to maintain on a moving campaign press circus than it had been back home in Texas. The sophistication of the Rove–Hughes Texas team was stretched to the point where the campaign fell back on intimidation. Traditionally, press secretaries assume that reporters are the enemy. When journalists wrote negative things about Ann Richards, her press secretary Bill Cryer says it "never occurred to me to punish them."[59] Bush's team thought differently. Around Rove swirls a storm of allegations of dirty tricks. At his gentlest, Rove is famous for calling reporters at home, berating them, often screaming.[60] Hughes was subtler, but she shared the same mission. In person, she was upbeat, friendly, smooth, but reporters who tried to seek an off-the-record relationship with her found that it just didn't happen. "Hughes on the record was exactly the same as Hughes off the record," says Wolffe.[61] And day after day, Bush dodged reporters' questions to spout identical soundbites.

In Iowa, the press got so fed up that they banded together. They lobbed question after question about abortion and, under pressure, Bush said that he supported the Republican Party agenda that sought a constitutional amendment to ban abortions without exception. It was a chink in the "compassionate conservative" armor. Afterwards, he told a Fox reporter it was "a gang-bang," and for the naughty journalists, there was a telling-off.

"We were basically bawled out," says Wolffe. Not by Karen, but by her minion, Mindy Tucker, who went on to work for the White House. Tucker explained in no uncertain terms that the Governor would stop holding daily news conferences. "We have a message a day and we want to stick with it," she said. "Clearly, they wanted to decide what the news of the day was, not us," remembers Wolffe. But he remembers another thing: Tucker wasn't subtle. "Hughes would never have made a decision that transparent."[62] Tucker was yanked off the campaign, and the press conferences continued.

With Bush's assumption of the White House, Hughes rose to become the most powerful woman in the land. Never has there been a woman whose job brought her into closer, more influential contact with the President. As "counselor to the President"—Bush created the position uniquely for her—she sat in on every meeting, oversaw the offices of press secretary, communications and speechwriting, and had the communications directors of every department reporting directly to her.

Her closeness to the President is famous. While the press's nicknames for Hughes are less than kind ("Nurse Ratched," "the Enforcer," "the Surgeon General of Spin"), Bush's name for her is "High Prophet" (supposedly a play on "Parfitt"). Especially on the campaign trail, Bush often seemed lost

without her. The best evidence to support the claim that Bush
knew nothing in advance about the attacks of September 11
2001 is that the President was so far from Karen Hughes when
they happened. It seemed to surprise no one, however, when it
was she, not he, who first addressed the nation after the events
of that day. As she had many times before, she conveyed a
misleading message: the federal government was functioning
and the President was in control, she assured the country. In
fact, Wall Street and the Capitol were shut down, the Pentagon
was evacuated and in flames, and the President was skitting
about the nation on Air Force One, from Florida, to Louisiana,
to Nebraska.

David Frum, who worked with Bush and Hughes as a
speechwriter in the first year of the administration, analyzes
their relationship this way: Bush's mother Barbara, ''can be a
difficult to please woman—and George W. Bush was a son it
would often have been difficult to be pleased by.'' Wife Laura
was a woman as unlike Barbara as Bush could seek out, writes
Frum. ''When he ran for Governor, he recruited Hughes—a
woman very like his mother, but who offered him the
unqualified admiration his mother never did. His wife was his
mother antidote. His aide was his mother substitute.''[63]

More interesting than Hughes's relationship with Bush,
however, is her relationship with democracy. Her candidate
rose to power not on the basis of his legislative record, ideas or
integrity, but thanks to skillful message-control, which was her
department. Ironically, as communications director, what
Hughes did best was not communicate.

Voters in Texas were fed a fake Bush (''successful businessman''), and a disingenuous platform (''compassionate conservative''). The nation was then fed the same, with the addition, ''successful Governor of Texas.'' (In 1999, Bush's state was ranked third in the nation when it came to toxic pollutants in water; 41st in spending on public education; 48th on spending on public health; and manufacturing wages stood at 14 percent below the average.[64] Hughes and Rove packaged Bush as a moderate on social issues, when his record reeked of Southern Fundamentalist Protestant. ''A new kind of Republican,'' she saw to it that he was dubbed, when in fact, the President and his team were exactly the old kind: ruthless, qualm-free, extremist.

''No one ever said that 'compassionate conservative' was anything to do with moderate or centrist,'' reflects Richard Wolffe now. ''But the campaign certainly never corrected that impression.'' In fact, the Governor meant something very specific when he used the word compassion. ''He meant Christian. He meant religious,'' says Wolffe. ''But they couldn't come out and say that.''[65] Or they didn't.

When, in April 2002, Karen Hughes decided to leave the White House, pundits lined up to praise her. Indeed, the very same reporters who had been manipulated for years by the ''Surgeon General of Spin,'' accepted her explanation at face value. *The New York Times*'s Elisabeth Bumiller identified with Hughes: ''In a rare moment for Washington Ms. Hughes' explanation for her resignation, to spend more time with her family, particularly her teenage son, was taken not as the usual spin, but instead as a painful truth about the difficulties women face in balancing family and work.''[66]

Hughes's decision, described as "noble," "courageous," and "sad," had meaning, the media told the public. "Hughes's flight from high office spoke to all of us," suggested journalist Robin Toner. "Suddenly there was another Rorschach test for a culture striving mightily to come to grips with mothers at work."[67] Reporters took the same line as conservatives who argue that ultimately work makes women miserable.

One man presumably feeling pretty vindicated was Marvin Olasky, the Austin professor who came up with the "compassionate conservative" tag so eagerly embraced by the President. Olasky is not a fan of high-achieving women. Women joining the workforce have had "dire consequences for society," he told a Christian magazine in 1998. Can women be leaders? "God does not forbid women to be leaders in society ... but there's a certain shame attached to it," he said.[68]

Hughes, a career woman, GOP leader and stay-out-of-the-home mom, spent years massaging a message that came from a man who believes in his heart that success like hers shames society. It makes her a great example of an ambitious political operator, but a dubious role model for women seeking to hold office with integrity, courage and ethics.

Hillary Clinton's catchphrase was "it takes a village." If it took a village to raise the Clinton administration, it took Karen Hughes to raise George W.'s. There is no doubt that without her, Bush is brasher, crasser, less aware of public impressions. She softened the candidate's crude edges, and urged the President to address issues such as environmental protection and energy policy that women and moderate voters cared about. She apparently did her best to discourage the President from vetoing a Patients' Bill of Rights. (He vetoed it anyway and it worked against him.)[69] It was she who took the lead in spinning the Afghan war as a war to liberate women.[70]

Before she quit, Hughes saw to it that the job of public relations for the administration was in what she considered good hands, those of one John Rendon. Rendon is the Bruce Willis of the public-relations industry. How did the people of Kuwait City, liberated in February 1991 after being held hostage for seven months, get their hands on little US flags to wave at US troops in the first Gulf War? That was Rendon's work.[71] He set up shop in Saudi Arabia to spin news on behalf of the exiled Kuwaiti emir. After that war's end, he was hired by the CIA to spin world opinion against Saddam Hussein, the Iraqi leader. Then, after the attacks of 9/11, Rendon joined top officials including Hughes and the Pentagon's spokeswoman Victoria Clarke every morning at 9.30 on a conference call that set the day's official war message.[72] Rendon, like Hughes, considers what he does a form of combat: ''information warfare'' is his name for it. Late in October 2001, Hughes worked with Rendon to create something called the Coalition Information Center (CIC), with offices staffed by information-warriors in Washington, London, and Islamabad. A fast-response network set up to respond to anti-US news that appears anywhere in the world, the CIC is Hughes's Austin fast-fax system gone global. It was her parting accomplishment.

Karen Hughes, like Karl Rove (and John Rendon, too), likes her media messages simple. Indeed, it's been a mark of her tenure as the President's communications director that the world's most powerful leader narrowed the terms of debate to

a few emotive words: evil v. good, for us or against us. It's
simple and it's profoundly undemocratic. Moreover, looking at
Hughes's career so far, it's hard not to feel some nostalgia for
Houston, 1977. When Hughes got her start, there was a whole
lot of discussion going on. Debates were rowdy, but it was easy
to distinguish the players. The International Women's Year
crowd occupied one end of town; Phyllis Schlafly's friends
gathered at the opposite. The Stop ERA team didn't pretend to
be *in favor* of the Equal Rights Amendment. Today's Schlaflyans
do just that and Karen Hughes is a virtuoso.

When she left office in 2002, the administration's need for
"the Enforcer" was less than it had been. The President had
declared that the nation was in an undefined war. Reporters had
volunteered to do as they were told. (Dan Rather, the host and
managing editor of the CBS *Evening News*, declared that
"George Bush is the President. He makes the decisions, and,
you know, it's just one American, wherever he wants me to
line up, just tell me where. And he'll make the call.")[73]
Besides, Hughes didn't leave work, she only left Washington.
As Matthew Miller pointed out in the *Sacramento Bee*, "The
conclusion that she's making a big sacrifice in leaving the White
House to head home for Texas with her family is way off base."
Miller calculated that "for nearly a decade, Hughes has given
George W. Bush 120 percent for a government salary that
doesn't top $120,000. Now she'll be in a situation that thou-
sands of equally accomplished (though lower-profile) working
mothers only dream of—the ability to work half time for ten
times the pay. Just do the math."[74]

With an unspecified retainer from the Republican National

Committee, some highly lucrative speaking engagements and a book contract worth "over $1 million" from Viking Penguin, Hughes is hardly your typical working mother. Moreover, more than a year after her ballyhooed "departure," Karen Hughes is far from gone. Her email address remains Karen@Georgewbush.com and, according to her colleague Mark McKinnon, she's still spending roughly three days a week in Washington. Starting in August 2002, the White House established a "White House Iraq Group," or WHIG, to coordinate strategy for the attack on Iraq. Among the regular participants in weekly meetings in the White House Situation Room were Karl Rove, Condoleezza Rice, Mary Matalin, and Karen Hughes.[75] Later that year, she was deployed to the campaign trail.

After all, the Republican Party is worried again about the women's vote. In 2002, Republican Senator John Cornyn faced trouble from moderate voters in Dallas County. Hughes virtually took over Cornyn's strategy. Before a midterm election in which every Senate seat was critical, Hughes campaigned for Cornyn, and made fundraising stops for candidates in Hawaii, Iowa, South Dakota, New Jersey, North Carolina, Minnesota, Ohio, and Georgia. Why? As one writer put it, "That's where Karl Rove's political operation wants her to go."[76]

Hughes campaigned for Jim Talent in Missouri and Norm Coleman in Minnesota—both winners. Jean Carnahan, who was heavily backed by NOW, and Walter Mondale (who took the place of Progressive Caucus leader Paul Wellstone) were defeated.

In 2003, Republicans walked into a majority in the House

and in the Senate, but there was another election looming. A clear sign that the White House was thinking ahead: Hughes was recalled to Washington to work on Bush's 2003 State of the Union address. Hughes appeared on television the Sunday before the speech, following the President out of church. When members of Congress filed into the chamber on speech night, Hughes was visible in the balcony, watching the proceedings. Six months, soaring job losses and one Iraqi occupation later, the President's poll numbers took a dive. In August 2003, Bush's job approval rating fell to 53 percent, close to where it was just before the attacks of September 11. Women, especially older women, and Americans who are middle-income or lower-income had moved away from the President, the Pew Research Center pollsters suggested.

Karen Hughes has said, "The rumors of my retirement have been greatly exaggerated."[77]

Believe her.

FLAVR SAVR

Ann Veneman

People who know nothing else about Agriculture Secretary Ann Veneman seem to have heard that she was brought up on her family's peach farm. It's a warm and (given the nature of peaches) fuzzy link to small-scale family farming that has served her well.

"I was born a poor little peach farmer's daughter," Veneman told the *Los Angeles Times* soon after her nomination. It's true enough, but she has spent her entire *adult* life taking big business's side in a battle that pits the largest corporations in the world against the smallest farmer. The battle lines were drawn years ago, in the California fields not far from Veneman's grandmother's farm.

Veneman was born in 1949 in Modesto. The Central Valley town lies south of the state capital Sacramento and north of Fresno, not far from the *Grapes of Wrath* world of Steinbeck's Salinas and Watsonville. Almond farms, dairies, fields of fruit and vegetables surround it, and they're still worked mostly by laborers. In Veneman's youth, the tide of history appeared to be drifting the workers' way—towards greater rights for those who tend and nurture the farmlands, and more responsibilities for those who profit from them.

The year Veneman turned thirteen, her father, John, became the first Republican to carry his district in twenty years. He took a seat in the California Assembly in 1962, the same year that César Chávez founded what would become the United Farm Workers of America. Farm laborers, the only group specifically excluded from the National Labor Relations Act, were out to win the right to unionize. With fellow organizer Dolores Huerta, Chávez held their group's first convention in Fresno that fall. Another rumble was in the air too, something called environmentalism. Rachel Carson's book *Silent Spring* was published.[1] Like the UFW, Carson made the case that food is different from other products. The condition of the land, the water, and the lives of the people who work the soil are connected to the lives of those who eat the product. What happens in the first link of the chain affects the rest.

John Veneman and Huerta met on several occasions to talk about healthcare. A Rockefeller, rather than a Reagan-style, Republican, he's credited with designing the MediCal program (which provides health insurance for low-income Californians) and coming up with much of Richard Nixon's domestic-policy agenda. In 1969, he was appointed undersecretary for health, education and welfare in Richard Nixon's administration, where he developed the idea of the Health Maintenance Organization (HMO) and floated a plan for basic minimum incomes as an alternative to welfare.

Always one to cut to the chase, the UFW's Dolores Huerta says John Veneman wasn't a bad guy: "He was a Republican, but not one of the evil ones.'' (She doesn't say the same about his daughter: "Talking to her is like talking to agribusiness itself," says Huerta.)[2]

In 1966, the UFW marched through Veneman's town. She was a junior at the local Downey High School when the ragtag collection, mostly of Mexicans and Mexican Americans, passed through. The farm workers were on a 340-mile trek from Delano to Sacramento to take their demand for a union to the law-makers. By the time Veneman was a senior at the University of California at Davis, environmentalists were marching too, in their own way. In San Francisco, and hundreds of other towns besides, people marked the first Earth Day in 1970, and heard speeches that used words such as "eco-system," and "sustainability," and "recycling" for the first time. Writing five months before the event, *The New York Times* had this to say: "Rising concern about the environmental crisis is sweeping the nation's campuses with an intensity that may be on its way to eclipsing student discontent over the war in Vietnam . . ."[3]

Veneman was becoming interested in politics, it seems—she went on to the University of California at Berkeley to study public policy—but her drift was not towards the Bay Area radicals, but back to the Central Valley. By the middle 1970s, her father had become an influential man with powerful friends and he connected her to most of them. In 1974, he made an unsuccessful bid for state Lieutenant Governor and his campaign was run by one Pete Wilson (later the Governor of California). John set Ann up with an internship in Wilson's office when Wilson was an assemblyman and she was still an undergraduate. After she returned to the Central Valley, she worked for a short while as a deputy in the Stanislaus County public defender's office. Veneman's next stop was Damrell, Damrell and Nelson, the Valley's most powerful private law firm.

"My father was not a partisan person," Veneman has said. "He had friends on both sides."[4] Pete Wilson was one; Frank Damrell, a well-known Democrat, was another. (Damrell entertained President Carter at his home in 1980.) But the central divide in Central Valley politics wasn't partisan; it was agricultural—growers v. farm workers—and Damrell, like Wilson, was on the side of the growers. The Damrells, Veneman says, became "family."

Also in the family, the biggest wine-sellers in the world: Ernest and Julio Gallo. Allegations about their bootleg past ignored, the Gallo family were Central California's local barons. In 1972, *Time* magazine had dubbed them royalty, "the Kings of Wine." Workers in their fields were treated roughly like peasants, and that's how the Gallos liked it. Their sales methods were infamous: Gallo salespeople used every trick to hook inner-city drinkers on their low-cost wine and fruit-juice mix.[5] Their anti-union tactics were just as notorious. For years, Gallo rebuffed vineyard workers' demands for a free union election, and when the pressure became too great, the company arbitrarily granted representation to the Teamsters Union (which agreed to a sweetheart contract). The Gallos would do anything to avoid the UFW. Frank Damrell served as the Gallo Winery's lawyer. His only sister married Bob Gallo, Julio Gallo's oldest son.

1976 witnessed a showdown. The UFW had grown in strength since 1966, and by the middle '70s, they were nearing their goal: the right to organize without reprisal. A single woman made all the difference. Her name was Rose Bird. The Bush administration likes to say that Ann Veneman was California's first female secretary of agriculture. It is not true. When Veneman was a law student at Hastings College, the chair of the Hastings College Board was Bird, the bona fide first woman to hold the position. Bird was appointed secretary of agriculture *and services* by Governor Jerry Brown (who somewhat redefined the responsibilities of the post and changed the title, hence the confusion about who was the "first" woman to hold it). The job had typically gone to a grower, but to the growers' horror, Bird was not only *not* a farmer, she was a farm workers' advocate.

Rose Bird saw to it that the state banned short-handled hoes, a torturous tool that broke bent-over workers' backs, and she supported the farm workers' right to organize. She also helped to draft the first farm labor relations law in the United States. The California Assembly just had to be persuaded to pass it. One more mass march tipped the balance. This time the UFW didn't just pass through Modesto, it was headed right there—to the headquarters of the E. & J. Gallo Winery. The turnout was ragtag no more; 15,000 people came, and along with the Mexican and Filipino and migrant farm workers were consumers, environmentalists, members of fellow unions, and the media. Such a show of strength was more than enough to persuade the Sacramento legislature that the UFW were a force to reckon with, and not long after, with the support of Brown and Bird, the union got its law. You could almost feel the farm fields quake.

Brown and Bird's Agricultural Labor Relations Act gave farm workers the right to vote by secret ballot, bargain collectively, collect unemployment benefit and earn a minimum wage. Finally, the poorest workers in the country had a way to defend themselves through something other than boycotts, hunger strikes, and marches. The ALRA was the first law of its kind, and Central Valley growers were determined it would be the last.

California agriculture was accustomed to having several huge things going for it. Hugeness for one thing. The state had inherited scale from the Spanish and Mexicans. Vast pre-revolutionary estates neatly evolved into the country's first agribusinesses. Massive wheat fields stretched for miles, ranches and dairies housed thousands-strong herds. The soil and climate were perfect, water was easy to get. What completed the picture was an abundant labor force—cheap, largely immigrant, all non-unionized. Cheap workers made even labor-intensive crops like berries and grapes and lettuces profitable. Mechanization and new technologies could help cut labor costs, but pro-union labor laws were a threat.

When Veneman signed on with Damrell, Damrell and Nelson, the biggest growers in California were getting very serious about politics. They weren't about to tolerate another Jerry Brown in office or, heaven forbid, another Rose Bird. Party affiliation was secondary; growers beefed up their contributions to friendly politicians of either party, and did whatever it took to kick out their enemies. Growers' groups tried to block Bird's appointment to the state's Supreme Court—the first female chief justice. When that failed, they embarked on a decade-long drive that finally got her ousted her from the bench.[6]

Giants in the farm fields wanted giant political influence. Especially, they wanted influence over the decisions that affected their business. Companies like Sun-Diamond Growers (a fruit and nut consortium comprising Sun-Maid, Sunsweet and Diamond Walnut), the California Grape and Tree Fruit League (one of the largest farm organizations in the state), and Dole Food Co. Inc., the world's largest fruit and vegetable company, gave generously to boost the campaign funds of their friends.

Grower-backed Wilson beat Jerry Brown in the 1982 race for the Senate. George Deukmejian, another grower-backed Republican, became Governor. Asked why he ran for office, Deukmejian replied, "Attorney Generals don't appoint judges—Governors do." During his eight-year term, Deukmejian appointed 1,000 judges. By the time he left office in 1991, the vast majority of the California State Supreme Court was made up of his appointees.[7]

The Gallo brothers were in on the campaign finance act, too. They became the largest corporate donors to local congressional candidates and rose into the top twenty nationwide. They were equal-opportunity givers: the Gallos were the single largest financial backers of Bob Dole's Senate career, and the fifth largest donors to President Bill Clinton. Locally, Gallo money showered on Democratic Senator Alan Cranston among others, and later, Senator Dianne Feinstein. In 1997, Feinstein nominated Frank Damrell to the bench. So it was that Bob Gallo's brother-in-law, the company's former lawyer, became a federal

judge with jurisdiction over land and water use, the imple-
mentation of environmental regulations, and labor law
enforcement.[8]

Central Valley influence was on the rise. After all, California
growers had helped to elect a Californian to the White House.
In 1986, Ronald Reagan returned the favor and appointed Dick
Lyng, a former Modesto feed-grain dealer, long time lobbyist
for the meat industry, and a colleague of John Veneman's, to
serve as agriculture secretary. Lyng, who had served in the
Nixon administration with John Veneman, reached back to
Modesto to hire Ann to come to Washington with him.

Trade was the issue of the day. At the Department of
Agriculture, the tiring Lyng (then almost seventy) made
Veneman deputy undersecretary for international affairs at the
Foreign Agricultural Service (FAS). There, she got a place on
the team negotiating the North American Free Trade Agreement (NAFTA), the US–Canada Free Trade Agreement, and
the Uruguay Round of the General Agreement on Trade and
Tariffs (GATT). It was a sweet spot for the peach-farm girl, at
the center of everything her Valley clients cared most about.

Ever since the Second World War, the nations of the world
had been developing open markets to exchange goods and
services, the ostensible goal being to provide stability and
ensure some degree of consistency in supply, quality, and
prices. At the heart of the system was a series of pacts that set
the rules. In the late 1980s, a set of new pacts was in the
works. NAFTA phased out tariff barriers between the US,
Mexico, and Canada. The Uruguay Round of the GATT talks
(which began on Veneman's watch and culminated in 1994)

created a World Trade Organization (WTO), a kind of global
trade-court.

In the post-colonial period, independent nations in Africa
and Asia, Latin America and the Caribbean were seeking
development. They were rich in land and low-cost labor, but
poor when it came to powerful corporations. From a US grain
trader's perspective, the time was ripe to grab a big new
market.

Ann Veneman wouldn't call it that, of course. In Veneman's
terms, the Uruguay Round instilled a ''dispute resolution
mechanism,'' and ''sound science'' into international trade
policies.[9] The negotiators, led by the United States, gave the
WTO the power to write trade rules, punish cheaters, investigate abuses and generally grease the wheels for members. Top
of the list of things traders wanted policed were tariffs—the
taxes nations impose on foreign imports—and subsidies—the
help they give their own producers.

Just as at the old Stanislaus County court, the people with
the most power wanted the most influence, and from almost
every possible perspective, they got it. As Veneman put it later,
''US agriculture got what it needed in the Uruguay Round
because the United States set the agenda and we led, pushed
and pulled the negotiations where we wanted them to go.''[10]

The Uruguay Round established ''free trade'' as the global
goal. The stated mission was for all countries to drop the
''trade barriers'' that protected domestic producers from foreign competition. Negotiators laid out the promise of a virtuous
exchange, where underdeveloped nations would import capital
goods from the developed world while wealthy nations bought

the developing world's agricultural produce. It didn't quite work out that way because the mission was not pursued anything close to equally. Powerful nations (who had the power to bargain, and whose farmers had the political strength to threaten their governments) played a game of chicken with each other, each blaming the other for not dropping their home-team protections.

"The United States will take only those actions . . . that are matched by the [super-protective] European Community," Ann Veneman promised the Senate in 1989.[11] Poorer, more desperate countries found it harder to resist outside pressure. For them, "free trade" wasn't free at all.

A decade later, then agriculture secretary under the second President Bush, Veneman led the US delegation to the UN World Summit on Sustainable Development, where UN officials and international trade groups reported on the decade of trade. Poorer nations had dropped their trade barriers at a rate three times that of richer countries, they reported, but when those countries tried to sell their own products abroad—or even at home—they could find few buyers. That was largely because, even as they preached "free trade," nations in the developed world had subsidized their own producers to the point where US exporters were able to flood world markets with their cheap foodstuffs. The US government even gave corporations export subsidies or "credits" to help them dump their food abroad. Tariffs on imports in the so-called developed world, meanwhile, had risen by 20 percent. While cotton farmers in Africa were forced to compete with products from affluent American agribusinesses, US trade laws refused to eliminate tariffs on, say, Turkish-made cotton fabrics.

Developed-world produce, flooding the global market, is "imperiling the very survival of producers in West Africa," a minister from Benin complained.[12] In Ghana, another minister reported that 40 percent of all rice was imported—from the United States. The US rice could undercut the domestic product because it was priced way below what it actually cost to produce, and US taxpayers were making up the difference by shelling out emergency grants and agricultural subsidies.[13] As US agriculture activist Kristy Dawkins explained, the system uses "US taxpayer dollars to subsidize international traders who are grabbing more and more market share and driving small producers out of business."[14]

To the world's largest producer-traders, however, none of this sounds bad. Those traders grabbing market share were disproportionately American, among them Philip Morris, ConAgra Foods, PepsiCo, Coca-Cola, Cargill, Archer Daniels Midland, and Dole Food Co. From their point of view, Veneman had done her job.

The Reagan and Bush administrations were certainly happy. Veneman rose through the ranks at the Department of Agriculture, becoming, in 1991, the first female deputy secretary. After her father's death in 1982, Frank Damrell had begun to assume the parental role. In 1991, he threw a swanky gala for the hometown girl to celebrate her promotion. Governor Wilson even came back from vacation to be on hand as the Mayor of Modesto declared "Salute to Ann Veneman Day." Ann Veneman was fast becoming the Valley's most valuable export.[15]

The local biotech industry was happy, too. For more than a

decade, biotechnology companies had been working up agricultural projects. Like the "free trade" negotiators, they
promised great things for the world. Food plants that would
taste better, stay fresher longer, contain more nutrients, grow
more easily in less fertile soil; technology would create crops
that discouraged weeds, grew with fewer pesticides, resisted
pests. Biotechnology supporters touted their wares as "the
single most promising approach to feeding a growing world
population while reducing damage to the environment."[16]

In 1987, a California-based company, Calgene, became the
first to receive a Department of Agriculture permit to field test
a genetically engineered food crop, an altered tomato. The
FLAVR SAVR was supposedly going to stay fresher longer, due
to an introduced gene that delayed ripening. In 1992, the
department freed Calgene to grow and ship its FLAVR SAVR
without further regulation. Veneman, then second-in-command
at the agency, flew all the way to Calgene's corporate headquarters in Davis to make the announcement at a promotional
press conference.[17] The company (and their shareholders) must
have appreciated the official vote of support. The very next
year, Veneman was given a paid seat on Calgene's board—and
in '94, the FLAVR SAVR hit the supermarket shelves.

"Increased trade will open the doors to opportunity,"
Veneman told Californians a year later, in a pitch for NAFTA.
"As trade barriers come down, American jobs and profits will
go up. The global community is open for business."[18]

Especially Californian business. The first few years of
NAFTA saw dismal results for the nation as a whole. Farm
income declined, consumer prices rose. The small growth in

US exports to the North and South was outpaced by the increase in Mexican and Canadian imports. In the first seven years of the pact, tens of thousands of small and moderate-sized farms disappeared from the US landscape. In California, small farmers were hit too, but in a state where large-scale agribusiness dominated, the news was brighter. In just one year, California's farm exports to Mexico doubled to $1 billion.[19] By 1997, the US faced a $16 billion trade deficit with Mexico (compared with a $1 billion surplus before NAFTA), but California's exports were up to $9.1 billion. Tri-Valley, one of Veneman's clients at Damrell, Damrell and Nelson, reported $1 billion in sales.[20]

"From our ports to our stores, California is without question one of the world's largest supermarkets," Governor Wilson exclaimed later. He could have added "and wine cellars." By 1998, wine was the state's fastest-growing export—sales were up 80 percent since 1995. In 1997, revenues hit $374.9 million, up 31 percent from the year before. NAFTA was good for the Gallos.[21]

The export-oriented economy had other consequences, too. As it turned out, government-appointed trade negotiators, in the name of free trade, could release the restraints on corporate agriculture with even more ease and authority than a senator or a judge in the courtroom.

At the Department of Agriculture under Bush Sr, Veneman had supported rolling back tougher local environmental protections (like those on the use of pesticides and fertilizers in California) to the less stringent federal standard, in the name of competition. Where labor and immigration laws threatened to push farm wages up, the administration approved a "guest worker" program that permitted growers to recruit foreign (non-unionized) workers, arguing that domestic producers needed to compete with low-wage growers in other countries. (The federal government approved granting growers the right to hire undocumented migrants, even as Congress passed the Immigration Reform and Control Act, 1986, which increased the penalties attached to being one.)

The first Bush administration came up with the notorious Freedom to Farm Bill, which slashed federally-set farm prices and cut tariffs to benefit corporate traders. When dairy farmers came to Washington for assistance because the price of their product had fallen by some 25 percent, Bush's USDA turned them away. The free market, they said, should be given free rein, but there was nothing free about it. Between 1993 and '98, the US lost some 26 percent of its dairy farmers but those that survived grew in size.[22]

Trade talks took Veneman all around the world—in a single year, she visited Geneva, Moscow, Paris, Tokyo, Montreal— but she never ventured to the family farms of the Great Northern Plains, or the hog houses of North Carolina. There, the downward pressure on commodity prices, coupled with the US system of subsidies and emergency payments, was putting family farmers out of business. Unlike welfare, there are no means tests on agricultural subsidies; direct payments go to rich and poor alike, based on crop-size, so the biggest farms benefit the most.[23] While tens of thousands of small livestock farms went bankrupt, corporate conglomerates mushroomed. The post-NAFTA period witnessed the merger of the nation's biggest pork producer, Smithfield, with its former competitor, Murphy Farms; top poultry producer Tyson acquired IBP, a meat packer. In three decades, the top four beef-packing firms went from slaughtering less than a third of all beef-raised cattle to killing 80 percent. As the size of the average hog farm quadrupled, pressure on the environment intensified. In 1992, in North Carolina, Smithfield began production at the world's largest slaughterhouse, designed to process 24,000 hogs per day. In the next few years it polluted the nearby river no fewer than forty times. When hurricane Floyd hit the state in 1999, hundreds of thousands of carcasses and millions of gallons of toxic manure spewed from flooded industrial farms, causing an environmental catastrophe.[24]

Ann Veneman was out of government when Congress ratified NAFTA, but in some ways, she was in an even handier place, working as a lobbyist—this time not only with Damrell, Damrell and Nelson in California, but also Patton, Boggs and Blow in DC. Dole Foods (which had taken to calling their business not "farming" but "worldwide sourcing")[25] snagged Veneman's services. Who better to work on their behalf during the debates over NAFTA and GATT than the woman who helped write the texts?

By 1995, when Pete Wilson, then Governor, was looking for an agriculture secretary he could hire fast after a conflict of interest scandal at the department, Veneman was not only an old family friend, a former intern and a powerful player in Washington, she also brought with her the goodwill and access to the deep pockets of agribusiness. The *Los Angeles Times* wrote: "Two of Wilson's major agribusiness supporters, Sun-Diamond

Growers and Dole Food Co., praised the appointment of Veneman (who has done legal work for Dole,) and that can only help as Wilson runs for President.''[26] Wilson made a point of administering the swearing-in-oath in person. It was noteworthy because he'd been virtually silent for months, following throat surgery.[27]

There were, of course, those who objected to Veneman's appointment as agriculture chief. ''I don't think she knows anything about crops,'' grumbled Ken Miller, a rancher who called the choice of Veneman ''strictly political.''[28]

In the view of her supporters, Veneman's critics were just sexist. ''Agriculture is very traditional, very slow to change, and slow to accept a woman in leadership,'' says Carole Whiteside, her longtime friend.[29] (It had been Whiteside, former mayor of Modesto, whom Pete Wilson dispatched to persuade Veneman to return to California.) ''You heard a lot of farmers complain that she didn't have enough dirt under her fingernails. But agriculture's not just about farming. It's also about trade, and agribusiness, and food safety,'' says Whiteside. ''And that's really where Ann's expertise lies.''[30] As Veneman herself put it: ''The farmer types kind of wondered who is this woman coming in here?''[31] But it was her agenda, not her gender, that worried many ''farmer types.''

As California agriculture secretary, one of Veneman's first acts was to reorganize the department so that the international trade staff reported directly to her. She toured Asia, pushing up sales of specialty exports to the Pacific Rim: exports like the fruits and nuts of Sun-Diamond and the wines of E. & J. Gallo. International trade remained her number one priority, even as the Asian economic crash began to cast a pall over the export euphoria, but there were other worries besides the failing Asian tiger.

Remember those FLAVR SAVR tomatoes? They flopped. Americans shunned the expensive, less-perishable perishables. In 1997, Monsanto bought out Calgene and successfully remarketed the same product under a different name, this time without letting the public know that the genetic composition had been "modified." The lesson Monsanto learnt from the market was that disclosure was bad for business. At the very same time, at the competing end of the market, the federal government moved to impose weaker, federal standards on states like California that had tough laws on what food could be certified organic. Monsanto argued that as organic farming and biotechnology were both evolving, "Making a clear distinction right now ... does not seem to be necessary or wise."[32] Organic farmers had to force Veneman to write a letter in defense of her California law. "She did it, but it shouldn't have been so difficult to get her to defend her own state's laws," recalls Bob Scowcroft, executive director of California's Organic Farming Research Foundation.[33]

Consumer groups weren't concerned because the Agriculture Secretary was a woman; they were worried about what Veneman's focus on unfettered trade might might mean for food safety. Likewise, farmworkers didn't care about Veneman's gender; they were worried about their health. A hepatitis scare hit the Mexican strawberry market in 1997. Veneman responded by eating a bowl of berries in front of television cameras and assuring consumers that fruit grown in California

was safe. But at the very same time, she opposed a bill that
would have stopped food imports from countries whose safety
standards were poorer than those in the United States. The
Safety of Imported Food Act might cause reprisals that could
hurt US exporters, said Veneman. Besides, "when you have so
much regulation it makes it difficult to do business."[34] The
Agriculture Secretary never addressed the fact that US markets
were trading with growers whose workers endured conditions
that made them sick. Closer to home, she and the Wilson
administration agreed to delay a state-ordered ban on methyl
bromide, a chemical that California's strawberry growers use to
"sterilize" their fields. Long recognized by the Environmental
Protection Agency as a "Category 1 acute toxin"—the EPA's
term for the most deadly substances, exposure to which can
lead to damage of the liver, brain, kidneys, even death—
"there's no question that exposure to the pesticide methyl
bromide can be dangerous, even fatal, to agricultural workers
applying it in the field," editorialized the *Los Angeles Times* in
January 1996.[35] (It also contributes to ozone depletion.) But
growers, complaining that they couldn't compete without it,
lobbied for a delay in phasing methyl bromide out, and that's
just what they got.

On the economic front, Veneman stood by as a new generation of migrant workers arrived to work California's fields
under the guest-worker program. Many were bankrupt Mexican campesinos, wiped out by a flood of cheap US corn. Their
desperation drove wages down. By 2000, some farm workers
in the state had seen their hourly wage drop by 50 percent since
1980. Still others were sharecropping (paid no wage at all), or

working illegally, unprotected and off the books.[36] In '96, the UFW started another organizing drive, and found their activists beaten back by grower-paid anti-union thugs.[37] This time there was no Rose Bird around, only Ann Veneman.

At her confirmation hearing for USDA, Ann Veneman laid out her priorities: "With 96 percent of the world's population living outside the United States, we need to expand trade and eliminate barriers to access for our products in what is an ever-expanding global market." Technology, ingenuity, and above all, "teamwork" would help American farmers to escape hard times, she told the senators.[38]

What discussion there was, in the Senate and the media, centered not on power politics—big farmer v. little—but on regional differences. With her support, farming in California had become a chemically dependent, technology-driven, big-farm, big-money business. John Whitaker, president of the Iowa Farmers' Union, called that "an entirely different face of agriculture" from that practiced elsewhere in the country, and said, "I don't want to see that face transferred to Iowa."[39]

Home state Democrats, Senators Barbara Boxer and Dianne Feinstein, enthused about the long list of firsts associated with Veneman's career. "The first woman to head California's Department of Food and Agriculture, the first woman to hold the post of deputy secretary of the USDA. She sits before you as the first woman ever nominated to be secretary of agriculture. It's a very proud moment." Boxer emphasized Veneman's bipartisan support. Leon Panetta (former Democratic Congressman, member of the Clinton administration) had praised the appointment, saying that Bush couldn't have

picked a more "moderate, hardworking, and intelligent candidate."[40] Veneman was "not an ideologue," said Panetta.
Generally forgotten—or never known—was the fact that
Panetta was hardly an objective observer. He had worked for
Veneman's father in the Nixon administration. Forgotten, too,
was the reality that US trade and agriculture policy is profoundly non-partisan. Clinton Democrats were just as
pernicious, business-friendly, and worker-exploiting as the
Republicans.

The point is, says Tom Buis, an Indiana farmer, and government relations officer for the National Farmers' Union,
"The rural economy is in a shambles—what is USDA going to
do?"[41]

The USDA has come a long way since the 1860s, when it
was established to make sure that enough food was available to
feed the country's population. Now the plan is for US farmers
to feed not only the country, but the world. As Veneman put it
at a biotechnology conference in October 2000, "We simply
will not be able to feed the world without biotechnology."
President George W. Bush is right behind this plan: "The
President gave some very clear guidance to Secretary Veneman
and I [sic] and that is that opening global markets for our farm
products is a top priority," US Trade Representative Robert
Zoellick told the press in July 2002, at a joint press conference
with the agriculture secretary. "What are we telling the
world?" he continued. "Well, we are telling them that we are
proud of our farmers."[42]

It doesn't feel that way to Rhonda Perry. Perry is a family
hog-farmer in Minnesota who works with the Missouri Rural

Crisis Center. Ann Veneman was "well suited for the Agriculture job," she says, "if the Administration had the sole goal of making sure that agriculture is being traded on a world market to the best interest of [grain dealer] Cargill. Low price, no controls, no anti-trust enforcement, all in the name of free trade . . ." Perry says that the Department of Agriculture may have signed up for the export agenda but the pig farmers where she lives didn't. The department, which used to be the place to which farmers like herself turned for assistance, now exists only to advance the profits of big producers. When Perry asks for government help now, she says she's told to produce her way out of her economic mess, "but the more we produce, the more saturated the market becomes." Besides, "we can't produce any cheaper just because the government cuts commodity prices."[43]

Kathy Ozer of the Family Farm Coalition fears that federal farm policy is breeding resentment—not only abroad, where struggling indigenous farmers find themselves priced out of the market by hugely subsidized US corporations, but also at home, where taxpayers get the impression farmers are greedy and lazy. "Farm subsidies are sold to the public as a way of helping struggling family farmers," says Ozer. "The general perception is that the farmers are getting handouts, which they are, but the benefits are transferred from the farmers to the corporations through the low pricing system. The debate becomes subsidies when it should really be prices. The price should reflect what the food costs to produce, not less than that to help out the traders."[44]

In 1999, Perry, Ozer, Huerta and the farmers' union joined

consumer groups, the country's largest trade union body, the AFL-CIO, and environmentalists to demand a voice at the World Trade Organization meetings then taking place in Seattle. The groups accused the WTO of endangering the public health, threatening the food supply, and engineering a race to the bottom in wages and environmental protections. Patented, genetically-engineered crops, aren't shrinking world hunger, they aren't even producing more than indigenous crops, and they are driving poor farmers deeper into debt and dependency, they argued.[45]

While the police beat back their rain-soaked parades with tear gas and rubber bullets, Ann Veneman was inside the meeting, urging negotiators to remove the last "technical barriers" to trade. At the WTO she wore two hats; that of a former high-ranking federal and state policy-maker, and also of a member of the International Policy Council of Agriculture Food and Trade, a policy group financed by Monsanto, Cargill, ADM, Kraft, and Nestlé.[46]

In her view, the time to "complete the reform process" is now. "Trade rule reform" in Veneman's vernacular means roughly what "welfare reform" meant in Clinton's. Food safety risks, says Veneman, "should be evaluated in terms of the product, not the production method."[47] That's a sophisticated way of saying that manipulating genes should be treated no differently from watering seeds. Food packaging and labeling laws must not "discriminate" against US exports (which is to say, identify them) according to this view. The so-called "precautionary principle" must be resisted. (Embraced in Europe, this approach requires that products be withheld from the market for as long as the scientific data on them is inadequate or inconclusive.)[48] The goal of the next round of trade negotiations is to "level the playing field," Veneman has said.

Veneman's language is right out of the civil rights co-opter's phrasebook. Far from level, the fields of US agriculture are sharply raked. With corporate agriculture giving huge sums to political candidates of both parties, not only is a fox guarding the henhouse, but there's only one henhouse, it's owned by a huge multinational business, and it sells billions of its factory-plucked broilers around the world every year at a fraction of what they cost to produce. The people getting discriminated against are the ones who don't happen to own a multinational business.

Veneman was an early supporter of George W. Bush's presidential campaign. At the 2000 Republican National Convention, she sat on the steering committee of Farmers and Ranchers for Bush and she co-chaired the California Bush for President Campaign. Among her co-chairs were Eloise Anderson, a right-wing African-American anti-welfare activist (the Heritage Foundation's favorite to head the Labor Department), and Condoleezza Rice, then Provost at Stanford. The committee did well, raising $15 million for a campaign that barely spent $1.5 million in the state. The Central Valley growers who contributed weren't paying for the President to come and win votes from Californians. They were paying to cast their vote in Washington, and the appointment of Veneman to head USDA was their first return on the investment.

Even before her confirmation, in late December 2000, "a select group" of twenty-two "national leaders" from the industry were invited to a private meeting in Austin with Veneman, the incoming head of the EPA, Christine Todd Whitman, and the President-elect. California Farm Bureau Federation President Bill Pauli came away delighted. "It's great news from a California perspective," he said. "I was able to engage the President-elect in a candid, free-flowing discussion about the issues and policies of greatest concern to our members." Better yet, Bush promised access. Pauli said, "Bush made it clear that he would continue to talk directly with key industry leaders and ensure easy access to his office and those of his cabinet members."[49]

At the Department of Agriculture, industry will already know the players well. The $1 billion department, with some 100,000 employees in forty-two separate agencies, is peopled by corporate agriculture's dream team. Veneman's deputy secretary is a former pork industry executive; her chief of staff is a former director of the National Cattlemen's Beef Association. A director of the Pork Producers' Council is undersecretary for food safety with responsibility for monitoring slaughterhouses and regulating factory farms. Undersecretary for natural resources and the environment, in charge of managing 156 national forests, is Mark Rey, who spent nearly twenty years working for "big timber" loggers.[50] Undersecretary for farm and foreign agricultural services is an agribusiness consultant formerly employed by ConAgra, Monsanto, and America's largest private company, the food processor and commodities trader Cargill.

As for rural development, the man put in charge of that agency is Tom Dorr, an Iowa farmer whom Senator Tom

Harkin has called a liar and a cheat. Dorr was forced to repay $17,000 in subsidies from the very agency at which he now works.[51] Dorr is on record attributing successful farming to racial and religious homogeneity. He's also shared his vision of farming's future with *The New York Times*: a "225,000-acre operation," run more by machines than men. It's a vision Veneman shares. She came to the Bush administration fresh from the board of Beeline Technology, an Australian-based firm that makes farm equipment to guide tractors with satellite global-positioning technology. The same guidance systems that served the US military in the Gulf War enables farmers to drive their tractors in a straight line, not for as far as the eye could see, but almost indefinitely. The Beeline website features testimonials, including this one from a Californian almond farmer: "[Tree planting] previously required 10 people working 2–3 days. Thanks to Beeline, this year's job was reduced to one man, one day, and one Beeline navigator."[52]

In 2003, the USDA played host to a "mini-ministerial" summit on "agricultural science and technology" that brought technology like this to the attention of ministers from every developing nation. In Sacramento, ministers who came to hear a government-to-government discussion of farming techniques were treated to an advertising and promotion blitz by the most powerful firms in industrial farming, courtesy of the Department of Agriculture.

While the department goes out of its way to help the most powerful people in farming, the least powerful have to sue to get the farm loans to which they're entitled. The USDA faces Clinton-era lawsuits brought by Native American, Latino, and

African-American farmers. Black farmers are going bankrupt at a rate three to four times that of whites. Once 14 percent of all family farmers, now they number less than 1 percent. A lawsuit brought by more than 21,000 black farmers in 1997 was settled for an unprecedented $1 billion under Veneman, but those who were compensated received just $50,000 for loss of land and livelihood, and under the strict terms of the settlement (black farmers had to find a "similarly situated white farmer" who had been denied a loan in the same year the black farmer's loan was denied) over 40 percent of the plaintiffs received no award.[53]

Women farmers have yet to find any relief from the first woman agriculture secretary in history. In claims brought during the Clinton administration, 102 named plaintiffs and thousands of other women farmers say they are involved in every possible kind of farming, but share virtually the same experience with the USDA's farm loan program. Lawyers in one of several large gender discrimination suits, RoseMary Love et al v. Ann Veneman, say that women who raise horses in Maine, sheep and goats in Oklahoma, vegetables in Mississippi, and cattle in California have all been denied loans without explanation, refused loan financing or given financing on unfavorable terms, and told to return to the USDA office with a male co-signer, or were blocked from even filing a loan application in the first place. The plaintiffs quote an Arkansas USDA official's comment to one class member, Glenda Anthony: "The farming business is too risky for women and I can't do anything to help you."[54] The business hasn't been too risky for Ann Veneman.

Veneman is a hardworking and dedicated person, even her critics say. On social issues, she's moderate, pro-choice, pro-equality for lesbians and gays. She certainly seems to work "farmer's hours"—she's got no husband or kids, although she's once divorced. When it comes to farming, however, her principles were all forged long ago, in that battle in the farmlands that put big business on a collision course with farm labor, small farmers, taxpayers, and the environment.

Within weeks of her arrival in office, the Department of Agriculture suspended a Clinton administration decision to ban commercial logging and road-building on 58.5 million acres of national land. (Disclosure forms released at her confirmation showed that immediately before joining the administration, Veneman worked for the Sierra Nevada Access Multi-Use Stewardship coalition, which existed specifically to oppose Clinton's "roadless initiative.") In a backroom deal, the USDA agreed not to terminate a mandatory contribution that hog-farmers make to the National Pork Producers' Council, even though, in a national referendum, farmers voted 53 percent to 47 percent to end the tax which they say disproportionately benefits the biggest corporations.

Although in testimony before Congress, Agriculture Secretary Veneman promised that her department would give farmers "the appropriate tools to continue to make the best decisions on how to protect the environment," an investigation presented by Democratic Congressman Henry A. Waxman of California found that USDA had imposed strict controls on the publication of information on agricultural pollution. Research into the health effects of factory hog farms on those who live near them was quietly reclassified as "sensitive," and top scientists were told to seek prior approval on all manuscripts pertaining to "agricultural practices with negative health and environmental consequences, e.g. global climate change; contamination of water by hazardous materials (nutrients, pesticides and pathogens): animal feeding operation or crop production practices that negatively impact soil, water, or air quality."[55]

While Veneman and the President talk about striking down farm subsidies and leveling playing fields, the administration virtually sat-out the congressional debate on the 2002 farm bill—which sets pricing and subsidy levels for the next half-decade. "That way she can go to trade conferences and say this was forced on us by Congress," says Kathy Ozer. Besides, with congressional elections looming, the GOP leadership didn't want to offend voters in Arkansas, Georgia, South Dakota, Iowa. The President duly signed a farm bill that set subsidy payments at a record high and provided $180 billion to American farmers over the next decade (the bill's critics said that of the country's two million farmers, fewer than a quarter received 84 percent of all federal subsidy payments.)[56]

In 2002, the thirty industrial nations of the Organization for Economic Cooperation and Development (OECD) spent $311 billion on domestic agricultural subsidies—more than the combined gross domestic products of all the countries of sub-Saharan Africa.[57] Even as the USDA props up these barriers to trade, it is determined to dismantle others. At the post-Seattle, Doha Round of trade negotiations (begun in Doha, Qatar), Veneman continued her crusade against "obstacles to trade."

The obstacle she was particularly agitated about was Europe's block on American GM products. There is no doubt an element of protectionism in Europe's moratorium on biotechnology (which is overwhelmingly American), but US consumers might reject GM foods too, if US law required products with modified ingredients to be labeled as such (an idea that is anathema to the biotech lobby). The scientific verdict is still not in. Britain's Royal Society, for example, expresses concerns about allergic reactions that could result from ingesting or even inhaling dust from biotech grain crops. Another study, by a coalition of health and consumer groups, worries that eating GM products could weaken the immune system.[58] Even in the United States, investors and insurers worry about liabilities due to the inevitable GM contamination of non-GM seeds.[59]

Veneman wants the WTO to take legal action against Europe's prevaricators. "The precautionary principle used in Europe is not based on objective science," she told a food safety conference in January 2002. "It forms a barrier to technological progress and could stymie efforts to help third world countries with biotechnology."[60] To force the issue, acceptance of American GM crops is quietly becoming a requirement for countries seeking hunger relief. In 2002, the USDA refused to supply the World Food Program with GM-free corn (despite the availability of hundreds of thousands of tons, in the US and elsewhere). When Zambia, one country in need, refused to accept genetically-modified grain, Tony Hall, the US ambassador to the United Nations, pointedly claimed that "people that deny food to their people, that are in fact starving people to death, should be held responsible for the highest crimes against humanity in the highest courts in the world."[61] It was rich stuff, coming from an administration which, at the United Nations Food Summit in Rome that same year, had caused a diplomatic dust-up when its delegation announced at the very start of deliberations that it wouldn't sign any document that referred to food as a human right.

Looking towards the 2004 election, the Bush administration faces a challenge. Not even five Supreme Court Justices and James Baker III could have delivered the White House for George W. and co, if hundreds of thousands of rural Americans hadn't voted Republican in November 2000. In 2004, George W. is unlikely to face an opponent who takes a strong stand against farm subsidies or for fairer prices, but Bush is still going to need every last farmland vote if he wants to be assured of a second term in office. White House policies please agribusiness (campaign contributions from agribusiness have tripled to almost $60 million since 1990, with 74 percent going to Republicans),[62] but people in heartland America are watching family farmers buckle under debt, and even conservatives are getting restive about subsidizing the world's wealthiest corporations to trade their wares abroad at a discount (the Heritage Foundation thinks all subsidies should be scrapped).[63] "Agricultural subsidies undermine our national security," by provoking resentment, wrote a former Republican congressman from New York in August 2003.[64] That resentment is not likely to wane any time soon and, on top of subsidies, the United States' reconstruction plan for Iraq is hardly going to win friends around the world.

In 2003, the British-backed US invasion of Iraq featured

bombing raids not only on power plants and presidential palaces, but also on farms and feedlots, irrigation systems, and fertilizer warehouses. (As reporter Jeffrey St Clair put it in May 2003, pesticide factories are the ''closest thing the US has come to finding Weapons of Mass Destruction.'')[65] The man put in charge of rebuilding Iraq's agriculture is Daniel Amstutz, an international trade lobbyist who served with Veneman in the USDA under the first Bush presidency, and, with her, negotiated agricultural trade issues at the Uruguay Round of the GATT talks. Amstutz is a former executive of Cargill, the world's largest supplier of grain. His appointment provoked Kevin Watkins, of Oxfam in London, to warn that ''Putting Dan Amstutz in charge of agricultural reconstruction in Iraq is like putting Saddam Hussein in the chair of a human rights commission.'' Amstutz, says Watkins, is ''uniquely well-placed to advance the commercial interests of American grain companies and bust open the Iraqi market, but singularly ill equipped to lead a reconstruction effort in a war torn country.''[66]

The same could be said of virtually every official in the USDA. After years of devotion to big business, the department is beginning to betray signs of inattention in other areas. In July 2003, USDA employees were sitting down to lunch in their main cafeteria when security guards ordered everyone out. It wasn't a bomb scare in the building; there were mice droppings, and (according to the Department of Health inspection report) dead mice in a trap—right there at the USDA, home of the Animal and Plant Health Inspection Services, the nation's meat and poultry inspectors.

"It's inexcusable for these conditions to be allowed," said Theodore J. Gordon, of the Health Department (who conducted the raid). "People are entitled to safe food." Perhaps the mice came to send that message.

As her father did, Ann Veneman talks a lot about health: ours is the "safest food supply anywhere in the world," she told her confirmation committee, yet her first year in office witnessed two major recalls: ConAgra distributed enough potentially contaminated beef to infect a quarter of the population with the E. coli bacterium, and the Aventis Corporation's genetically engineered STARLINK corn— approved only for use in animal feed—showed up in ready-to-eat Taco Bell taco shells.[67]

Veneman's response was consistent: blame the victim. Although food producers stonewall every effort to control their methods, Veneman tends to blame consumers, not corporations for bad food. "People who are preparing food at home do not remember or have a memory of their grandmother teaching them . . . basic food safety," she told Californians after a food scare in '98.[68] Elsa Murano, her undersecretary for food safety, told Americans the same thing after the E. coli threat in 2001. "If people just cooked their food correctly, a lot of outbreaks would not take place."[69]

The same administration that embraces the logic of "precaution" when it comes to waging war on Iraq, because that country just might someday produce nuclear weapons, calls the "precautionary principle" heresy on the food front. Those who favor importing a European precautionary model to the United States, and want it applied not only to biotechnology but to all the chemicals we use on our land and water, Veneman calls "irrational," and "emotional." It would be awkward for a man to accuse consumers of all the traits commonly wrapped up in the misogynist term "hysteria." In the cynical world of the Bushwomen, that's best left as women's work.

In 1962, Rachel Carson warned that "as crude a weapon as the cave man's club, [a] chemical barrage has been hurled against the fabric of life."[70] Industry called her crazy, but the public outcry that followed the publication of her book *Silent Spring* forced the banning of DDT (at least in the United States), and spurred a generation of research. Now the link between environmental degradation and human health is well established. Many doctors, researchers, and people grappling with disease think that certain cancer types may be especially directly linked. Breast cancer tops that list. Rachel Carson died of it in 1963. Rose Bird succumbed in 1999. In 2001, George W. Bush announced that Ann Veneman too, suffers from the disease.

At a White House press conference, she was a featured guest as the President announced a "Healthy Us Initiative." Regular exercise, a nutritious diet, and "smart choices" can help prevent many serious health problems, "including cancer," declared George W. Bush between lots of jokes. Environmental protection, toxic clean-up, and responsible corporate behavior never got a mention. The consumer, in this case the cancer patient, was the only player admonished and told to shape up.

Veneman has undergone radiation treatments and says she's doing well. She's proud to say she hasn't missed a day of work. The 50,000 women who die each year from her disease are not so lucky. Stopping those deaths is within our grasp, say activists. One smart choice would be to take a long, hard, critical look at the effects on people of our agricultural policies. ''The predator and the preyed-upon exist not alone, but as part of a vast web of life, all of which needs to be taken into account,'' wrote Carson.[71] In twenty years of service to farming driven only by profit, that is not a choice Ann Veneman has ever made.

FIRST DAUGHTER FOR THE FIRST SON

Elaine Chao

When it comes to one's personal history, it sometimes suits a politician for the public to know very little. Better yet for the public, the media, and fellow politicians to know little, but assume much. Such has been the happy fate of Labor Secretary Elaine Chao.

"Elaine Chao believes deeply in the American dream because she has lived it," effused George W. Bush when he announced her nomination to his cabinet in 2001. "Her successful life gives eloquent testimony to the virtues of hard work and perseverance and to the unending promise of this great country."

The Organization of Chinese Americans welcomed the first Asian American to hold a cabinet position. Chao, they said, would help the Bush administration "represent the diversity of the nation." Union leaders John Sweeney and Morton Bahr supported Chao because they'd worked with her when she ran the charity United Way. Conservatives in the Bush administration were reassured because Chao stood a good chance of getting an easy ride from labor. And Chao's colleagues in the right-wing Heritage Foundation were delighted, for reasons they kept all to themselves.

As far as the members of the Senate health, education, labor, and pensions committee were concerned, one of the best things about Elaine Chao was that she was relatively unknown. (She wasn't Linda Chavez, for example, Bush's first choice for Labor Secretary. Behind Chavez blazed such a fiery trail of civil rights controversies that six national groups signed up to testify against her within hours of her nomination being leaked to the press.) Chao is married to a powerful GOP fundraiser, Senator Mitch McConnell of Kentucky. Decorum would rule out any tough questioning of this nominee in the Senate chamber—and outside it, Chao had a powerful personal story, and that's about all the public would hear.

Republican Senator Jim Jeffords of Vermont gaveled the proceedings to order with the announcement that Chao's life "epitomizes the American dream—a concrete example of the consequences of opportunity and hard work and talent . . . A positive role model for America." Chao "knows first-hand the experience of minorities," chimed-in the committee co-chair, Democratic Senator Ted Kennedy. "Her career is a vivid example of the American dream." Apart from a brief inter-jection of skepticism by the late Paul Wellstone (Democrat of Minnesota), the only point of contention among the senators was over Chao's relationship to that "American dream." Did she "epitomize" it, or "embody" it? Chao's home-state Senator Bunning of Kentucky broke with the pack when he declared, "Elaine is living proof that the American dream is alive and well."[1]

Ironically, while the Bush administration opposes affirmative action, and claims that every appointee is named on his or her merits alone, Chao's merits, as laid out by Bush, and then by senator after senator at her confirmation hearing, had very little to do with her experience as a banker, a GOP fundraiser, and corporate bureaucrat, and everything to do with her gender and race. What qualified Chao to oversee 125 million workers, 10 million employers and the enforcement of 180 federal laws? The senators on her confirmation committee never asked. It was enough that Chao had, as one senator put it, this ''compelling'' and ''poignant'' personal story. Even if no one knew what it was.

One of the few observers informed enough to voice an opinion called Chao ''ideologically similar to Chavez, but [without] the paper trail.''[2] But it's not strictly true that nothing has been written by or about Chao; it is rather that the *same thing* has been said and written about her, again and again and again.

''Elaine Chao began her life in this country with nothing,'' wrote the *Christian Science Monitor* in 1997.[3] Her family came to America with ''little more than the clothes on their backs,'' declared the Heritage Foundation in a 1999 profile.[4] ''The rigors of assimilation still seem fresh in Chao's mind,'' wrote the *Los Angeles Times* in a 1992 piece; ''her hard-driven father . . . helped her get by.''[5]

With her mother, father, and two sisters sitting behind her in the Dirksen Office Building, Chao beamed a loving look her family's way, thanked the committee for their welcome, and noted the auspiciousness of the occasion. It was Chinese New

Year, she pointed out. It was indeed: the beginning of the year of the snake.

Chao's statement began:

> Surrounded by so many special people who have played such significant roles in my life, I am reminded that even though I'm personally honored to have been nominated for this position . . . I know that this is not just for me. This is also for all those immigrant families who have come to this country with nothing but bare essentials and unswerving faith in themselves, the promise of America and in God.[6]

So who is this woman whose elevation to Bush's cabinet honors all immigrant families and whose life embodies, epitomizes and is living proof of the American Dream?

Elaine Chao was born in Taiwan in 1953, to a family who fled from Shanghai after the Chinese revolution in 1949. These were difficult years for Chinese anti-communists, but Elaine's father, James, had had the luck not only to attend one of his country's finest universities with Jiang Zemin, the future leader of the People's Republic, but also to fall in with the immensely powerful Shanghai-born family the Tungs, who shifted their operations to Taiwan for a time. The Tung dynasty is powerful in Chinese politics and business to this day. Hong Kong's first chief executive after reunification with mainland China was Tung Chee Hwa, the first child of the magnate Tung Chao Yung, in whose Maritime Trust company James Chao got his start. James Chao married into another powerful family: the Hsus (pronounced "shoe"). His wife's family would later operate a shipping empire in Hong Kong. Did James Chao arrive in the US with nothing? Quite possibly, but Chao had, as one who knows his history put it, "access to plenty."[7] Chao was connected to powerful families in Taiwan—the center of US–Sino relations during the embargo against mainland China—and in trade, connections translate into freight.

James Chao came to the United States in 1958, an assistant in one of the Tungs' merchant-shipping outfits. At a time when immigration to the US by Chinese from anywhere in the world was strictly limited to 102 people a year (the quota for Britons was 65,000), and the FBI was aggressively pursuing potentially disloyal "Red Chinese," James Chao was somehow able to navigate the system and, within three years, send for his wife and daughters.

In the Chaos' adopted land, the racism of the immigration system was just then becoming a target of the burgeoning civil rights movement. Asian Americans put pressure on the Congress and, a year after the passage of the Civil Rights Act, Lyndon Johnson's administration ended almost a century of legal exclusion and discrimination against Chinese, Japanese, Filipinos, Koreans, and other Asians. The Immigration Act of 1965 finally set the same cap on immigration from every country in the world.

As a new American, Elaine's star was already rising, thanks to the civil rights movement—which was eliminating obstacles that had blocked the paths of generations of Asian Americans before her—and thanks to her industrious parents, who made hard work and study top priorities. Her talents clearly stood her in good stead, as did the New York City public-school system. A non-English speaker, she entered third grade at a public school in Jamaica, Queens, and by fourth grade, she'd been taught well enough, and fast enough, to be elected class president.[8]

In 1964, James Chao founded his own shipping company, called Foremost, to carry goods between the US and Taiwan. It was a turbulent decade for traders. Organized labor was flexing its muscle, and no sector saw more dramatic industrial action than transport. In 1966, New Yorkers like the Chaos witnessed a thirteen-day transit workers' strike, which bedeviled commuters and held the brand-new administration of Mayor John V. Lindsay to ransom. (Lindsay was the city's first Republican mayor in twenty years.) The strike was settled with a 15 percent wage hike for workers. The very next year, in the most extensive rail strike ever, members of the AFL-CIO's International Association of Machinists downed tools, idling some 600,000 railroad workers and affecting 95 percent of the nation's railroad tracks. In 1970, four unions representing close to half a million railroad workers began a walkout. This too was ended, under President Nixon, with a pay increase.

One can imagine that the conversation around the Chao table was none too friendly towards unions. No shipping-company owner likes to see smooth distribution of goods come under threat. James Chao's company was doing fine. After years of isolation from post-revolution Beijing, the most ambitious men in Washington had their sights set on opening up US relations with mainland China, and Chao, with his personal and professional connections already established, was in a perfect place to take advantage. In 1971, Congress lifted the trade embargo on the People's Republic of China. A year later, President Nixon made his famous trip to Beijing, arranged by then foreign policy advisor Henry Kissinger. Former Congressman George Bush Sr of Texas became the chief US liaison officer in the Chinese capital from 1974–75. Full diplomatic relations were established in 1979 by President Jimmy Carter. Secretary of State Kissinger went on to become "Mr China," so-called for his long list of Chinese clients seeking influence in Washington, and his US clients (such as Coca-Cola, Chase Manhattan Bank, and the insurance conglomerate American International Group) looking for introductions to deal-making Chinese. The value of US trade with China grew, from some $95 million in 1972 to $120 *billion* in 2002, and the vast majority of all imports came by sea.[9]

The Chao family moved from the city to the suburbs, and a series of larger, more expensive homes. From Queens, they moved to Syosset, Long Island, and from there to Harrison, in New York's affluent Westchester County. Elaine, the eldest of six daughters, clearly had the coveted role of First Son. James Chao taught her plumbing, as well as house-painting. As she tells the story, one year the family painted their massive Westchester house themselves, "even though the family could afford to hire painters." Another long summer project was to tar their long circular driveway.[10] It is here, as Elaine Chao's up-by-the-bootstraps story turns to talk of circular driveways in Westchester, that one begins to get a sense of the quality of the bootstrap leather.

There's nothing wrong with Chao's family's success. There are plenty of immigrants from every land who arrive in the

United States with the right stuff, in the right circumstances to get ahead. The problem arises when Chao generalizes from her own experience to draw conclusions about the "immigrant" experience. The very word "Asian" spans a vast array of countries, traditions, and routes to the United States, yet Chao permits her personal tale to function not as an interesting case history, but as a symbol of what all immigrants can, and by extension should, achieve. In particular, she likes to suggest that her success is predetermined by her "culture," as if some cultures more than others push people forward, or hold them back. To see poverty or its opposite as a function of "culture," as opposed to policy, fits in neatly with the conservative view of government's proper role ("nonintervention" they call it, when it's really about sustaining the status quo), but Chao's story is very much her own.

Unlike many young Chinese immigrants, Chao had to beg her father to let her take a job after high school. In a 1996 interview, she said, "I had to convince him that to be American I had to get a summer job." (One was an unpaid internship.)[11] There were no long hours toiling in the family business for Chao.

Consider, too, the Chinese culture she misses no opportunity to eulogize. Of the vast array of so-called "Chinese" values, Chao emphasizes what she learnt from her father about hard work, perseverance, and more hard work. But it was lucky for Elaine that her family's embrace of tradition did not extend to that patriarchal part of some Chinese culture that discourages daughters from seeking anything but an early marriage and motherhood. Whether her father, who ruled the household, was innately enlightened, or influenced by changing women's roles in the US, Elaine not only received permission to pursue a college education, but was permitted to leave home to study, put off marriage for decades, and was sent to one of America's very best schools—a proudly feminist institution at that—Mount Holyoke in leafy South Hadley, Massachusetts.

She applied as a wave of Asian-American student activism was spreading East from California. In 1969, East Coast students founded a network of Asian-American student associations and added their weight to the pressure on universities to open their campuses to a diverse student body, and new fields. (The first Asian-American studies departments were established as part of the new phenomenon, Ethnic Studies, in 1968.)[12] Mount Holyoke, a highly selective, liberal arts establishment, the oldest continuously-run institution of higher education for women in the United States, offered Chao a place. With no more than 1,200 to 1,300 students at that time, the college boasted "equestrian studies" (horse-riding), and golf at the world-class Orchards Club. A classmate recalls lessons with a rather quiet and standoffish Chao on the campus's championship eighteen-hole course.

By way of contrast, it's worth comparing Chao's experience with that of another immigrant who forged a career in politics: Geraldine Ferraro (who ran for Vice-President in 1984), the daughter of an immigrant from Italy. Her father owned a restaurant, she went to a small college (Marymount in Manhattan), and she taught grade school in Queens while attending law school at night.

Elaine Chao graduated from Mount Holyoke in 1975 with a

BA in Economics and was immediately snapped up by Harvard Business School. From there, she worked for a spell at the Gulf Oil Corporation (which owned a Taiwan-based petrochemical subsidiary at the time), and at Citicorp, a massive international investment bank. Her area of expertise was shipping, her father's business. At Citicorp she became a loan specialist, working in the ship-financing department in New York City. In 1983, she applied to be one of thirteen White House Fellows, and was accepted, working as special assistant in the Office of Policy Development in the first administration of Ronald Reagan.

The national political scene was in uproar. That August, 250,000 people demonstrated on the Washington Mall to mark the twentieth anniversary of Dr Martin Luther King Jr's March on Washington for Jobs and Freedom. A few months later, the Rev. Jesse Jackson declared his candidacy for the 1984 Democratic presidential nomination, and launched his "rainbow coalition" of women, people of color and other minorities oppressed by Reagan's policies.

Taking stock of the new alliances being forged, the Radical Right was evolving. Gone was the anti-integrationist rhetoric of the Barry Goldwater era; in its place was the cynical embrace of "diversity" in pursuit of the very same goals. While officially opposed to affirmative action, for example, the Reagan administration actively practiced it. Reagan appointed the first woman, Sandra Day O'Connor, to the Supreme Court, and the first woman, Elizabeth Dole, to run the Department of Transportation. Over tremendous opposition from fellow commissioners, conservative Mexican American Linda Chavez, a protégé of William Bennett (then secretary of the Department of Education), was made chair of the federal Civil Rights Commission. Clarence Thomas, a conservative black judge with no government experience, was brought in to lead the Equal Employment Opportunities Commission.

The New Right's agenda was to use their activists' time in federal office to eviscerate the powers of the government agencies they didn't like. People like Chavez and Thomas provided a more acceptable face for the plan. While Pentagon spending soared, funding to the agencies dried up, with the willing cooperation of their directors who set the budgets. The branches of government that in the 1970s had forced open the education system and the workplace to women and people of color were pruned back, redirected, and, in relation to the movements they had served, cut off.

In 1984, President Reagan visited China, and Elaine Chao did too (later that same year, in an exchange program). The focus of her fellowship in the Office of Policy Development was almost entirely international shipping and maritime unions.[13] She used the time in Washington to make friends outside the office, striking up an acquaintance with Sandra Day O'Connor and Linda Chavez. In 1985, Chao joined BankAmerica in San Francisco, as a vice-president with a focus, again, on shipping, but in 1986 she was hired back into government, this time as deputy administrator of the Maritime Administration (MARAD) in the Department of Transportation, under Elizabeth Dole. The administration celebrated her status as one of the highest officials of Chinese ancestry ever to serve in the department, but the shipping industry was equally well pleased.

Shipping companies loved Chao. After only seven months in office, the trade magazine *American Shipper* put her on the cover. It wasn't a matter of ethnic pride; Chao had salvaged their favorite government loan program. The US merchant-ship construction loan program authorized in Title XI of the 1936 Merchant Marine Act guaranteed shippers millions of dollars a year in cheap, fixed-rate loans. In the 1980s, several ship-owners had defaulted and critics in Congress began howling for the program's cancellation. Chao helped overhaul it, and the loans were refinanced. No wonder shippers were pleased.[14]

Chao and MARAD were a perfect match; her expertise and family connections ideally suited her to the tasks at hand, and much as she denies that it had anything to do with her appointment, her ethnicity had advantages for the administration, too. There's no denying that the Republican Party was wooing Asian-American voters. An influx of Asians had followed the opening up of immigration in 1965; still more had arrived in the 1970s and '80s from Laos, Vietnam and Cambodia, fleeing war, poverty and genocide. All told, more than a million Southeast Asians came to the US after 1975—nearly doubling the existing Asian-American population. Their numbers grew from 3.5 million in 1980 to 7.3 million in 1990, making Asian Americans the fastest growing minority in the country.[15]

Politically, they were unspoken for. Unlike African Americans, who stuck with the Democratic Party, and Hispanic and Latino populations, who also tended to favor Democrats, Asians remained relatively independent, with the anti-communist small business owners among them tending to be conservative. They were active (in 1984, Asians became second only to the Jewish community in the size of political campaign contributions they made per capita), but as a young and extremely diverse population they had yet to gel into a single voting block. In key electoral states such as California, where Elaine Chao kept a legal residence, Asian Americans counted for 10 percent of the population. The Republican Party was out to win them over.

Although Chao's passion was clearly business, trade, and shipping, she was willing to get involved in identity politics for the sake of her party. In 1989, Chao told a reporter that she did not like to describe herself as an Asian American (''I'm an American first,'' she told the *Washington Times*; ''I've never viewed myself as an Asian American,'' she said in October 1989)[16] but she served as national chair for Asian Americans for the Bush–Quayle campaign.

Early on, George Bush Sr began including the Elaine Chao/ American Dream story in his speeches to Asian and Asian-Pacific Americans. ''I think of Elaine Chao . . . who was eight when she boarded a freighter and made the long slow journey across the Pacific . . .'' said Bush in the Asian-Pacific American Heritage Week Proclamation of 1988. He made a point of mentioning that just a week before, the administration had elevated Chao to chairman (*sic*) of the Federal Maritime Commission—the first American of Asian-Pacific heritage ever to hold the position.[17]

Not long before the election, Ronald Reagan signed legislation that gave apologies and reparations to Japanese Americans who were interned in prison camps during the

Second World War (the declaration used the word "mistake" and granted each surviving internee $20,000). Chao was an active campaigner, primarily among Asian Americans in California, and she gave one of several seconding speeches for Bush's nomination at the Republican National Convention in New Orleans that year.[18] Come November, Bush–Quayle won by a landslide, and among Asian-American voters, Republicans secured a 54 percent edge.

Bush went on to name 150 Asians to positions in his administration, including Wendy Gramm (wife of Senator Phil Gramm of Texas) and Elaine Chao, whom he nominated to head the Peace Corps in 1991. It was not, according to any observer, a post Chao wanted. She had her heart set on secretary of transportation—as deputy secretary (at thirty-five, the youngest deputy secretary in the administration), she had certainly done dogged duty.

Chao was on hand when the department had to deal with the San Francisco earthquake; she flew to Scotland to honor the victims of Pan Am Flight 103 at Lockerbie; she visited Alaska in the wake of the *Exxon Valdez* oil spill.[19] She was also on duty during the US invasion of Panama. The 12,000-troop action shut the canal to shipping for the first time in its seventy-five-year history.[20] An early Bush family foray into the business of "regime change," the 1989 invasion was justified in part by Bush Sr by the need to keep international shipping routes secure. Human rights observers say the invasion claimed thousands of Panamanian lives.[21]

The advantage of the job at the Peace Corps was that it inched Elaine Chao closer to foreign policy. She was still not involved in the making of foreign policy, but she got a chance to model it. The Peace Corps is a benign-looking, federally-funded operation, founded in 1961 by John F. Kennedy. It sends American volunteers abroad, traditionally to developing countries. The Corps' critics on the Left see it as a tool of US colonialism. On the Right, they complain it's a liberal '60s relic. Ronald Reagan proposed abolishing the Corps in 1995 but it never happened. In 1991, when Chao took over, Republicans were just figuring out how to turn it in a new direction.

Chao oversaw the dispatch of the first American volunteers to the former Soviet Union. Headlines like this one (in *Money*) appeared in US financial magazines: "Want a capitalist job? Try going to Russia." The Corps offered American MBAs free language training, housing, healthcare, and a stipend to spend two years either teaching or "developing small businesses" in the former Soviet republics. US taxpayers, in effect, paid for a horde of bankers, stockbrokers, and experts in advertising, marketing and finance to get their foot in the door in the post-communist states. "Memories of living in a developing nation are part of who I am today and give me a profound under-standing of the challenges of economic development," Chao told the press. What was needed in the former Soviet Union, she said, were "managerial skills."[22]

What Russia really needed at the time were doctors and scientists and anyone who could have stopped an impending catastrophe. Life expectancy for men was plummeting (from 64 years in 1991 to 57 by '95). Infant mortality was rising by 15 percent a year. Fifty percent of all schoolchildren suffered chronic illness, and those rates were going up. Russians needed experts in heart disease, alcoholism, cancer, radiation poisoning, and wife abuse; what they got, courtesy of the Peace Corps, was a state-funded capitalist vanguard.[23]

The Corps was sending volunteers to China, too. In a controversial move, Bush's National Security Advisor Brent Scowcroft had pushed Beijing to accept Peace Corps volunteers when he met the head of the People's Republic just three months after the massacre in Tiananmen Square. The Peace Corps concession was a sop to Scowcroft's critics—of whom there were many—who said he should never have gone to Beijing at all. Bush insisted it showed the power of what Reagan had once called "positive engagement." Americans were not convinced. They had been glued to their television sets in June 1989 when student poets and others inspired by the opening up of politics in the Soviet Union gathered in a festive encampment in Beijing's central Tiananmen Square. The world watched, horrified, as army tanks rolled in and over the protestors, killing scores of nonviolent students and rounding up hundreds more for arrest. The public reaction to such scenes threw Washington politics into turmoil.

During the Reagan administration, following Nixon's lead, Cold War anti-communism had gradually given way to capitalist realpolitik vis-à-vis China. Red or not, the country had a vast population of compliant low-wage workers, and a massive, undeveloped market. US companies (like those still represented by Henry Kissinger) wanted in. Human rights crimes such as what happened in Tiananmen Square soured American public opinion on the whole project. Tie trade and diplomacy to human rights improvements and progress towards democracy, said US trade unions, human rights groups, and a large portion of the Congress—or reinstate the embargo.

This was hardly a matter on which Elaine Chao had no views. Chao's family's interests were directly tied to US relations (and trade) with China. In 1988, making a bet on the likely turn of the tide, James Chao moved his business from nationalist Taiwan to Hong Kong (which was due to revert from British hands to Chinese, in 1997). He renewed his ties with Beijing and his college chum, Jiang Zemin. According to research by John Judis of the *New Republic*, Chao contracted to build two ships with China's state-owned shipyard in Shanghai in these years, when Zemin was party secretary of Shanghai. After Zemin became the Chinese head of state, James Chao began visiting Beijing regularly—meeting with Zemin and the head of China Shipbuilding in August 1989, just three months after Tiananmen Square.

In Sino–US relations, the Chaos straddled a critical world divide: father James took tea with the powerful in Beijing, and daughter Elaine went out for coffee with their Washington counterparts. It was around this time that Elaine met George W., or as she has referred to him, First Son.

According to Chao, Asianness and gender, not her political connections, explain her success. She was appointed to the Peace Corps, she says, because she understood poverty. As a child in Taiwan she played with "red earthen clay" because that was all there was, she told the *Los Angeles Times*.[24] At United Way, she says she drew on her natural female predispositions. As she told a women's group in 1997: "We're better at building alliances, better at listening.'' The ''traditional women's managerial style is very emblematic of how Asians manage,'' she added, deftly folding two stereotypes into one.[25] Chao doesn't give herself credit. Political *savoir faire* is the secret to her success, not her mild-mannered Asian femininity. But unlike Linda Chavez, for example, who's made no bones about her hardcore ideological bent, Chao clouds her political choices in lots of talk about personality and race.

In the 1990s, her personal and political life came together in a whole new way. She got married, to Kentucky Senator Mitch McConnell, and dug herself still more deeply into the Washington Republican scene. McConnell and Chao met in '87. When she was appointed to the presidency of United Way, he became what *The Washington Post* called her ''social walker.''[26] On February 6 1993 they married (seven weeks before her fortieth birthday, and on Ronald Reagan's birthday, in fact). She'd done a good deal of dating, mostly with influential men. Among her beaux was C. Boyden Gray, then White House counsel. ''I thought I would marry a nice Chinese boy, but I'm too tall,'' she told the *Straits Times*, in 2001. Mitch McConnell is the ''love of my life,'' she has said. He also ''takes care of his own laundry. He picks up his own dry cleaning, he enjoys shopping and he cooks, too.'' She does the plumbing.[27]

Republican heaven must have been smiling. In '93, McConnell, a widower, was rising in the Senate leadership. ''The meanest junkyard dog in the Republican Party in Kentucky,'' his home state Democratic Party chair has called him. McConnell had been building up the coffers of the Kentucky

GOP to the point that his party was making gains back home, and he had a million-dollar campaign fund himself—more than all but a handful of big-state senators. In the Republican sweep of 1994, McConnell picked up the chairmanship of two key committees, one of them a critical subcommittee on foreign operations and export financing. The Israeli lobby (the American Israel Political Action Committee, AIPAC) was, and still is, his second largest contributor. Speaking out on world affairs was serving him well, and with Elaine Chao, he was about to do a whole lot more.[28]

Like a successful '80s merger, the McConnell–Chao partnership was greater than the sum of its parts. Together, the two had connections to die for. Few Washington weddings boast a guest list, for example, that includes officials of the world's two most powerful states. China's United Nations representative attended. Chao's family showed up too, of course. With the wedding, the Chao–McConnell relationship became familial, but there was already a financial link.

Right after the Tiananmen Square massacre, McConnell began to receive campaign contributions from James Chao and people associated with Foremost Maritime. Chao hoped for influence in the Senate and, as their closeness grew, the Kentucky senator began to receive money from other influential Asian Americans too. These were tricky times for Sino–US connections. In 1996, Republicans launched a veritable witchhunt against Asians in politics after a concerted effort had mobilized Asian-American votes and campaign dollars for Clinton–Gore. The so-called "Buddhist temple scandal" (so named because of a fundraiser that occurred at the Hsi Lai temple, in LA) resulted in the conviction of Maria Hsia and John Huang on charges of laundering money from abroad, and became a rallying cry for the Republican Right who didn't like President Clinton's fundraising powers.[29]

But McConnell had received donations from John Huang, too. In fact, he was one of only two Republicans who did, and it was at least partly due to his wife. According to reporter John Judis, McConnell and Chao traveled to Los Angeles shortly after their marriage, to attend a fundraiser thrown by the same Pacific Leadership Conference to which Hsia and Huang belonged. "[Chao] was a very distinguished Chinese-American leader then," Huang told a House hearing in 1999.[30] In December 1993, Chao and McConnell accompanied James Chao to Beijing where they met Jiang Zemin. They attended Hong Kong reunification ceremonies with a delegation from the Heritage Foundation when Chao was a fellow at the institution, and in 1997, when Zemin visited Washington, he met McConnell and Chao in private, just before a VIP state dinner.

Ask McConnell about his "Asian connections" and he is apt to fly into a rage. McConnell described a newspaper editorial about his campaign contributors as "xenophobia" and "an outbreak of yellow fever."[31] But neither he nor his wife did anything to slow the swell of the GOP's rhetoric after the Gore affair (or stem the effect on Asian and Asian-Pacific Americans who once again became suspect citizens in its wake). Apparently racism against Democrats was different. Chao, too, knows the routine: when CNN's Al Hunt quizzed her about her family's business with China, she burst out, "That's not true . . . And if my last name were not Chao, it would never have

. . .'' Hunt followed up: "Have you spoken out on labor conditions in China?" She dodged the question.[32]

What was Chao doing at United Way all this time? By her admirers' account, she was "turning it around." Contributions to the charity were, as one observer put it, "in the toilet" after an embezzlement scandal. Chao fired a third of the staff, got the finances back on track, then left. There was a tricky moment when she failed to reveal a $300,000 "gift" that some board members wanted to give her upon her departure. Once word got out, she turned it down in rather a huff.[33] But her critics say the big-dollar gift was emblematic of Chao's way of doing business. To recoup lost dollars, Chao focused not on United Way's traditional base of worker-contributors, but reached out instead to major donors (those who gave $1,000 and more). She turned the outfit around, all right; she turned it upside down, says Kevin Ronnie of the National Council on Responsive Philanthropy, a longtime critic: "Chao left United Way a very changed organization, and not a more stable one."[34]

A turn-around may be just what is in store for the Department of Labor. It wasn't her beat in 1996, but the Heritage Foundation was pushing a big plan for the department when she arrived at the think-tank that year. Heritage published a major paper by Dixon Mark Wilson, who argued that since its creation in 1913, the DoL has become one of the "most pervasive regulatory agencies in the federal government . . . presenting a barrier to the formation of firms and their ability to create jobs." Their plan was to do away with the whole thing. The title of Wilson's paper? "How to close down the Department of Labor."[35]

Created to "foster, promote and develop the welfare of wage-earners, to improve their working conditions, and to advance their opportunities for profitable labor," the department sets rules and standards governing working hours, workplace health and safety, the employment of children. In the 1920s, it set up a Woman's Bureau to promote the status and job opportunities of women. Congress passed the Davis-Bacon Act, the Wagner Act, which guaranteed the right to collective bargaining, and the Fair Labor Standards Act (FLSA), which set a mandatory minimum wage and maximum working hours. Under the law, employers were to give their workers a break after a forty-hour week, or pay extra called "overtime."

Every day when she crosses the threshold of her office, Elaine Chao is reminded of this history. The department building is named after the woman who pushed the FLSA into law, the first woman member of any cabinet. Another Mount Holyoke graduate, Frances Perkins had a "poignant" personal story too, and one that contradicts any notion that family is destiny in the United States. Born into a comfortable Republican household from Maine, she was moved by the conditions of life for working women, especially immigrant workers in New York. In 1911 she was having tea one Saturday afternoon near Washington Square when she heard fire engines roar by. Perkins went out to investigate and watched, horrified, as women trapped in overcrowded workplaces jumped to their deaths from the top floors of a factory building—146 women textile workers died in the Triangle Shirtwaist fire. "It seared on my mind as well as my heart—a never to be forgotten reminder of why I had to spend my life fighting conditions that could permit such a tragedy,'' wrote Perkins.[36] She was Franklin Delano Roosevelt's choice for Labor Secretary in 1933 (in fact, FDR was urged on by his wife, Eleanor).

The FLSA, like the whole Department of Labor, was now outdated, and a huge burden on employers and industry, argued Wilson. ''Workers are demanding more flexible hours, working conditions and compensation packages than current laws and regulations allow,'' he alleged.[37] Now Wilson is a deputy assistant secretary in the Employment Standards Administration, a division of the Labor Department under Chao. And Chao, who has talked in generalities for years about ''Asians'' and ''women'' and ''immigrants'' and ''Chinese Americans,'' is talking in the same generalities about ''workers.''

She's no expert on workers and the working life, but that's no impediment to her advancing policy about them. She's not an expert on race or gender issues either, and that never stopped her speaking out against civil rights. Chao opposed the 1991 Civil Rights Act on the grounds that it would harm Asian Americans, even though the need for new legislation was exposed by the Supreme Court's decision in Wards Cove Packing Company v. Antonio, a case involving what one dissenting justice called ''plantation-style'' treatment of immigrant Filipino workers at a salmon-packing plant.[38] She spoke out against the confirmation of Bill Lann Lee for US assistant attorney general for civil rights because he had been an advocate for affirmative action. And for a decade and more she collaborated with the Right as they used her own success as a stick to beat poor immigrants and other less successful minorities. If Chao is the model of anything, it's this: she's the model of the "model minority" myth.

If Asian Americans can make it, goes that line, then so can others, or it's just their own fault. That being said, there's no need for social change, affirmative action, workplace regulation, anti-discrimination law. Such is the position of the American Enterprise Institute, Heritage Foundation, Chao, Chavez, and the rest. American Enterprise scholar Charles Murray goes further. In his book, *The Bell Curve*, Murray claims that racial minorities cluster at the bottom of society's ranks because of genetic differences.[39]

For a variety of historic reasons, Asians in America are particularly vulnerable to exploitation in this regard. For centuries, immigrants from one Asian country—the Philippines, or Japan, Korea, China, or Taiwan—have been used as a wedge against other Asians, and against other ethnic and racial groups, especially poor whites and African Americans. Faced with obstacles, it is said that "Asians" overcome them: "I think of Elaine Chao," said George W. Bush's father. "Her life gives eloquent testimony to the virtues of hard work," said First Son.

Chao is said to be "living proof" of the American Dream, which is to say, proof that access and opportunity are available to all, and American society needs no institutional adjustment. A few success stories pale in contrast to the statistical picture, but the statistics are not as "poignant." Or they're poignant in a different way. In 2001, according to the Department of Labor's own data, a woman working full-time is twice as likely as a man to be paid less than the federal minimum wage.

African-American women are even more likely to be paid a sub-minimum wage.[40] White women earn only 75 cents for every (white) man's dollar; Asian-Pacific women earn even less than that.[41] And a machine operator who deals with metal is still paid more than a machine operator who deals with textiles—the former are disproportionately men, the latter overwhelmingly female.[42]

Discrimination is nothing that can't be overcome by dint of personal effort, ethics, hard work, and "character," say Elaine Chao and her colleagues. Affirmative action, which seeks to counter contemporary discrimination and repair the legacy of hundreds of years of slavery, exclusion and disenfranchisement, is not only unnecessary, it's stigmatizing, opponents claim. It can even harm some minorities, they say, such as—you guessed it—Asian Americans, who are homogeneous, according to this view, and doing great.[43]

This is the argument Elaine Chao made to President Clinton. In 1997 Chao joined Linda Chavez and Ward Connerly (the African-American University of California Regent who led the campaign that banned affirmative action in California), to form the Citizens' Initiative on Race and Ethnicity, the sole purpose of which was to challenge the President's Initiative on Race. The Citizens' Initiative did very little except to provide a media platform for powerful people of color who opposed affirmative action. In December, they met President Clinton, and Chao, by then a successful and powerful woman, claimed that Asians like herself find it hard to get ahead, "because they're not aggressive ... there are cultural differences." She joked, "We're just learning rules and goddamn it, they change them on us."[44] It wasn't quite the party line, neither did her story bear any resemblance to her own life, but not one reporter said a disparaging word.

With Linda Chavez and Abigail Thernstrom, Lynne Cheney and others, Chao hopped aboard the anti-feminist bandwagon, too. It was just then undergoing a remodeling. No more the dowdiness of anti-ERA crusader Phyllis Schlafly. In the wake of the Clarence Thomas/Anita Hill debate, frustrated right-wing women founded the Independent Women's Forum. The IWF was stylish, sassy and oh so media friendly, thanks to financing from the same foundations that bankrolled Ward Connerly's anti-affirmative-action campaign, and the Heritage Foundation. (According to 1994 foundation records, the IWF received $100,000 in start-up funds from the Carthage Foundation. The Bradley Foundation granted them $40,000 to produce a media directory of conservative women to distribute to the media.)[45]

Journalists, who were mandated to provide "balanced" reporting on such issues as sexual harassment, affirmative action, and the pay gap, got into the habit of interviewing a representative from NOW or 9to5 (a national women's organization focusing on workplace issues) with a representative from the IWF for the "other side." They weren't exactly equivalent organizations, but they looked that way in the media. (NOW and 9to5 each represented tens if not hundreds of thousands of dues-paying members, while the IWF comprised a few hundred carefully-selected female figureheads.) The IWF offered no services other than media services. Its office in Washington specialized in press conferences. Gender disparities can be explained by the frailties and talents of the individual, argue the women of the IWF. Poverty among women, they say, is explained by women making poor choices—just look at us.[46]

Does Chao misconstrue her own family history? She's been caught in a few "mix-ups," as one headline writer put it, such as where she first "set foot" on US soil (she told the *Los Angeles Times* it was Los Angeles; she told New Yorkers it was New York).[47] In 1991, an enterprising reporter asked Chao why she had never volunteered in the Peace Corps herself, given her professed concerns for countries in development. "If you're of a minority background, you have obligations to your family to support them financially," she replied.[48] It is possible that Chao meant helping with the Westchester tar-the-driveway project, but for the girl who had to "beg" her father to let her take a summer job, it seems like a stretch.

And some Mount Holyoke staff and graduates are irked by her relentless argument that "hard work" is the only legitimate route to success. It wasn't true in her case, they allege. Shortly after her appointment to the Bush administration, word from the campus started to spread. In her senior year, Chao was accused of plagiarism, several sources claim. They further allege that there was intervention by "powerful people," such that her degree was ultimately secured. Three of Chao's classmates were willing to talk about it off the record. A former professor of Chao's said, "I have a pretty good idea what you are calling about but I will not discuss it." Chao herself will not respond to questions about the affair, and the school, citing student privacy rules, will neither confirm nor deny that it occurred. Chao's name does not appear in Mount Holyoke's

1975 commencement program; Chao's office refuses to explain why. And that is where it stands. A lot of people seem unwilling or afraid to tell what they know.

That suits Chao fine; public ignorance has served her and her allies well. They refer to her origins as an eight-year-old not speaking English, and let a pre-existing stereotype do the rest. "Asian immigrant" conjures up a story quite different from Chao's. It does not typically feature shipping executives, for example, let alone shipping executives who are on close personal terms with the leaders of not one, but two of the world's most powerful nations.

As Sonia Shah, author of *Dragon Ladies: Asian American Feminists Breathe Fire*, puts it, "Chao has shrouded her right-wing stances and hard-core corporate mindset in soft-core identity politics."[49] In fact, Chao is an expert, with much experience and a long track record, at serving the very interests she's now advancing at the Department of Labor. The interests belong to business, however, not to labor. She has served on the board of directors for Northwest Airlines, Clorox, Dole Food Co., NASDAQ, and HCA-Healthcare. Her goal, and the goal of her Heritage Foundation friends, is to turn the department around to be more business-friendly. A second spin on the 1980s project, the new "New Right" plan is not only to cut the budget and diminish the power of regulatory agencies, but to shake them up and dedicate them to new purposes.

In August 2002, Elaine Chao shared her vision for the department with the American Legislative Exchange Council (ALEC), a national grouping of far-right legislators. She began by crowing about cutting the DoL's budget (7 percent in

2003). Making it trimmer, she said, was a "victory," given some of the silly things the department's come up with. She mentioned "child labor restrictions on baseball batboys, enforcing overtime requirements for Salvation Army [bell] ringers, putting federal health and safety inspectors in private home offices."[50] By picking on trivial examples, it's easy to make federal child labor, wage and workplace regulations sound silly. It's also a way to build antipathy to the fundamentals—Heritage has used the very same examples for years.

Chao didn't talk to ALEC about "shutting down" the Department of Labor, she talked about "transforming" it. Chao fancies turning it into something called the "Department of the Workplace," where distinctions between workers and managers, bosses and employees would be ignored (even if power disparities remain). Like her husband, who has talked about this on the floor of the Senate, she wants the Labor Department to "transform" itself from being an advocate for workers to being a watchdog on unions.

In a budget that cut funding for enforcing health and safety laws, child-labor regulations, and the minimum wage, Chao has proposed dramatically increasing spending on auditing and investigating unions. In virtually every other realm of life—the environment, trade, civil rights—the White House is bitterly opposed to regulation (of air and water quality, food safety, and business practices), but the organized workforce is different. In December 2001, the Department of Labor issued new regulations that require unions to itemize every expense over $2,000; every outlay spent on organising workers, striking, and any other legislative or political activities.

More reporting by trade unions will be matched by less reporting by the government. In a time of mass lay-offs— 700,000 in the months immediately following 9/11 alone— Chao's department laid off the mass-lay-off statistics program that reported the number of firms laying off fifty or more workers every month. If it had still been in effect, the statistics program might have registered the laying-off of close to 100,000 airline employees, who received next to no government aid even as the White House lobbied vigorously and successfully for a $15 billion bailout for the airlines, including Chao's friends at Northwest. Since 2001, the unemployed workforce has grown by 1.6 million; the number of Americans "outside the workforce" has gone up by 4 million.

With regard to mining safety, it's hard to know even where to begin to define "conflict of interest," when the federal government's top regulator is married to the number two man in the Republican leadership. It may not be illegal, but it's probably not good for miners. Assistant Majority Leader Mitch McConnell's funders include some the country's biggest coal-mining companies. Jeff Young, a public radio correspondent, received unedited notes from a meeting between federal Mine Safety and Health Administration (MSHA) personnel and coal operator Robert Murray, a contributor to Mitch McConnell's campaigns. According to Young's report, Murray made repeated threats to have MSHA employees fired over agency enforcement actions at his mines.

"Mitch McConnell calls me one of the five finest men in America," Murray said to the MSHA representative, adding, "And last I checked he was sleeping with your boss."[51] Young says he doubts the public would be surprised to hear about a coal company owner exerting pressure ("but they might be surprised by the colorful language"). What's more important is what happens afterwards. In this case, the inspector in question was removed from Murray mines. MSHA denies that political pressure played any role.[52]

While Chao claims to care deeply for working people's families, she never visited the miners of Quecreek. In 2002, nine miners at the Quecreek mine in western Pennsylvania came within a few hours of dying in an accident involving outdated maps and lack of oversight at a non-union mine. For seventy-seven hours, their families waited, and agonized, while the rescue mission was underway. Chao, so conscious of her image in other contexts, never put in an appearance. Davitt McAteer, former assistant secretary for mine safety and health in the Clinton administration, says that's the least of what she did wrong.

"This was the most public of rescues," says McAteer, but afterwards, the administration balked at calls for a public hearing. The decision not to hold one was "silly," he says. "It could have done a tremendous amount of good in the public mind." Moreover, a hearing would have given officials at MSHA subpoena power to obtain mine company documents and witnesses, the best way to find out just why the accident at Quecreek occurred. "Some in this administration seem to have a problem having any grasp of their public responsibilities," McAteer reflects.[53] Today, he says, the administration would rather focus on assisting mine owners with meeting the letter of the law than forcing them to comply with health and safety rules. McAteer was reassigned shortly before the Bush administration took office. The man who holds his job now, David Lauriski, says McAteer is off base on all counts. "I think everybody forgets our mission is to reduce injury and illness, not to write citations," Lauriski told the press. Lauriski admits his department has seen budget cuts in some areas, but "We're not lessening enforcement. We stepped up our enforcement compliance efforts." Mining fatalities, he says, are down. [54]

As peaceful rhetoric has come to frame the arms trade—Peacekeeper missiles, Patriots, and so forth—so too at Labor the talk is all about "flexibility" and "options" and "freedom" (and "lessening citations"). Who better to front such talk than a woman whose own success "epitomizes" the notion that left to their own devices, even the most lowly American can rise to power and influence. [55]

Almost immediately upon taking office, the George W. Bush administration eliminated workplace-safety rules that had been twelve years in the making. Investigation into the ergonomic protection regulations, signed at the last minute by Bill Clinton in 2000, began under Elizabeth Dole. With the sweep of a pen, they were declared null and void under an obscure congressional rule employed by the incoming Bush team. No debate, no paper trail. The hard-won rules to protect workers—disproportionately women in sweatshops, meat-processing, computer work and other jobs requiring hours of repetitive motions—had to be eliminated, argued Chao, so that businesses could have more "freedom" to address workplace safety in their own ways. The Occupational Health and Safety Administration ended 2002 without having cited a single employer for ergonomics injuries. ("Apparently the administration's reliance on voluntary guidelines amounts to simply letting employers do it their way whether it's effective or not," reported the Louisville *Courier-Journal*.)[56]

On Chao's watch, the Bush administration tried to close ten regional offices of the Women's Bureau, which gives women information about harassment, discrimination, family leave, and childcare and the rights they have in the workplace. On the minimum wage, Chao doesn't talk about eliminating it—she says she supports raising it—but she wants to make it voluntary for the states, so workers and employers have more "options." As US troops entered Baghdad in 2003, 90 percent of them with just a high-school diploma, from low-income families earning on average $33,000 a year,[57] Chao and her administration colleagues set about rewriting the nation's wage and working-hour laws, just as the Heritage Foundation paper proposed in 1995. The initial legislation is called the "Family Time Workplace Flexibility Act." Unions say it could eliminate overtime pay for many of the 80 million workers entitled to it under the existing legislation. The department says the real number is a tenth of that. Regardless of the numbers, unions see the "Flexibility" Act as a first step to doing away with the Fair Labor Standards Act altogether. "It should be called the Flexibility for Bosses Act," says Ellen Bravo, president of 9to5.[58] The administration's overtime rules were even too much for some Republicans. In a rare move, six GOP senators joined with Democrats to oppose the administration's proposal in September 2003. After months of unity, it was the first sign of dissent in Republican ranks.

The administration has become adroit at linking worker obedience to "national security." After the attacks of 9/11, Bush bailed out the airlines in the name of "national security." He used the power of injunction to end strikes at two major airlines in the name of "national security," too. In 2002, Elaine Chao claimed national security concerns prompted the administration to invoke the anti-union 1947 Taft-Hartley Act and force 10,000 longshore workers at twenty-nine West Coast ports back to their jobs after a lockout. Members of the ILWU (International Longshore and Warehouse Union) were in negotiations over a new contract when they were locked out by management for several months. Where her predecessor Frances Perkins had staked her political career on defending the rights of ILWU leaders to organize a powerful, coastalwide union, and a historic general strike in 1934, Chao considered sending troops in to quell the ILWU, then supported the President in invoking Taft-Hartley. The move was reminiscent of Ronald Reagan's tough stand, firing the striking air-traffic controllers of PATCO in 1981. Taft-Hartley had been used before, but never against a management lockout.

Publicly Chao stated, "We have been patient, but now other workers, small business owners and farmers are being affected by this dispute." In fact, those being affected were powerful Chinese and US shipping interests whose fates have been tightly tied to Chao for decades. Piling up on the West Coast's docks were tons of ship-bound cargo. Shippers and retailers were panicking about profit losses and cargo damage, and none worried more than those who insure cargo, and those who trade with China. In 2002, the US imported $42.29 billion worth of goods from China and 90.8 percent of it went through West Coast, ILWU ports. Even before the lockout, shippers had formed a coalition with some of their largest customers, mostly large retail chains such as WalMart and Gap, and they had met a task force from the Bush administration to prepare strategy. Included in the shippers' lobby, the Pacific Maritime Association, was one of James Chao's clients, the China Shipping Company or Cosco, a company controlled by the Chinese government.

Also relieved when one of the country's most powerful unions was forced back to work was a major maritime insurer, American International Group, a Henry Kissinger client that does big business with China. AIG's chief executive officer, Maurice "Hank" Greenberg, is one of the Heritage Foundation's largest donors and a major contributor to Senator Mitch McConnell. He must have been very proud of Chao.

Chao was one of George W. Bush's "pioneers" in 2000— the people who pledged to bring in $100,000 worth of donations to his presidential campaign. She gave a prime-time speech at the RNC's "multi-culti" convention in 2000. Again, she rehearsed her month-on-a-freighter, traveling to America story, but by now religion was a big part of it: "Strengthened by faith in God and family, we knew in our hearts that with hard work, perseverance and the help of newly found neighbors and friends we could indeed achieve the American dream."[59]

One person who wasn't cheering Chao's appointment to the Department of Labor months later was Dan-Thanh Nguyen, of the National Asian Pacific American Women's Forum, which represents women workers, including sweatshop workers, in the Seattle area. When Chao came to Seattle to introduce herself to the local Asian community after coming into office, Nguyen and her group picketed the meeting. As she put it, ''Chao opposed Bill Lann Lee, she opposed affirmative action. She's affiliated with the Independent Women's Forum, she's anti-union, and Asian Americans are supposed to be glad because she's Labor secretary?''[60]

Elaine Chao is somebody's American Dream, for sure. ''But not ours,'' says Dan-Thanh Nguyen. ''Not everybody's.''

DON'T CRY FOR CHRISTIE

Christine Todd Whitman

It was December 22 2000 when George W. Bush named Christine Todd Whitman to head the Environmental Protection Agency (EPA), but from the media coverage, you would have thought Christmas for moderates had come early.

"Liberal," "moderate," "pro-choice"—the words appeared inextricably attached to Christine Todd Whitman's name. Elevated only by presidential fiat, not law, the post was cabinet-lite, but heavy with political significance. The selection of "moderate New Jersey Governor Ms Christine Todd Whitman" was a "balancing" maneuver, reporters said, part of the incoming President's effort to "construct a broad team" and "placate" his progressive wing. United Press International called Whitman a "Republican-liberal," brought in to balance Bush's nominee for Attorney General (John Ashcroft).[1] "Whitman brings GOP's liberal wing to EPA," declared ABC TV.[2]

Twenty-nine months later, with pollution levels up and environmental clean-ups down, the media trotted out the same conventional wisdom in May 2003 when Whitman announced her resignation. "An unsurprising exit," "a voice of reason leaves Washington," declared the editorial writers. *The New York Times* worried that Whitman's departure left the environment "without a single reliable defender" in the administration. Given the White House vendetta on the Clean Air Act, the Clean Water Act, the Kyoto Protocol on global warming, and so much more, the duties of her office had finally become too distasteful for the moderate, environmentally-friendly, pro-choice former Governor of New Jersey. So went the mantra.[3]

Whitman told a different story: "I'm not leaving because of clashes with the administration," she said on CNN "I haven't had any."[4] There's no reason to doubt her. She may have differed with the White House style, but "clash" she never would. One only has to look at her history. Over years of loyal service to a party that has lurched to the right on the social issues she claims to care about—abortion, gay rights, religious orthodoxy—the moderating she's done has all been of her own voice. As for taxes, corporate conduct, and the environment, she's no white hat in a bad crowd, she's a Bushwoman. Ask the people who worked with her at the EPA.

On September 11 2001, Robert Martin was in Washington. Martin was the EPA's ombudsman. It was his job to investigate complaints brought to his office by disgruntled businesses or community groups. That morning, there was chaos in the capital, and the TV was broadcasting scenes of devastation from New York. No one at the EPA had ever seen anything like 9/11 before. That's why Martin was taken aback when, two days later, Whitman, the nation's top environmental watchdog, went to Ground Zero and gave New York's air and water a preliminary all clear. "EPA chief says water, air are safe," ran the headline in the *Daily News* on September 14.[5] On September 16, John L. Henshaw, assistant secretary of labor for the Occupational Safety and Health Administration (OSHA), was quoted in another press release as saying, "Our tests show that it is safe for New Yorkers to go back to work in New York's financial district."[6] The very next day, Wall Street reopened for trading. On the 18th, Whitman issued her official assessment: "I'm glad to reassure the people of New York that their air is safe to breathe and their water is safe to drink."[7] Business and government leaders exhaled a huge corporate sigh of relief. "But it was not safe," says Martin. "You can't have good science without good facts."[8]

In the days that followed, tens of thousands of workers got the go-ahead to return to their jobs. In downtown Manhattan, secretaries spluttered their way to their desks. Construction crews rinsed rust-colored dust off their skin and resumed digging at the burning disaster site. Wall Street traders returned to the trading floor, and local inhabitants mostly returned to their homes. But an acrid taste in the air left a sourness on the tongue, and a light, gray silt penetrated every piece of upholstery, salted every windowsill, and settled on every jacket, every eyelash, every leaf.

Hugh Kaufman, the ombudsman's chief investigator, and a thirty-two-year veteran at the EPA, says that Whitman's reassurances were based on a handful of tests: statistically, "no data at all."[9] Cate Jenkins, a hazardous-waste expert with twenty-two years' experience at the EPA, says the agency's

statements were simply wrong, and they didn't follow standard
EPA procedure. "At the time of the disaster, based on past
experience, we knew there would be at a minimum an asbestos
hazard," she says. "EPA did take measurements. All of their
filters were clogged. It was so heavily contaminated we could
not even get a reading in the laboratory, so we knew it was bad
even from the preliminary tests." In such circumstances, the
EPA has certain "standard" hazard warnings it releases. But in
the messages sent by Whitman after the attacks on New York,
"the EPA did not follow its own regulations," Jenkins says.[10]

It turns out that Whitman was clearing every statement with
the White House. "All statements to the media should be
cleared through the National Security Council in the White
House before they are released," she wrote in a memo to her
staff.[11] According to an investigation by the EPA's own
Inspector General (released in August 2003), the White House
altered the draft statements coming from EPA scientists. One
draft statement was edited to delete a warning that homes as
well as businesses should be professionally cleaned. A draft that
stated that asbestos levels in some areas had been found to be
three times higher than the national standard was changed to
read "slightly above the 1 percent trigger for defining asbestos
material." The comment from OSHA about it being safe to
return to the financial district was inserted into the September
16 press release by the White House.

What the EPA told the press about the "1 percent trigger"
for asbestos was "totally untrue," says Jenkins, who prepared a
440-page memo for the Inspector General. The typical trigger
for concern is enough asbestos to cause one possible cancer case

in a million people. Whitman's reassurances used a standard of one in only ten thousand, Jenkins says. The last time Jenkins worked on a comparable case, it was a building in California. "They didn't take tests to prove it was safe or unsafe. They just evacuated everybody in a five mile radius."[12]

If ever there was a time to clash with the White House, EPA staffers say this would have been it. The man in charge of editing the agency's statements at the National Security Council was no scientist, he was a lawyer, James Connaughton, chairman of the White House Council on Environmental Quality. Connaughton formerly represented the asbestos industry. After the release of the Inspector General's report, which came out after Whitman had left the EPA, she denied she had experienced pressure from the White House. "We were not told to lie," she told *Newsweek*.[13] She has suggested that the criticisms impugned her staff, whose integrity and efficiency she defends. But in the months after the attacks of 9/11, Whitman came into direct conflict with several EPA staffers, including Kaufman and Robert Martin, now the *former* ombudsman.

In the weeks after the attacks, New York Democratic Congressman Jerry Nadler and Senator Hillary Clinton clamored for hearings. "Whitman misled the public," said Nadler, whose district includes Ground Zero. "I decided that her representation to the people of New York was simply wrong, and if it was the last thing I did, I would bring that out to light," says Martin. "It *was* the last thing I did."[14] The hearings revealed that in the days after the attacks, the EPA's own tests of air and water did not support what Whitman had told New Yorkers. Hudson River run-off water showed elevated levels of asbestos, dioxin, PCBs, and heavy metals.[15] A US Geological Survey team found dust from the World Trade Center site that was as caustic as drain cleaner because of the concentration of powdered cement. The team sent their conclusion to the EPA, but the agency kept it to themselves.[16] In October, when the administrator informed parents that it was safe to return their children to Stuyvesant High School, just a few blocks north of Ground Zero, experts from the University of California were telling the EPA that pollution in the air near there exceeded the toxicity of Kuwait after the Gulf War oil fires.[17]

An EPA report released in December 2002 declared that Ground Zero workers were "unlikely to suffer serious short or long term health effects from the terror attack," but a study of Ground Zero workers who came forward for physical examinations at the Mount Sinai Medical Center showed that nearly three-quarters had ear, nose or throat problems more than ten months after the World Trade Towers attack. More than half still had lung complaints.[18] And almost two years after the attacks, another Mount Sinai Study showed that women who were exposed to the dust, ash and smoke were more than twice as likely as other women to give birth to babies in the lowest 10 percent for birth weight.[19]

The worst part of the picture, say Martin and Kaufman, is that, at the very least, there was the appearance of a conflict between Whitman's responsibility to the public and her own family's financial affairs. As the former Governor of New Jersey, Whitman owned bonds worth between $15,000 and $50,000 in the New York/New Jersey Port Authority—the owner of the World Trade Center site and the major liable party in the affair. Her husband, John Whitman, formerly a Citigroup vice-president, manages hundreds of millions of dollars of the banking giant's assets, and Travelers Insurance, a Citigroup subsidiary, stood to lose multiple millions in Manhattan medical claims. The Whitmans were deeply invested in Citigroup (owning up to $250,000 in stock). At his company Sycamore (a Citigroup-spin off), John Whitman received a six-figure bonus from Citigroup as recently as 2000.[20]

Federal law requires officials to recuse themselves from affairs in which they have a direct or perceived personal interest. "If the EPA had revealed to citizens the same information that Martin revealed in subsequent hearings," says Martin's lawyer, Tom Devine, of the Government Accountability Project, a whistleblowers' support organization, "it would have been financially painful to her husband's company. She had no business going to New York at all."[21]

Four months after Martin opened his investigation into the World Trade Center clean-up, he found himself out of a job. One Friday afternoon in April, while he was in New York, Whitman, who had been trying to redefine the ombudsman's responsibilities since she first came on board at the EPA, ordered that his office be closed and his job transferred. Louise Hall, Martin's seventy-six-year-old secretary, watched as, late into the evening, EPA agents carried Martin's files away in boxes. Shortly afterwards, Martin resigned in protest.

"The press has taken it easy on Whitman," says Kaufman, who was shifted to a desk job under the Whistleblower Protection Act. "They like to talk about her as a liberal because of her stand on abortion. But on the environment, she's one of them . . . She's a piece of work."[22]

Welcome to Whitman's world. With friends like that, moderates are in sad shape. She rose to prominence in her party on account of a tax cut. She ran for Governor in 1993 on a pledge to balance the state budget and slash income taxes by 30 percent in three years—which she did. She inspired tax-cutters everywhere. When it comes to economics, she's an extremist whom the Republican Right adore, but because she favors a woman's right to an abortion, she earns the "moderate" tag. If the US media gave economics the same attention they give to social issues—or if abortion were safe, legal, available, and uncontested—the Whitman-mobile would have no gas and without Whitman, the Republican Right would lose a powerful decoy.

Call her the Mighty Mouse of the GOP. When the party's in an awkward spot, it's Whitman they call to save the day. In 1996, she co-hosted the Republican convention when an anti-right-wing backlash was in full swing. After the Right swept to power in both houses of Congress in '94, it was Whitman whom the GOP chose to be their public face. Asked why the victorious GOP leadership chose a freshwoman Governor instead of one of their own to offer the response to President Clinton's State of the Union address that year, House Speaker Newt Gingrich, author of the *Contract with America*, explained: "She is clearly just a very articulate and attractive advocate of our cause."[23]

What she is, in fact, is an attractive shill, a lure for liberals and moderates. She didn't support the incoming Congress's

Contract with America. Asked if she'd sign it, she declined. ("I don't usually sign things like that," she told *The New York Times*.)[24] She opposed the Human Life Amendment called for in the official Republican Party platform, or manifesto, in 1996, but that didn't stop her headlining at the Convention. She was willing to go along to get along.

January 2001 was another Whitman moment. "The environment is probably the single issue on which Republicans in general—and President Bush in particular—are most vulnerable," Republican pollster Frank Luntz wrote later in a memo. The party, he said, had been waging the same uphill battle for years. "I don't have to remind you how often Republicans are depicted as cold, uncaring, ruthless, even downright antisocial."[25] In this context, who could be better at the EPA than a woman whose public image, if not the substance of her policies, could allay those crazy fears? Luntz urged Republicans to attend to the "environmental communications battle." Whitman has been waging it for years—and winning. Hence all the talk about her environmental credentials.

She came to the EPA touting her record as a saver of open spaces and a lover of wilderness. She and her husband, John, are horse and country people; they also love to sail, and they love to hike. Shortly before leaving office as Governor of New Jersey, she backed a $1 billion bond-issue to preserve a million acres. She also supported a suit brought by eight East Coast states seeking relief from pollution by Midwestern power plants. But when it comes to policing polluters close to home, and protecting the public health, especially of people living near industrial sites, Whitman quit New Jersey leaving a trail of deregulation, and a sharp dip in enforcement. Fines of polluters were down by 70 percent, even as New Jersey ranked near top in the nation for dirty water and air, and top for the number of toxic, so-called Superfund clean-up sites.[26]

Asked how she ended up in the Bush cabinet, Whitman was clear, even if the media were not. She said it had had nothing to do with "balance," it was because she was tough. "George Bush knows what he wants to accomplish. He knows my record as Governor," she told *The Washington Post*. "He knows how I make decisions, and one of the things he keeps saying is this is one of the toughest agencies so we need somebody tough here."[27]

The Bush team needed somebody tough all right. Whitman fitted the bill. At the Environmental Protection Agency she was the perfect choice: a cut-throat "moderate," an "appealing" anti-regulator. She is even an oil "man." Her financial report, produced in advance of her Senate confirmation, revealed that she and her husband own holdings in oil wells run by the Hunt Oil Co. of Houston.[28] Whitman is a pro-choice woman who is 100 percent Good Old Boy.

She was born into the GOP. Her parents met at a Republican convention. She attended her first at the age of nine. Her father, Webster Todd, was chairman of the Republican state committee in New Jersey for eleven years and claims to have known personally every Republican president since Eisenhower. Her mother, Eleanor Schley, chaired the New Jersey Federation of Republican Women and was a Republican national committeewoman for a decade. In the 1950s, the *Star Ledger* of Newark speculated that if New Jersey were to elect a female Governor, Eleanor Schley would be qualified to run.[29]

"Politics really is the family business," Whitman told her biographer, Patricia Beard (an editor at *Town and Country* magazine),[30] and from the very start, Christine Todd wanted to go into it. She told her husband when they married in 1974 that being Governor was her goal. The tricky thing for Whitman has been keeping the business of family and public apart.

It's not by whim that she retains the family name—hers is one of the GOP's grand old families. John R. Todd, Webster's father, restored colonial Williamsburg in Virginia for the Rockefellers and built Rockefeller Center for John D. Rockefeller. According to family lore, it was he with his son "Web" who "personally jack hammered" Mexican artist and socialist Diego Rivera's mural off the Rockefeller Center wall and dumped the pieces, including those bearing Lenin's face, into the East River at night.[31] On her mother's side, grandpa Reeve Schley was no slouch either. One-time Mayor of Far Hills, Schley headed up Chase Bank and he too served for a spell as the New Jersey Republican Party finance chair.

The Schleys and the Todds lived near each other in New Jersey's western hunt country. Reeve's wife, Kate, was head of the Federation of Republican Women in the state and a Republican national committeewoman. So was their daughter, Eleanor. The parents literally fixed their children up at the 1933 Republican National Convention. As a wedding present, the Schleys gave Eleanor and Web their 250-acre estate, Pontefract, in plummy Hunterdon County. The wedding was preceded by a breakfast hunt in which 150 of the 500 guests took part.[32]

"Christie" arrived in 1946, when Web was forty-seven and Eleanor thirty-six. "It was a household of dictatorial men and complicated women," writes Beard. Icy Eleanor terrified Christie's chums. Web was famous for taking his sons upstairs and whipping them hard enough that guests could hear the lash of his belt from the dining-room below. Beard quotes a letter that Web sent his daughter when she was in boarding school. He talks about her pet animals:

> Drummer Boy is fine. I expect to shoot him any day. Angel, if she keeps barking every morning, will also get shot. Next on the list will be the ducks ... All of which means that when you come back you won't recognize the place. I may decide to shoot both horses ... over the week-end. Angel I will save until you arrive home, and probably the old woman the week after.

"Old woman" refers to Christine's mom. This, Whitman calls "jocular." Analysts might find in it explanation enough for her apparent dedication to a party that seems to push her around. She's certainly used to men—and women—who play rough.

When George W. Bush and Christine Todd Whitman's children meet, they can say their family's friendship spans three centuries. W.'s grandparents—Senator and Mrs. Prescott Bush—and Whitman's maternal grandparents were colleagues. Web and Eleanor inherited and built up the relationship. (By Beard's account, Eleanor and Barbara Bush were especially fond of each other.[33] It's the only time the word "fond" comes up in connection with either of these daunting women.) In 1980,

Whitman's mother chaired and Christine co-chaired committees on George Bush's presidential campaign in New Jersey.

How did the old-boy and—to be fair—old-girl network serve Christine Whitman? Straight out of college, with what she admits were embarrassing grades,[34] her impeccable Republican ties opened up a spot for her on President Nixon's transition team. Cast by the media as a fish out of water in the Radical Right realm of the Bush administration, the fact is that Whitman and several of her fellow cabinet members have known each other for decades.

In 1972, Christine Todd Whitman worked for the US Office of Economic Opportunity (OEO). Donald Rumsfeld was director; Dick Cheney his right-hand man.[35] The OEO was established to carry out Lyndon Johnson's "War on Poverty." It funded legal defense as well as social-welfare projects in marginalized communities. Rumsfeld and Cheney were trying to figure out how to run the office in reverse.

Instead of funding community groups and poor people's organizations, their goal, according to *The New Yorker*'s Nicholas Lemann, was to "put an end to political protesting, on the government's nickel, by recipients of OEO grants."[36] Cheney came to Rumsfeld's attention for work he'd done spying on Students for a Democratic Society (SDS) meetings and jotting down the members of the teaching staff he saw involved (for example, at the state-funded University of Wisconsin; the college would then face questions about the use of funds).

Christine Todd invented a different sort of listening project for herself. With her father's help, she talked the chair of the RNC into paying her to listen to voters in minority communities to see what the party could do to win their support. Whitman, who had grown up chasing foxes with hounds and shooting skeet at Pontefract, set out, as Beard puts it, "to interview ghetto blacks, college radicals, and whoever else seemed like a prospect for Republicanism."[37] She was twenty-three, a graduate of the most exclusive private schools—Wheaton college (outside Boston), Manhattan's aristocratic Chapin, and a Virginia finishing-place called Foxcroft (where girls showed up with luggage trunks, and horses too). Her lack of experience was matched only by her enormous sense of her own entitlement. From Hunterdon County—which still in the year 2000 had a population that was 93.9 percent white—Whitman sallied forth to Chicago and fifteen other cities to "listen" to "ghetto blacks." (Interestingly, Newark, New Jersey, never got a visit. The place had just two years earlier exploded into riots in response to racist policing and an oblivious white leadership, but there's no mention of Newark in Whitman's travels; perhaps it was a tad too close to home.) She wrote up a report. The party needed to become more diverse "if we want to continue as a viable party," she argued. To her credit, Whitman was onto something party strategists are still grappling with today.

Concerned about her party's reputation, she was remarkably insensitive to her own. While Whitman has never been charged with breaking conflict-of-interest laws, perceived conflicts abound. In the 1980s when she served on the Somerset County Board of Chosen Freeholders, questions came up after she voted to deposit county funds in the Somerset Trust Company, a bank her grandfather bought, members of her family still owned, and in which she herself owned shares.[38] The same criticisms were raised again after Governor Tom Kean hired her as President of the NJ Public Utilities Board. The Keans were old friends of the Todd family (in the late '80s, Eleanor Todd started calling the Governor about finding "Christie" a cabinet job. "I'm sure Mother drove Tom crazy," says Whitman).[39] In Kean's waning hours as Governor, Whitman approved the sale for development of 290 acres of watershed land owned by Hackensack Water Company. In their 1993 race, Democrat James Florio's campaign accused Whitman of having succumbed to pressure from Kean whose brother was a director of the water company at the time of her vote.[40]

Environmentalists were wary when Whitman geared up for the Governor's race, but they had no idea what was coming their way, says Bill Wolfe, who worked at the New Jersey Department of Environmental Protection (DEP) from 1985 to 1995. Wolfe served under Governors Kean, then Democrat Jim Florio, then Whitman, who came to office in '93. "There's a perception out there that she's a moderate," he said, after Whitman moved to the EPA. "But I categorically deny that that's the case. I wouldn't even call her mainstream."[41]

The Hackensack deal was eventually reversed by litigation, he says. Midnight deals, no public review, "She did it without public notice and hearings, with total disregard for the public interest. They tried to stuff it, but they got caught," says Wolfe. But the Hackensack deal set a tone.

Her heart set on the governorship, Whitman won her party's support in 1991 to take on what was assumed to be a long-shot campaign against the hugely popular incumbent senator,

Democrat Bill Bradley. She did not get the White House assistance she sought (from her parents' old friend George Bush Sr, the President, whom she asked to campaign with her in New Jersery), but she did have some high-powered help from none other than Richard Nixon. The former President, who lived in New Jersey, gave Whitman a private two-hour foreign policy briefing on the day of her first debate with Governor Bradley.[42] With Nixon's help, she came on strongly when asked about the Gulf War, an area about which she wasn't expected to know much. Asked how she'd boost morale among troops still stationed in the Gulf, she said she'd tell soldiers that "they're there to stop a megalomaniac who would have gone next to Saudi Arabia and Israel." On Iraq, she said, "We will not let raw aggressive force go unchecked." Bradley came off weakly, suggesting he'd ask what food they wanted sent from home.[43]

Grossly outspent, Whitman came within a single percentage point of beating the beloved Bradley, and a shocked and startled party started paying attention. Soon after that, she formed a political action committee—the Committee for an Affordable New Jersey—and in 1991, pal Nixon was the star attraction at a $500-a-plate fundraiser. The event made over $80,000 for Republican candidates around the state, and the committee became the launch pad for Whitman's bid to be Governor.

For a Republican, Whitman benefited from unusual support from pro-choice women's groups, but it didn't come without a struggle. In 1993, Elizabeth Volz, 2003 state chairwoman of the National Organization for Women (NOW), represented a relatively conservative NOW chapter in southern New Jersey, and she remembers the heated debates over whom the organization should endorse: Whitman, who would be the first female Governor in state history if elected, or Democrat Jim Florio. Both candidates were pro-choice and pro-civil rights for gay and lesbian people, both supported a relaxation of mandatory sentencing laws, and both, it turned out, employed undocumented immigrants as domestic help. (At Pontefract, Whitman employed a Portuguese couple for whom she paid no taxes.) Whitman's most dramatic promise was a 30 percent state income tax cut over three years. The NOW membership was dramatically divided.

"I won't say that her being a woman didn't come up. Of course it did," says Volz. The group was committed to electing more women to high office, but the debate, says Volz, centered on whether Whitman would be an effective women's rights advocate. "Would she be willing to go to the mat for our issues?"[44]

On one position Whitman stood out. She said she would consider changing the so-called "family cap" passed by Governor Florio, which limited benefit payments to mothers who had additional children while on welfare. That, and her potential to break the all-male lock on the Governor's mansion, tipped the balance. By the slimmest of margins, NOW in New Jersey voted to recommend (rather than endorse) Christine Todd Whitman. It was the first time in its history that the organization had supported a Republican for Governor.

Come election day, every vote made a difference. Whitman slid into office with just a one-point victory over Florio. She didn't win over the majority of women—Florio did, by 6 percent—but she won more than your average Republican. Whitman subsequently hired Myra Terry, New Jersey NOW president (and a Whitman supporter) to join the Governor's transition team. Soon after, Whitman appointed the state's first woman Attorney General, and Terry enthused: "We're all standing a little taller."[45]

Other NOW members were less impressed. While Whitman's commitment to legal abortion has a valiant glow within her party, being pro-choice was hardly a heroic stand in New Jersey. "There hasn't been an anti-choice Governor in the state for thirty years," says Volz. "Anti-choice candidates don't just lose, they get trounced."[46]

New Jersey has had its share of feminist heroes, after all. Consider Alice Paul, founder of the National Women's Party. An uncompromising women's rights advocate, Paul and her fellow suffragists picketed President Woodrow Wilson in the middle of the First World War with a bedsheet banner proclaiming him "Kaiser Wilson." Paul was arrested, went on hunger strike, was force-fed and incarcerated in a psychiatric hospital—all to win votes for women. She dedicated the rest of her long life to the passage of the Equal Rights Amendment. Christine Todd Whitman is no Alice Paul.

As Governor, she stood firm against a Republican-supported abortion ban, and appointed not just the first female Attorney General, but the first African American to the state Supreme Court, but the Governor reversed her position on the so-called "family caps." They stayed in place. And tax returns revealed that in the early 1990s, when she was courting New Jersey Roe v. Wade supporters, she was at the same time contributing to the campaigns for seventeen anti-abortion Republicans. She contributed a measly $50 to Planned Parenthood according to her 1992 return.[47]

In her first year as Governor, she took time out to campaign in Texas on behalf of George W. Bush against Governor Ann Richards. (Bush didn't say it very loudly, but he favored a constitutional amendment overturning Roe.) She chose, and re-appointed, her state's Republican Party chairman, Chuck Haytaian, even after he was accused of sexual harassment by a female aide. (He agreed to settle.)[48] She didn't win NOW's support a second time, and in 1999, after resisting such measures for years, she signed a parental-notification law that left pro-choice groups enraged.[49]

"The Governor had a strong circle of powerful women around her in office," says Sherryl Gordon, of AFSCME, the public employees' union, but "abortion is not the only women's issue."[50] Whitman's tax-cutting budget disproportionately affected women workers. In the first year of downsizing and privatizing, three times as many women as men lost public-sector jobs. Some 271 workers, about 86 percent of them women, lost work in one agency alone, when the state turned the Department of Motor Vehicles over to private hands. A network of state-run daycare centers was privatized. Hundreds of unionized women workers lost benefits and pensions overnight. Gordon remembers women calling her office in a panic. Wages that had been $18 per hour for licenced daycare-providers were dropped to the legal minimum, and positions shrank from full- to part-time, she says.[51] Under Whitman, the Department of Labor changed the rules to make it easier to deny unemployment benefits to temporary workers, and a ten-part exposé by the Bergen County *Record* revealed that of the jobs Whitman claimed had been created since she took office, a disproportionate number were for part-time workers. Even the state, under Whitman, hired increasing numbers of temps.[52]

On the environmental front, Whitman didn't so much shake up the state as shake it down for corporations, say environmentalists. Within months of taking office as Governor, she cut the environmental protection budget by 30 percent. In her first three years in office, 738 employees at the state Department of Environmental Protection (DEP) lost their jobs, and the remaining staff found themselves on a four-day week. The only obvious jobs created were new ones at the Office of Dispute Resolution, which she established to mediate conflicts over environmental issues (usually resolved business's way), and the Office of Business Ombudsman, which Whitman created to help businesses navigate environmental laws.

Foreshadowing the behind-closed-doors meetings of Dick Cheney's Energy Task Force, Whitman's DEP director invited corporate executives to private meetings, at which no environmentalists were allowed. "We had quarterly meetings," a manager at Schering Labs told the Bergen County *Record*. "Sometimes we need his influence, if you will, to kick a little ass . . . just to get motivation."[53]

Her motto was a rhetorical shingle that would hang perfectly well outside the Bush administration's door: "open for business." At the same time, Whitman's DEP eliminated the office of Public Advocate. A famous survey of state workers found that Whitman's environmental staff thought the biggest problem facing New Jersey's Department of Environmental Protection was the Governor herself.[54]

"She comes off as such a sweetheart, and behind the scenes she's a knee-capper," says Bill Wolfe, then of the DEP. "She will not tolerate dissent."[55]

Wolfe resigned in 1995 in a dispute over the state's water-pollution laws. During Whitman's first term, explosive and poisonous chemicals were among some 2,000 substances removed from the state's mandatory "right to know" laws. Whitman said the new policy was designed to ease the regulatory burden on businesses by allowing them to focus on their most dangerous substances, but community activists and emergency workers complained that the program was their only way of knowing what toxins were in their neighborhoods. In 1992, the Chemical Industry Council of New Jersey had backed a bill sponsored by Assemblyman Robert Shinn that would have cut much of the list. The bill failed, but in '94, Whitman appointed Shinn to head the DEP. He cut the list by two-thirds using regulatory powers that avoided the legislature altogether.[56]

Wolfe became concerned when the Academy of Natural Sciences (ANS) found clear links between garbage incinerators and coal-fired power plants in the state, and dangerous levels of mercury in freshwater fish (contamination that posed a particular threat of neurological damage to breast-feeding women and fetuses). Whitman's DEP delayed the release of the ANS report while refusing to issue any regulation on mercury emissions from the relevant power plants. The DEP continued

licensing incinerators, disbanded the civilian "Mercury Task
Force," and commissioned a new study, while Wolfe's complaints and the ANS findings languished in the files. In
frustration, Wolfe disclosed some internal memos on the
matter to the press, and Whitman's lawyers came down on him
hard, accusing him of criminal theft of government property.
("The precedent the Attorney General used was Nixon v.
US—the case of the missing Watergate tapes," he says.)[57]

"If you were a business, and you wanted help from DEP,
there was a welcome wagon for you there," says Amy Goldsmith, director of the New Jersey Environmental Federation.
Goldsmith says she battled Governor Whitman nonstop for two
terms. "But there was no mechanism for citizens or environmental groups to get wrong-doings addressed because that was
not in her interest." Watching the hoopla over Whitman's
appointment to the EPA, Goldsmith winced. "They call her a
feminist; but going around destroying the environment isn't
very feminist to me," she says. Besides, her appointment is no
accident, adds Goldsmith. "On the environment, Bush was
clear about wanting to dismantle environmental protection. In
New Jersey, Governor Whitman did just that."[58]

There were those in New Jersey's African-American community who were wincing even before Governor Whitman hit
Washington, DC. In November 2000, the GOP sent her to
Florida to oversee the contentious vote count. While GOP
leaders Trent Lott and Tom DeLay's congressional staffers
showed up undercover, in mobs that intimidated vote-counters
behind the scenes, Whitman appeared before the cameras,
talking earnestly to election workers and saying gracious things

about every vote's importance. It was a classic GOP/Whitman double-play, but New Jersey's black community didn't buy it.

"Minorities here would view her as a conservative, not a moderate," says the Rev. Reginald Jackson, executive director of New Jersey's 600-plus Black Ministers' Council. "She bases most of her decisions on what's expedient."[59] The RNC sent Whitman to put her "moderate" face on an election in which the GOP did everything it could to suppress the (disproportionately Democratic) black vote. But Whitman's appearance in Florida recalled nothing so much as her own New Jersey administration's founding black-vote scandal.

Whitman hired two veterans of the Reagan administration to direct her 1993 campaign for Governor. One was Larry Kudlow, associate director for economics and planning at the Office of Management and Budget during Reagan's first term. (Kudlow co-chaired, with Whitman's childhood friend and neighbor Steve Forbes, her Economic Recovery Council, which is credited with devising the 30 percent tax cut.) Her campaign manager was Ed Rollins, who hadn't had much work since orchestrating Reagan's 1984 re-election campaign.

Under Rollins's leadership, the campaign stumbled its way through New Jersey's racial politics. Whitman was endorsed by radio host Bob Grant, whose favorite term for African Americans was "savages." After community groups spoke out, Whitman declared she would never appear on his show again, but when he subsequently attacked her, she went on his show to explain why she wouldn't appear on his show. Then she hired Larry McCarthy, the man who had written George Bush's race-baiting Willie Horton commercial, to help with her TV ads. After that link was discovered, Whitman fired McCarthy on the spot with an almost audible ''oops.'' But no sooner was the election over and won than the news broke that Rollins claimed to have paid half a million dollars to local black ministers to suppress black-voter turnout.

Asked by journalists about his ''winning strategy'' in New Jersey, Rollins said he'd urged black ministers who supported Florio not to make their usual get-out-the-vote speeches from the pulpit. ''We said to some of their key workers, 'How much have they [the Florio campaign] paid you to do your normal duty? Well, we'll match it; go home, sit and watch your television.' And I think to a certain extent we suppressed their vote . . .'' Rollins said.[60]

Investigations were never able to substantiate Rollins's claim, and no minister came forward to admit having received money. A few days later, he sheepishly retracted his allegation.[61] Nonetheless, black voters, or rather the lack of them, were a critical factor in the 1993 race—black turnout was unusually low.

''Whitman came in under a tremendous cloud,'' says the Rev. Jackson. The cloud went from gray to worse.[62] Rarely has a woman come into high office with greater personal wealth and power or more secure political influence. ''She was one of the most capable politicians we've ever had,'' says the Rev. Jackson. Yet ''she blew it,'' he growls. It was worse than that.

Jackson recalls hearing her speak at a black issues convention during her gubernatorial campaign. One of the matters that came up was racial profiling. ''She talked about racial profiling then,'' he says. ''Everyone did.'' The anecdotal picture was already stark. Although the use and possession of drugs and guns spanned all races and socio-ethnic groups, it seemed to many as if the only arrests New Jersey troopers made on the state turnpike involved minorities. For close to her whole time in office, Whitman and her Attorney General, Peter Verniero, her close associate and former chief of staff, vociferously denied the problem existed, even long after it had been brought to light in court.

William Buckman, a criminal and civil rights attorney in Moorestown, represented nearly two dozen minority drivers stopped on the turnpike in Gloucester County in the early 1990s. In 1996, after a six-month trial, with extensive pre-trial hearings, a Superior Court judge ruled that the troopers did indeed practice profiling: black drivers were five times more likely than whites to be stopped by state troopers. Instead of dedicating taxpayer dollars to investigate and stamp out the problem, Whitman instructed Verniero to appeal.

"I hold her personally accountable for the extended length of time that this problem of profiling festered," says Buckman. "And for the countless thousands of people that were victimized."[63]

Laila Maher and her friend Felix Morka were two of the victims. In January 2003, they were awarded $400,000 when the state settled their case, part of a suit brought by the American Civil Liberties Union (ACLU) on the part of twelve motorists.[64] In 1997, they were driving home from Washington early one freezing January morning when New Jersey turnpike troopers pulled over their Mercury Capri. According to Maher, who has testified to the same effect in court, when

Morka, who is Nigerian, took a few seconds too long to find his driver's license, one of the troopers reached through the car window and started banging Morka's head against the steering wheel. The trooper then dragged him out of the car by his sweatshirt collar, while a second put a gun to Maher's head. Five foot two inches tall at the side of the highway as traffic whizzed by, Maher recalls, "That was it. I was sure I was about to die. I was sure they were about to kill us."

People talk about Americans losing their sense of security after the attacks of 9/11. "For me," she says, "it happened on the New Jersey turnpike in 1997." Talking about the incident, Maher, six years on, still weeps. "For years, to hear Governor Whitman say it wasn't happening ..." she murmurs. "They say Whitman's good for women. Which women?"[65]

Buckman's 1996 Moorestown case should have been enough for New Jersey to stop the troopers' abuses. The Justice Department certainly thought so. When Whitman ordered an appeal, the DoJ started an investigation. With pressure on her police force mounting, instead of coming down hard on the police lobby, she chose to amp up her image as police-pal. This was no subtle thing on her part. She performed her loyalty for all to see. One night in the spring of 1996, for example, she decided to go for a ride in a squad car in inner-city Camden. In a bulletproof vest and special shot-proof Kevlar gloves, she agreed to pose with a so-called "suspect," while someone (supposedly a cop) took a snapshot. Smiling as she did it, she patted down the young black man as he stood, unarmed, spread-eagled against a wall. "She made that man a human prop for a photo op," says Buckman. "She wouldn't have thought to do that with a crony or a colleague wearing lime-green golfer pants.''

In 1998, a turnpike shooting of three unarmed minority men by troopers—and a federal Justice Department investigation—turned up the heat on the "driving while black" phenomenon, and in '99, New Jersey officials finally released 91,000 pages of documents. Racial profiling was revealed to have been the standard operating procedure of the New Jersey State Troopers for years. Not every highway search involved a Latino or black driver—but 80 percent did.[66] For over a decade, the documents showed, New Jersey police brass ignored calls to improve training and data-collection and engaged in a practice of aggressive obfuscation, denial of evidence, and intimidation of those who spoke out. The Governor and her Attorney General led the way in at least the first two of these.

When Whitman arrived at the EPA, the Rev. Jerry Falwell, founder of the Moral Majority, was pleased as punch. Interviewed by *The Washington Post*, Falwell declared himself happy with President Bush George W.'s appointments: ''We're going to like President-elect Bush the way we loved Ronald Reagan.'' Asked specifically about the pro-choice Governor, Falwell said he had warned Bush that her support of abortion rights should disqualify her from any social policy post, but ''Governor Whitman will have zero voice on social policy at EPA,'' Falwell said, adding, unnecessarily, ''I don't mean that in a negative way.''[67]

Whitman would balance Attorney General Ashcroft the way
that sheep's clothing balances a wolf. Falwell only had to look
at Whitman's history with the party to be confident of that. The
tax-cutting, budget-shrinking, attractive Northeastern Governor was at one time well placed to wield some influence.
Whitman has a net worth of over $14.4 million. She's a GOP
giver.[68] But she has never used her influence within the party to
much effect.

Whatever she thought of the *Contract with America*, she performed to Newt Gingrich's bidding, rebutting Clinton's State
of the Union address in 1995, and in '96, when moderates
were infuriated by the 104th Congress's battle with the President over social spending, a spat that actually shut the
government down, Whitman loaned the party her reputation
again and agreed to co-chair the RNC in San Diego.

Whitman told *The New York Times* shortly before the RNC
that the party would be "more inviting to all voters without an
anti-abortion plank." In 1992, that plank (manifesto pledge)
stated that "the unborn child has a fundamental individual right
to life which cannot be infringed" and called for "a human-life
amendment to the constitution" and the "appointment of
judges who respect traditional family values and the sanctity of
innocent human life." But when she could have gone to the
mat to support some pro-choice colleagues, Whitman stuck
with Gingrich.

Pro-choice Republicans sought to remove the party's anti-
abortion position. Whitman, to whom many looked for solidarity, did not even show up at a pro-choice demonstration,
and inside the convention hall, she sold out two pro-choice

Governors who tried to make a stand. Massachusetts Governor William Weld and California Governor Pete Wilson refused to address the convention rather than bow to party officials' orders that they did not talk about their support for abortion rights. Whitman said not a word from her coveted role as RNC co-chair, and even insisted on CNN that Weld and Wilson's absence had nothing to do their pro-choice stance.[69] Her co-chair at the '96 convention was that other up-and-coming young Governor, George W. Bush.

To be fair, while Whitman says that she believes abortion is a "very personal decision between a woman and her doctor," and the government has no business telling a woman what to do with her body ("it's actually a very conservative position"), she's also made it very clear that she won't stand or fall by it. "While it's an issue of importance to me, it's not my major issue," she says. "It's not the definition of who I am."[70]

It's the media, not the woman herself, who have cast Christine Todd Whitman as akin to a pro-choice Joan of Arc. It's the same way with the environment. In New Jersey, Whitman became an expert at saying one thing and doing another. On Earth Day 1996, she took schoolchildren on a celebratory canoe trip down the Rancocas Creek on the very same day that new regulations came into effect allowing the dumping of more pollutants into the state's waterways. She approved the closing of a state lab that discovered the cause— illegal toxic dumping—of a juvenile cancer cluster in the town of Toms River, and she turned up to tout her administration's hard stand against toxins wearing a white lab coat.

"It's not our ideas that need changing, it's our delivery,"

Whitman is famous for saying about the Republican Party's approach.[71] It's a line she almost wore out at the EPA. Almost immediately on coming into office, the administration dumped last-minute changes set in place by Clinton that set new standards for arsenic in drinking water; President George W. Bush reversed a campaign pledge to reduce carbon-dioxide emissions, and he withdrew from the Kyoto Protocol on global warming. On the afternoon before Thanksgiving, Whitman announced a change to the Clean Air Act, shortly followed by a change in the Clean Water Act that lifted the limits on how much mining refuse mining companies could dump in rivers and streams. "It's not a giveaway to the mining industry," said Whitman. It was, of course, just that.[72] Her favorite words were "streamlining" instead of "weakening," "freeing" instead of deregulating.

A chorus of voices went up, claiming that Whitman was held captive by the White House. Connecticut Democratic Senator and presidential contender Joe Lieberman urged her to resign: "Out of principle and protest." She has "a good record and good intentions," said Lieberman, chair of the Senate environment and public works clean air subcommittee.[73]

But after her resignation, Whitman said she had never disagreed with Bush's environmental policies, she just wished they'd been handled in a different way. On "climate change" (a phrase Republican pollster Luntz advises Republicans to use instead of "global warming"), Whitman said "It was a question in those early days of not articulating the message ... Because we weren't ratifying the [Kyoto] protocol, we were telling the world we weren't interested. In fact, the opposite is true.'' As for the arsenic in the water débâcle, the policy wasn't wrong, Whitman said, the problem was public relations: ''It was a PR disaster,'' she told *Newsweek*.[74]

Several high-level EPA officials did choose to resign in protest at what was taking place. The EPA is ''fighting a White House that seems determined to weaken the rules that we are trying to enforce,'' wrote Eric Schaeffer, the head of regulatory enforcement, in his resignation letter. Reflecting on his experience a year later, he said, ''The message was, 'there's been too much enforcement. We want less of that.' '' Whitman, he says, is ''a Republican first and an environmentalist way down the list.''[75]

Her last big job as EPA Administrator was to release the agency's 2003 *Draft Report on the Environment*. It represented a ''comprehensive roadmap to ensure that all Americans have cleaner air, purer water, and better protected land,'' Whitman explained.[76] According to leaked EPA memos, however, the report was driven by politics as much as by science. White House officials heavily edited the draft to remove all mention of research that demonstrated sharp increases in global temperature. The President's staff even tried to replace quotations from an NAS report on the human contribution to global warming with references to a study by the American Petroleum Institute that questioned evidence for climate change.[77] In the end, the report contained no information whatever on global warming, stating simply, ''This report does not attempt to address the complexities of this issue.''[78]

To some, this was the latest last-straw humiliation of good Governor Whitman. ''Christie Todd Whitman has been a fish

out of polluted water from the minute she stepped into the
Bush cabinet," Democratic National Chairman Terry McAuliffe
declared. Whitman, he said, was "paying the ultimate price for
being a moderately pro-environment administrator." Carl
Pope, executive director of the Sierra Club, said, "Under the
circumstances, Christie Whitman did the best she could at
EPA."[79]

The President, of course, held a different view: "Christie
Todd Whitman has served my administration exceptionally
well," he commented.

Indeed, there's every reason to believe that it wasn't the
hard time she was having with the Bush team that sent Whitman packing. It was the bruising she was receiving from
environmentalists and her own staff. Coming down the pike
was the Inspector General's report on the clean-up operation
after 9/11. There was also another scandal about to break. In
Anniston, Alabama, citizens were investigating the pollution of
the community by carcinogenic chemicals. Court documents
revealed that a multi-million-dollar verdict against the chemical
company found liable (Monsanto) was changed in Monsanto's
favor just days after Whitman received a forty-five-minute
"briefing" on the case. On the eve of Whitman's departure
from the EPA, a former EPA attorney who had testified in the
Anniston case came forward and said that inspectors general at
the EPA and at the Department of Justice had pressured her not
to testify. Janet MacGillivray, formerly a Superfund attorney,
said a high-ranking EPA official told her Anniston didn't make a
list of national clean-up priorities because Monsanto didn't
want it to.

Mike Casey, vice-president of the Environmental Working Group, said he had been on the fence about Whitman during her tenure at the EPA. ''I started off thinking she didn't give a crap about EPA, and was mostly a sideline tool of the administration,'' said Casey, but by the time she resigned, he'd changed his mind. ''She's an active part of the Presidential wrecking ball.''[80]

In April, Whitman came under fire for diverting EPA agents from their normal investigative work to provide her personal security and even to make restaurant reservations, a charge which she denies. Agents also complained that the former New Jersey Governor instructed them to call her ''Governor,'' rather than ''ma'am'' or ''Administrator.''[81]

And then there was the unpleasantness in Tampa, Florida, when word reached town that the federal government intended to reduce the reimbursement value of senior citizens in official calculations of the cost of life-threatening pollution. Whitman arrived, all excited about a series of ''listening sessions'' she was scheduled to hold around the country. At the kick-off event, she was besieged by organized elders, all calling her plan the ''senior death discount.''[82] After repeat performances in Pittsburgh, Iowa City, San Antonio and Los Angeles, Whitman took to the podium in Baltimore and announced quickly, before any elder could get a word out, that the EPA would no longer assign less value to the lives of the elderly. ''EPA will not, I repeat, not, use age-adjusted analysis in decision-making,'' Whitman said.[83] After that, it's easy to understand why a former governor who's attached to her ''moderate'' and ''compassionate'' reputation might call it a day.

In her resignation letter of May 22 2003, Whitman wrote that she had been proud ''to lead the EPA in its effort to leave America's air cleaner, its water purer, and its land better protected than it was when this administration took office.'' EPA documents showed that the number of officially defined smoggy days had increased by 32 percent from 2001 to 2002. The completion of clean-ups at Superfund sites was down by close to half.[84]

In August 2003, the President announced his nomination of a faithful Western governor, Michael Leavitt, to replace Whitman at the EPA. A major GOP fundraiser, Leavitt holds the distinction of having secretly negotiated two controversial deals with the Department of the Interior to open up millions of acres of Utah wilderness to road-building and development. He was even the proud recipient of a ''Golden Shovel Award'' for his efforts to keep roads open on federal lands. A group of protestors gave him a shovel they had used to dig an illegal road through an endangered species habitat. ''It means a lot to me to receive it,'' said Leavitt. (The road-diggers were federal trespassers at the time.)[85]

Anonymous insiders told *The New York Times* that the White House had ''given up a little bit on the Eastern-industrial-urban-environmental base.'' The administration, reported *The New York Times*, ''had believed they could mollify swing voters with Whitman . . . But she never managed to appease the President's critics.''[86]

She didn't appease the President's critics. (When she left the EPA, polls were still giving Democrats a two-to-one advantage over George W. Bush.) She doesn't seem to have had any

influence either, on the administration's position on reproductive rights. Perhaps to shore up their religious Right voting
base well in advance of the 2004 election, Senate Republicans
approved a new federal abortion ban that the President promised to sign. Constantly misrepresented by its advocates as a
ban only on late-term, so-called "partial birth" abortions, the
measure's deceptive wording actually has the effect of overturning Roe by criminalizing a whole array of midterm abortion
procedures and omitting any exceptions to protect a woman's
health. At the time this law was passed in the Senate, the
public's understanding of the abortion ban was as clear as a
cloud of smog. Christine Todd Whitman did nothing to clear
up either one.

MARLBORO WOMAN

Gale Ann Norton

Once upon a time, Gale Ann Norton campaigned *against* the national security state. An ambitious young lawyer with a radical world view, she wanted to legalize marijuana and end the censorship of porn. As for troops abroad, she backed a presidential candidate who would have brought every last soldier home. He opposed Ronald Reagan, called for a ban on nuclear weapons, and pledged to dissolve just about every acronym agency in Washington, including the EPA, the Department of Energy, and most definitely the FBI and the CIA. Two decades later, the same Gale Norton is a federal agent herself, a cabinet secretary in a Republican administration that has expanded federal police powers as never before. Spying, infiltration, even military tribunals are back. The young Norton would have scoffed at any attempt to call an occupation abroad and Big Brother at home patriotic, but Gale Norton, Secretary of the Interior, seems quite happy to play little sister to George W. Bush's Big Bro.

In January 2001, Ruth Bennett watched her friend's Senate confirmation with a smile. "Gale always was very bright, ambitious and hardworking,'' says Bennett, a Libertarian who lives in Washington state.[1] Bennett's the sort of Libertarian who supports the transfer of federal lands into private hands. On that, she and Norton once agreed. From 1979 to '80, they toiled endless hours on the presidential campaign of Ed Clark, the great presidential hopeful of the fledging Libertarian Party. Norton coordinated Clark's Colorado state campaign. It was, as Bennett puts it, an ''all-out'' affair. The Libertarians were determined to rattle the monopoly interests of the entrenched two-party system, raise a banner for individual liberties, and evict Washington from the public's property.

That Norton should come to join the Republican Party, assume a spot in a cabinet next to a Christian moralizer like John Ashcroft, and become the nation's largest landlord—with control over some 500 million acres of parks, wilderness, and wildlife refuges—is ironic, Bennett admits, but it is not altogether a surprise.

''People change, beliefs change. I think she saw a way to get into a position where she could wield some power,'' Bennett reflects.

Ron Arnold agrees that Norton has been through what he calls ''a series of metamorphoses.'' Arnold, executive director of the Center for Defense of Free Enterprise, is the official biographer of Norton's mentor and predecessor at Interior, James Watt. Arnold authored the 1988 ''Wise Use'' agenda, which called for the opening of the Arctic National Wildlife Refuge to oil drilling, and the selling off of public parks. ''Gale started out as a super-duper attorney fighting for the property rights issues I care about,'' he says. But then she went astray:

"She went to work for the government and took an oath to serve. You never keep a friend when they move to Washington," he sighs.[2]

The good news for Arnold (if not for Bennett) is that in Norton, so-called "property rights" advocates still have a friend. She has not given up on the Wise Use agenda, she has just found a way inside government to pursue anti-government goals. Sure enough, she told the Senate confirmation committee that she looked forward to managing the "untamed wilderness of Alaska" as a "beautiful and special place."[3] But once confirmed, a beautiful place for oil drilling turned out to be what she had in mind. She still talks about individual freedoms; it's just that they tend to be the freedoms of the miner, the driller, the corporate rancher. The freedom of the pot smoker or the war resister are long forgotten.

Gale Norton was born in Wichita, Kansas, in 1954, a baby boom child, daughter of Dale and Anna Jacqueline Norton. Her father received his professional training at public expense, learning aviation mechanics in the US Army. He parlayed his skills into a lifetime of jobs in private business, working for the aviation firms Cessna, Beech Aircraft, and, for more than a decade, Learjet. When Gale was five, the Nortons moved to Thornton, a liberal suburb outside Denver. These were the days of population growth, city sprawl and construction-boom galore. The demand for power and energy was rising, and private companies working on government contracts made out like bandits with backhoes. As far as families like the Nortons were concerned, they weren't rich (they lived in a trailer when they first moved to town), but the American Dream was alive and well; it was playing at the movies, too, and John Wayne starred.

Sprawl and growth had some people worried, however. David Brower for one. An ex-mountaineer, who had become the director of the Sierra Club, Brower mobilized voters to oppose the damming of the Upper Colorado River and helped to found Friends of the Earth, the League of Conservation Voters, and the Earth Island Institute to protect United States wilderness. Brower wasn't alone. Michael Harrington's *The Other America*, Rachel Carson's *Silent Spring* (both published in 1962), and Ralph Nader's *Unsafe at Any Speed* (1965) expressed a growing concern that unmitigated growth could have its drawbacks.[4] There were dangers posed, they said, by the concentration of wealth and the growth of poverty, the spread of pesticides and pollution; the cozy relationship corporations enjoyed with government might not be good for consumers, the planet and other living things. In fact, progress in itself just might not serve the long-term national interest, not without careful stewardship, they said. In a parallel development, Native Americans, through the Red Power movement, were demanding fuller control over the resources on their lands, which were defined as separate nations.

Growing up in a Denver home, in the family of a Goldwater Republican who worked for a private firm fed on government contracts, Gale Norton is sure to have heard grumbling in 1961 when Stewart Udall, a Coloradoan (then secretary of the interior under John F. Kennedy), raised concerns about "uncritical acceptance of conventional notions of progress."[5] And if there were grumbles heard about Democrats, they can only have become louder when a Republican, Richard Nixon, started sounding a bit like Brower.

At the height of the Vietnam War, eager to distract from the environmental devastation and human carnage in Southeast Asia, President Nixon took the temperature of the times and hit a Green-note in his 1970 State of the Union address. "The 1970s absolutely must be the years when America pays its debt to the past by reclaiming the purity of its air, its waters and our living environment," Nixon told Congress. "It is literally now or never."[6]

Gale Norton was sixteen, a high-school "A" student, an outspoken kid, according to her teachers, who "wasn't Miss Popularity by any means."[7] She spent little time on dating, but did take time off to demonstrate against the Vietnam War. Born in the same year as her cabinet colleague Condoleezza Rice, Norton was a few years behind her in college but they both attended Denver University. In 1975, Norton received her BA and graduated with a degree in political science, and a husband, Harold Everett Reed, a man four years her senior.

Norton's parents had moved back to Wichita by this time, where Dale had scored a top job, in charge of Learjet's military contracts. Norton took the LSATs, received a perfect score, and headed off to DU law school, away from the rambunctious campus. DU law was located in downtown Denver in those days, not far from the city and county courts which were about to become her arena.

Marci Albright knew Norton then. Albright attended DU and DU law alongside Gale. In the 1990s, she served as her friend's chief deputy in the state Attorney General's office and, in 2003, she followed Norton to the Department of the Interior.

"Gale was always extremely bright," says Albright now. Norton worked on the transportation law journal, rather a dry area of the law, Albright agrees, but says, "You have to understand. Gale was always very interested in policy."[8]

Norton's marriage with Reed was on the rocks. Personal differences and changed priorities drove them apart, Norton has said. (Reed was outed in 1993 by a local gay magazine, *Out Front*, which described him as "having been seen over the years in a variety of leather outfits."[9]) It was really tough everywhere for women in law school in those years, and "Denver was no exception," says Albright. Norton was not only a woman, but she was married, heading for a divorce, ambitious and alone. No wonder she fell for Ayn Rand.

Norton has said that it was Rand's 1943 novel *The Fountainhead* that turned her away from the collectivism of the antiwar set and on to libertarianism.[10] "I liked the philosophy based on individuality," said Norton. One assumes she's talking about the male individuality in *The Fountainhead*. The heroine in Rand's classic is "taken by force," by Rand's hero, Howard Roark. A brilliant, ambitious architect, he was played by Gary Cooper in the film. Roark's "taking" of Dominque Francon is all part of his struggle against the forces of obscurity and conformism. He gains individual recognition and acclaim. (Francon, for her part, comes to submit to his power and brilliance.)

Something clicked, says Norton. At the time, Norton and the rest of the females in her class were in an uphill battle for recognition. "We all wondered if firms would hire us when we got out, or if we'd be shunted off to paralegal work," says Albright. The firm that hired Albright had never hired a woman before. Once in the workforce, success depended, she says, on differentiating oneself from other females.

"We felt compelled to wear the same business suits and Oxford shirts as the men, and those loopy feminized ties . . . We had to fit in with the male establishment to distinguish ourselves from the legal secretaries."[11]

It came as no surprise to Albright when Norton signed up with the new policy shop in town, Mountain States Legal Foundation. James Watt, an outspoken Denver lawyer, was the group's first President. He claims Norton "sought us out."[12] They were a perfect match. Norton wanted influence in the policy world and nothing to do with the public interest outfits that were just then absorbed with equal opportunity issues of collective rights of women and minorities. And she suited MSLF's agenda. A smart, male-identified, blonde, blue-eyed woman, Norton was an attractive spokesperson for a New Right movement that was eager to distinguish itself from its ineffective brothers in the supremacist Old Right.

Watt told the *Denver Post* that Norton interviewed well. "I was so impressed with her, but I didn't know what a Libertarian she was," he said. A colleague of Watt's told him that "a Libertarian is just a conservative Republican who smokes grass." When he asked Norton about it, Watt says, she laughed. "She said she didn't smoke grass but it gave the right connotation."[13] If she didn't smoke grass, Watt should have been especially impressed. Avoiding marijuana in Norton's circles at the time was quite an accomplishment.

The Libertarian Party was founded in Denver in 1972. Stressing individual freedom above all else, Libertarians favored an unregulated economy, an end to all laws governing private behavior between consenting people, a return to the gold standard, "freedom of choice" in abortion, quitting the United Nations, and opposition to the draft.

For years, the party attracted a hodge-podge mix of civil libertarians and isolationists. In the mid-1970s, they received an injection of funds that helped them to get serious. Charles Koch, a Wichita native, inherited hundreds of millions of dollars from his father's Koch Industries. One of the country's biggest conglomerates, Koch dealt in cattle, chemicals, real estate, but above all oil. Companies like that don't tend to get where they are by sharing profits with their workers. Charles's father, Fred, was a big-time funder of anti-union causes and a member of the national council of the anti-communist John Birch Society. Son Charles, a reader of Rand, became a Libertarian. It was a hipper, more '70s way to pursue the same anti-regulatory, anti-tax, anti-union plan.

When the possibility of the military draft was revived in 1978, the party's youth membership swelled. A tax revolt in California got Libertarians very excited about their prospects at the polls. In the same election in which Californians embraced Proposition 13, a voter-initiative that put a cap on property taxes, a Libertarian, Ed Clark, received 400,000 votes in the gubernatorial race, the best showing for a third-party candidate in California for more than three decades.

Norton coordinated Clark's Colorado campaign for president in '79. Charles Koch's brother, David, was the vice presidential candidate.[14] Norton herself was chosen as a state delegate to the party's national convention. Alan Crawford, a conservative journalist who was present, described it this way: "Their 1979 convention was a boisterous affair at the swanky Bonaventure Hotel in Los Angeles; marijuana circulated freely at the banquet honoring the presidential nominee, while delegates discussed esoteric matters of economic policy and the wickedness of the CIA."[15]

"It was the best campaign we ever ran," says Bennett.[16] Clark won almost a million votes, just over 1 percent of all votes cast. If you're going to run a third-party candidate for federal office, it really helps if the running mate is a millionaire. Koch's money helped the party avoid tricky campaign contribution limits. The Cato Institute (also funded with Koch money) contributed staff. Soon after, Cato learnt they had to distance themselves from electoral politics if they wanted to keep their tax-exempt status. Clark's 1980 1 percent remains the largest proportion the party has ever won in a national race. Bennett stuck with the party. In 2000, she ran for Lieutenant Governor on the Libertarian Party ticket in the state of Washington, where she lives. But Norton chose a different path.

"Yes I was an active Libertarian," Norton told a reporter in '94. "But then I decided to go into practical politics."[17]

Exactly what was practical, however, was just then getting sorted out. Ultraconservatives entered the 1970s with a problem. As the director of Mountain States Legal Foundation puts it, "Federal courts rarely heard arguments in favor of the right

to own and use property, individual liberty, limited government and the free enterprise system.''[18] It wasn't quite true,
but it was the case that lawyers working with the ACLU, the
NAACP, and the National Organization for Women were
bringing key lawsuits, enabled by new federal legislation that,
among other things, limited the ability of private employers to
discriminate. Native Americans were making gains in the areas
of religious rights, and protecting sacred sites.[19] At the same
time, congressional laws were making it harder to get away
with contaminating water, polluting soil, or spewing toxins
into the environment. For example, the 1969 National Environmental Policy Act (NEPA) required the government to
conduct an ''environmental impact'' survey before it under-
took any project or activity. The Marine Mammal Protection
Act had passed into law, along with the Endangered Species
Act, the Safe Drinking Water Act and the Clean Air and Clean
Water Act.

To make the picture even worse for the ultra Right, it was a
whole lot harder after 1973 for oil drillers and corporate
millionaires simply to buy a President. The Federal Election
Campaign Act of that year imposed limits on how much money
a person could invest in a single federal race. Instead of being
able to pay for the favor of a single powerful politician,
therefore, millionaires who wanted influence had to sway a
mountain of real-life voters. That presented a challenge.
Republican and Democratic Presidents alike were signing
environmental legislation in the 1970s. There was a popular
movement among voters, and the Radical Right was out of
step. When two million Americans massed in cities and towns

nationwide to mark Earth Day in 1970, the best response the Right could muster was a smear campaign launched by the John Birch Society, who alleged that Earth Day was a devious ruse to celebrate Lenin's birthday. It sounded not only silly but out of touch (and it failed to budge the President). Turning Americans against clean air and water was going to take some work.

Some wealthy businessmen were worried enough to pay out cash to anyone who could foment a better-than-the-Birch Society backlash. The Radical Right didn't want to change its agenda, but clearly it needed new arguments, new media skills, and new talent. It wouldn't hurt if those new faces looked different from the sour-faced supremacists of the pre-civil rights era. Above all, it needed a new strategy and the mechanism to carry it out.

One Colorado-based beer brewer made all the difference. Joseph Coors, a chemical engineer who had built up the third-largest brewery in the country, decided to open his pockets (and those of some of his employees)[20] to bankroll a revival on the Right. In 1973, he invested a quarter of a million dollars in the Heritage Foundation, a non-profit think-tank in Washington. A year later, he provided the start-up money for a political action committee, the Committee to Save a Free Congress (CSFC), and took a seat on its advisory board. In 1977, he founded Mountain States Legal Foundation. Coors became its first chairman; its first executive director was James Watt.[21]

The Heritage Foundation's job was to produce propaganda—they called it research—to inform a movement they dubbed the New Right. ("New" sounds better than "ultra.")

Coors' allies in Washington were Paul Weyrich, former press secretary to Colorado Republican Senator Gordon Allott, and Richard Viguerie, a fundraising genius from the 1964 Gold-water campaign. Viguerie had figured out how to raise big bucks for political causes and candidates in legal, bite-size contributions elicited in urgent appeals mailed direct to voters' homes.

"Research," lobbying, direct mail—gradually, it all came together. In 1976, Jimmy Carter won the presidency, but the New Right scored significant victories, among them the election of Orrin Hatch in Utah. Hatch, who was anti-union, anti-regulation and absolutely anti-abortion, was up against a veteran consumer advocate, Senator Frank Moss, a Democrat. Hatch took to declaring that the feds were "waging war on the West." It was a clever way of tapping into an ancient Westerners' notion—that those who had heroically settled the West were being robbed by eastern legislators, who wanted Westerners' land, their minerals, their oil.[22]

The brilliance of the "war on the West" rhetoric was that it sidestepped the question of clean air and clean water altogether. Federal regulators weren't waging war on big polluters or corporate poisoners; they were after John Wayne. The slogan had a little-guy appeal that never hinted at the fat-cat interests that had paid for it. New Right groups, their coffers filled by Viguerie's mailings, delivered Hatch to victory.[23]

"We are different from previous generations of conservatives. We are no longer working to preserve the status quo. We are radicals working to overturn the present power structure in this country . . ."[24] said Weyrich. Mountain States translated the same approach into legal strategy. James Watt's lawyers didn't just defend their clients from government prosecution under the new environmental laws; they attacked the government's right to regulate at all—and sought to make law enforcement costly, time-consuming, and wherever possible, politically dangerous. (Direct mail solicitations work best when the tone is sensational and personalized. New Right political action committees like Coors' CSFC drew up lists of politicians they targeted for defeat on account of their votes on select, "litmus test" issues. It's right-wing direct mail, not civil rights, that ushered in the era of "single issue" politics.)[25]

A "senior attorney" at Mountain States at the age of twenty-five, Norton helped file lawsuits disputing Interior Department grazing permits and Environmental Protection Agency clean air rules. With Watt, she submitted an amicus brief to the US Supreme Court that challenged the constitutionality of the Surface Mining Act. She represented the state of Louisiana's bid to repeal the Crude Oil Windfall Profits tax on oil companies, which passed during the Carter administration. She worked on the case with Professor Richard Epstein of the University of Chicago Law School, an up-and-coming libertarian legal scholar.[26]

Policy-wonk that she was, Norton also immersed herself in what was then a rather obscure backwater of property rights debate. She took up what is called the "takings" issue, and helped to craft an argument that the Fifth Amendment of the Constitution requires the government to pay polluters not to violate environmental laws, and "compensate" timber companies for the old-growth trees they are not allowed to log. The advantages to the corporations, like Coors, that underwrote such work were obvious. (In fact, a study published in the *Yale Law Journal* in 1984 revealed that in twenty-four of the cases on their docket, Mountain States advocated positions that "directly benefited corporations represented on their board of directors, clients of firms represented on its board of litigation, or major contributors to the MSLF's budget.")[27] The contradictions were just as clear. If the state should compensate private owners for losses incurred by government regulations, those owners should pay the government when regulators improve the value of land by improving water quality, say, or air. If we're arguing about value, Norton's clients who leased public land for mining or grazing should have been asked to pay fair market rates—instead of the giveaway rent the government charged for public-land leases. Ignoring those sorts of issues, Norton kept her focus where it suited her clients. With "takings" they believed they were on to a gold mine, legislatively speaking. In a 1985 book on the subject, Norton's mentor Epstein argued that along with environmental laws, minimum-wage laws and labor codes, building permits, even income taxes, were a form of "takings" for which private-property owners and employers should be compensated.[28]

Norton's work at Mountain States was rewarded in 1983 by a fellowship from Stanford University's Hoover Institution. There, again just like Condoleezza Rice, Norton was given free time to explore new policy possibilities and legal loopholes in the environmentalists' rules. Among other things, she studied what was then the novel idea of changing air-pollution laws to permit industries to exchange "emissions credits." Under

George W. Bush, the idea was written into the Clean Air Act.[29]

Her year-long fellowship at Hoover was followed by another at the Political Economy Research Center (PERC) in Bozeman, Montana, an outfit whose website displays the motto "Free Market Solutions to Environmental Problems." PERC advocates selling off national parks to private firms (Disney, perhaps?) and publishes a "parent's guide" to teaching children about the environment that is intended to counter the environmental movement's indoctrination of the nation's youth in public schools.[30] One of PERC's major funders is David Koch.[31]

By the time the Louisiana "Windfall Profits" case (US v. Ptasynski) came to be heard in Washington, Norton's former boss Watt was serving in the Reagan administration. Busy at the Department of the Interior, he made time to watch his former employee argue her case. Norton lost, but she attracted the eye of Washington, and Watt says he lobbied for the administration to bring her on board. "The first position [we] put her in was over at [the US Department of] Agriculture," he told the *Denver Post* in 1994.[32] She arrived in 1984. By then, things had become pretty hot for Reagan's anti-regulatory regulators. Watt himself was burning up.

Fresh from Mountain States, Watt came to the DoI with both barrels firing. Among other proposals, he suggested putting thirty million acres of public land out for private bidding. But the privatization of public land, which had sounded so grand to the Mountain States folks, provoked a firestorm from environmental lobbyists in Washington. Even real-estate lob-

byists were against the idea of so much property entering the
market. Bruised but not beaten, Watt announced he'd open up
the billion acres of the outer continental shelf, along with 100
million acres of Alaskan land, to offshore oil leasing and drilling. That, too, went over like a ton of toxic bricks.

Watt was not the only Mountain States alum bumping up
against the real world in Washington. Anne Gorsuch-Burford,
head of the EPA, quietly encouraged a Southwestern gasoline
refiner to break the EPA's own unleaded-gas regulations. When
it was discovered (in a preview of Dick Cheney's approach to
congressional oversight), she refused to hand over EPA documents on Superfund enforcement to the House Energy
Committee and, on an order from the White House, claimed
"executive privilege." During the delay, the subpoenaed
documents began to disappear into the EPA office shredder.[33]
Gorsuch was an MSLF graduate, as was her husband, Bob
Burford, who ran the Bureau of Land Management, from which
spot he handed out huge concessions to the ranching and
mining lobby.[34]

Ham-handedness just wasn't going to cut it. The Burfords
were forced to resign under a cloud. Watt was "run out of
town on a rail," as journalist David Helvarg puts it, "with a
stake driven through his heart by a very image-conscious Nancy
Reagan."[35]

Norton came to Interior not long after Watt's exit. The
Interior Secretary was Don Hodel (future leader of the
Christian Coalition). While at Interior, Norton helped to write
a report that reinforced Watt's plan to open up the Arctic
National Wildlife Refuge—a huge wilderness area—to oil

exploration.[36] In her role as associate solicitor for conservation and wildlife, she also questioned whether, in federal water rights litigation, "the Reagan administration might want to seek greater deference to state courts and to state water law in the determination of federal water rights." Like "takings" theory, certain claims of "states' rights" were becoming a theme of New Right legal strategy.[37] From 1985 to '88, Norton served on the President's Council on Environmental Quality, a paradoxical position for a lawyer who had at one time contested the very notion that the President had any business regulating the environment.

In 1987, Norton quit Washington DC and returned home, as did many of the Right's most virulent property rights activists. The first George Bush looked likely to be no Reagan when it came to "takings" and "states rights," and the "war on the West" agenda. Bush even called himself "an environmental president," when he ran in 1988. It was only a campaign ploy but it didn't go down well with the resource industry and its pals.

"We had more access to the Clinton administration than we did to the first Bush administration," says Watt's biographer, Ron Arnold.[38] At the end of the Reagan term, Arnold headed the Center for Defense of Free Enterprise, a group that grew fat on anti-tax direct mail appeals, developed by Alan Gottlieb (a one time partner of Richard Viguerie). He had seen all sides of the anti-environmental movement thanks to Paul Weyrich, who hand-picked Arnold to write his biography. Arnold had watched the workings of lobbyists and legislators, and he knew the grassroots realm of direct mail. Industry lobbyists and New

Right lawyers had been collaborating for years for their own purposes, but Arnold knew that "regular folks" could get very agitated about things like "property" and "privacy" and "freedom," too. Environmental regulations lay at a fault line in the culture: right where John Wayne cowboys ran up against bureaucrats with books of rules.

A 1988 meeting in Reno, Nevada, kicked off what would become the Wise Use movement. The 250 delegates invited by Gottlieb and Arnold represented two main groups—industry and lobbyists. Mountain States Legal Foundation, the NRA, Pacific Legal Foundation were there, as well as some big corporations and industry lobbyists including the American Mining Congress, the National Cattlemen's Association, the DuPont Co., Exxon Co., USA, and Louisiana-Pacific lumber. While seemingly "grassroots" groups of bikers and snowboarders gave Wise Use its "little guy" public face, the policy hacks framed and adopted the "Wise Use Agenda." On the list of goals—the immediate development of the petroleum resources of the Arctic National Wildlife Refuge in Alaska, the logging of three million acres of the Tongass National Forest in Alaska, the opening up of seventy million acres of federal wilderness to commercial development and motorized recreational use, the opening of all public lands "including wilderness and national parks" to mining and energy development, and the right of pro-development groups "to sue on behalf of industries threatened or harmed by environmentalists."[39] There was something there for everyone.

Fresh from Washington, Norton picked up more movement-funded fellowships—at the libertarian Independence Institute,

and another at the Pacific Research Institute for Public Policy—
and she became active in the Federalist Society, a conservative
legal organization that links individual right-wing lawyers with
each other and recruits private lawyers for *pro bono* work.
Federalist Society bulwarks include Kenneth Starr, Robert
Bork, and Edwin Meese (US Attorney General under Reagan).
Norton sits on the Board of Advisors of the society's criminal
law and procedure practice group with Meese. The Federalists
once named her their "Young Lawyer of the Year."[40]

"How do we restore a regime of property rights?" Norton
addressed a legal forum at the time. Property owners should be
compensated when their property lost value due to wetland-
protection or endangered species law, she argued. Such compensation requirements would cripple environmental
enforcement, she acknowledged, but "I view that as something
positive." Citing a 1987 Supreme Court decision by Justice
Antonin Scalia which asserted an "actual," rather than "government granted," right to build on one's property, Norton
argued that "We might even go so far as to recognize a
homesteading right to pollute or make noise in an area."[41]

In an article for the Federalist Society about "takings," she
argued that "economic rights are clearly not protected today.
Land is owned subject to the whims of one's neighbors on the
zoning commission. Prices of goods and services are controlled
by a plethora of governmental and regulatory bodies. Selective
taxation hampers the growth and innovation of industry, and
subsidizes some sectors of society at the expense of others." An
update on Hatch's "war on the West" speech, Norton's
complaint appealed to anyone who feels held back by faceless

regulators, government—or even their own neighbors.

James Watt claims Norton left DC because ''she never fit into that Washington bureaucracy.''[42] She was apparently itching to get into Colorado's. In 1988 she enrolled in the Republican Leadership Program, a statewide seminar that teaches future GOP insiders the basics of free-market economics and the conservative bent on other issues, and at some point in that year, Watt says Norton called him to discuss her interest in running for state Attorney General.[43]

Norton was ready to run for office: she was immersed in anti-regulatory theory, trained in voter-friendly argument, and her campaign coffers were filled by a Republican Right that was determined to beef up its presence—if not in Washington, then in the states. Moreover, in the election for Colorado's Attorney General the GOP was spitting mad at Norton's opponent, a two-term incumbent Duane Woodard, who had switched his party affiliation from Republican to Democrat. Enraged by what they considered Woodard's treachery, they wanted him out and Norton in, and they got what they wanted. Norton scored an upset victory, raking in 54 percent of the vote, thanks mostly to a blistering campaign of slick TV ads that linked Woodard with the state parole board's decision to release a convicted felon, Gary Davis, who later committed a murder. Norton's ads came straight out of the Willie Horton campaign-book. The Attorney General didn't sit on the parole board; he couldn't even advise executive agencies without being asked. Davis was released under a mandatory parole law. The ad was ''a lie,'' complained Woodard.[44] No matter. Norton had almost four times as much money for the race as he did:

$230,000 in political contributions, all but $30,000 of which came from the state GOP, which brought Presidents Reagan and Bush to Colorado to fundraise. In '91, Norton was sworn in, the first female Attorney General in Colorado history, and in '92, she duly appeared on the Republican National Convention stage, another grateful female star of the Radical Right's revival.

As Attorney General, she quickly dispelled any hopes local civil libertarians might have had that she would bring any freethinking ideas to the job. She was, as one Coloradoan Libertarian who knew her during the Clark campaign put it, "a truly repressive, conservative Republican, no longer suspicious of government power because she was the right sort to exercise it."[45] She supported the death penalty, tougher juvenile detention centers and chain gangs—"to combine hard work with humiliation." If she had ever had a beef with the war on drugs it didn't show.

Tough on some criminals, she tiptoed around corporate felons. Almost the first thing Norton did as AG was cut by a third her department's spending on environmental enforcement, and then she let others enforce the rules. When a gold mine spilled cyanide into a local river killing all aquatic life along a seventeen-mile stretch, Norton declined to press criminal charges and stalled for so long that the federal government intervened. She refused to act while the Sierra Club secured a $130 million clean-up settlement from a power plant, after a federal judge ruled that Hayden Power had violated the Clean Air Act 19,000 times. In another memorable episode, Norton testified against her own citizens in a case involving heavy-metal emissions. Residents who went to court won a clean-up order thirty times larger than the settlement the company had negotiated with the AG. Citizens had to act for themselves again when Norton refused to intervene in the case of a Louisiana-Pacific mill that was fouling the air. Louisiana-Pacific was sabotaging record-keeping and covering up violations too, but Norton's office refused to pursue any criminal penalties. Federal prosecutors stepped in, winning $37 million in fines—$31 million for fraud and $6 million for Clean Air Act violations.[46]

When Norton's name came up for Interior Secretary in 2001, Kevin Hannon, an attorney who had worked on several of these cases said, "I would have grave concerns about Gale Norton's aggressiveness in enforcing environmental compliance and protecting citizens from environmental damage."[47]

In spite of the mountain of evidence of corporate malfeasance and non-compliance by business, Colorado state legislators passed a landmark self-audit law in '94. What the Bush team would call a "voluntary compliance" program, it permitted polluting corporations to decide for themselves whether they were in compliance with environmental law, and exempted them from prosecution and fines if they blew the whistle on themselves. As AG, Norton supported this law against strong opposition by the federal Environmental Protection Agency, which argued that it violated Colorado's obligations under the Clean Air and Water Acts.

Even as she went easy on private polluters, she scored points with environmentalists for pursuing the federal government to clean up an Army weapons arsenal. (Making the feds pay up for despoiling local property fit well inside her "takings" agenda, in any case.) When it came to taking private industry to task, her enthusiasm was, at best, under control. When attorneys general from twenty-three states launched a suit against the biggest tobacco companies, Norton refused, saying that the cost to Colorado taxpayers would be exorbitant. (Not to mention the potential cost to her campaign coffers: in 1994, the largest contribution to her re-election campaign came from Philip Morris, with more flowing in from R.J. Reynolds, the Smokeless Tobacco Council, and the Tobacco and Candy Political Action Campaign.) Norton even testified against the constitutionality of the suit in Congress, earning her the honorific "the Marlboro Woman" in the Denver press.[48] At the last minute, she caved in to public pressure and joined the litigation in time for the pay-out. As Rep. Ken Gordon, a Democrat from Denver, said in '98, "She basically sent out a letter saying that if you are giving out money we want some."[49]

Norton advised Governor Romer not to defend a state affirmative action program when several of her Federalist Society colleagues challenged it in court (Adarand v. State of Colorado). She hadn't advised defending the program because she thought the state law would lose in court, she told her confirmation committee in 2000. But when Amendment Two, an initiative passed by Colorado voters which banned anti-discrimination laws that covered homosexuals, was ruled unconstitutional, Norton appealed against the verdict not once or twice but four times, and then took the fight to the Supreme Court. Under Norton's direction, Colorado spent over a million dollars defending an indefensible law before it was finally struck down.[50] Tim Tymcovitch, Norton's Solicitor General, who actually handled the Amendment Two appeals, went well beyond his duties as the representative of the state. Tymcovitch hired Paul Cameron—whom the American Psychological Association had dropped from their membership for ethical breaches in the 1980s—to be the state's "expert" on homosexuality. Cameron was the author of a salacious pamphlet, "Medical Consequences of What Homosexuals Do," which the Colorado for Family Values coalition distributed en masse the week before the '92 election in a bid to pump up the hysterical homophobe vote. (It was a good bet: "Gays are an octopus of infection stretching across the world. Fresh, undiluted pathogens are its daily food and excrement. Most gays are veritable Typhoid Marys," screeches Cameron's pamphlet.)[51]

Some in Colorado's gay community give Governor Romer the benefit of the doubt: "He may have been seeking a definitive defeat of the Amendment in order to set the precedent," says Pat Steadman, of Equal Rights Colorado, a group that grew out of the anti-Amendment Two resistance.[52] But even after the fact, Norton criticized the Supreme Court's verdict, as did Tymcovitch. (When asked if her fervent defense of Amendment Two was motivated by personal animosity towards her ex-husband, Hal Reed, Norton told the Denver weekly *Westword* that Reed's sexuality was "not an issue in the case."[53] She had married again in 1990.)

As for watching the state's budget, Cameron, proved too wacky to take the stand but he still received $15,000 from the AG's office for his service. If Norton had any doubts about the good judgement of her comrade Tymcovitch, she kept them well under wraps. An active member of the Federalist Society and a former member of the Independence Institute, Tymcovitch worked on Norton's first campaign for Attorney General. He returned to party activism after 1996, when he became Colorado co-chair of Lawyers for Bush–Cheney; he assisted Norton during her Senate confirmation, and in 2003, he was confirmed to the Tenth Circuit Court of the Appeals with her support.

When she campaigned for election as Senator in '96, Norton played the gender card: "I think it's a plus for the party to have a woman in this campaign," she told the press. "In the past I have been successful in attracting Democratic and independent women voters."[54] But Norton's record on women's rights was clear: she was pro-choice when her Democratic opponent was not, but she was aggressively anti-affirmative action (she sent private memos to colleges and universities ordering them to stop enforcing federal affirmative action laws). She defended an amendment to the Colorado constitution that required the state not to fund abortions in cases of rape and incest, despite a clear conflict with federal Medicaid law. And as AG, she spent upwards of $700,000 defending Colorado State University's decision to drop its women's softball team, in violation of Title IX.

At the 1996 summer symposium at the Independence Institute, she had this to say about the Americans with Disabilities Act: it required the state to build "this really ugly addition to the state capitol" (namely, a wheelchair ramp); and the Violence Against Women Act: "Is it interstate commerce when you're talking about domestic violence? I don't think so!

Is it national defense? Not exactly.''[55] Also in her Independence Institute speech, she marveled at the bravery of Confederate soldiers who were willing to die for state sovereignty. Slavery was a ''bad fact,'' she said, but with the defeat of the Confederacy, ''We lost too much.''[56] In 2002, Trent Lott was stripped of his Senate leadership position for less.

By 1996, not even Karl Rove (who worked on her campaign) could induce Coloradoans to elect her Senator. Her Senate star fizzled and died in the primary. ''She's just not much of a campaigner,'' says *Denver Post* columnist Diane Carman. ''She acted as if she wanted to wash after shaking hands with people.''[57]

Journalist David Helvarg says Norton's communication skills improved very little after returning to Washington in 2001. ''I've never seen a political figure so uncomfortable in public, especially among people with whom she might expect to disagree,''[58] he comments. Perhaps that's because Gale Norton has spent three decades among friends—in the legal, lobbying, and advocacy circuits of the anti-environmentalist, ''Wise Use'' Right. Ron Arnold, of CDFE, hailed Norton's appointment, calling her ''a longtime ally.''[59] Over at the Cato Institute, they said they were ''popping champagne.'' But Republican Martha Marks of Republicans for Environmental Protection (REP) says Norton's spent too long away from real-life Republicans.

''Her agenda betrays the proud party tradition of Republican environmentalists, dating back to Theodore Roosevelt, Goldwater, Richard Nixon,'' says Marks. In 1997, REP went head to head with Norton over a group Norton had formed with the help of Grover Norquist of the anti-tax group Americans for

Tax Reform. The Council of Republicans for Environmental Advocacy (CREA) was nothing but "a green scam," Marks told the media.[60] In 1998, Norton was co-host at a CREA gala to honor Newt Gingrich. Sponsors were the Chemical Manufacturers Association, the National Mining Association, the Chlorine Chemical Council, and the political consulting firm of Karl Rove. "All I have known CREA ever to do was have that $100,000 fundraiser," says Marks.

"The Republican leadership is on the wrong side of this issue," she says. It seems clear that they know it, too. The same research company, Luntz Research, which advised Gingrich on his *Contract with America* warned the administration that after two years in office, the Bush team's anti-environmentalism was showing through, and their language needed to improve. "First assure your audience that you are committed to 'preserving and protecting the environment,' but that it can be done more 'wisely and effectively,'" Luntz advised.[61]

During her confirmation to head the DoI, Norton did just that. Although, as Colorado Attorney General, she had once prepared an amicus brief against the Endangered Species Act, she swore to uphold it as Interior Secretary. She came to the office straight from working as chief lobbyist for a lead-paint manufacturer facing numerous lawsuits.[62] Yet she was deeply committed to prosecuting corporations that broke the law. She managed to get confirmed, despite years of opposition to most of the federal laws she was being hired to enforce. She'd base her land-management decisions on "sound science," not ideology, she promised.

Once in office, it was a different story. When scientists in her own department announced that drilling in the Arctic National Wildlife Refuge would pose significant risks for caribou, musk oxen, polar bears, and snow geese, for example, Norton ordered underlings to produce a revised report that came to the opposite result.[63] She withheld from Congress information that caribou herds were shrinking near oil developments, then called her distortions a "mistake."[64] As her special advisor on the Arctic refuge she appointed Camden Toohey, director of the pro-oil development group Arctic Power. And why not drill? The refuge in winter is "a great white nothing," Norton told the House Resources Committee in 2003.

Norton came into office with a catchphrase: "communication, consultation, cooperation in service of conservation." She toured the country making high-visibility stops at national parks, and let it be known that she and her husband, real-estate lawyer John Hughes, loved to hike. Norton had herself photographed with an American condor, an endangered species, on her arm. Out of public sight, however, the administration developed a plan to contract out National Park and Forest Service jobs to private, pro-profit companies, and Norton's legal team has been gutting environmental rules in deals with—you guessed it—lawyers working on behalf of the resource industry.

Backed by the White House, the Forest Service announced that it intends to conduct fifty large-scale timber sales in the Tongass National Forest, prime habitat for the endangered grizzly bear. Norton's deputy, J. Steven Griles, stations in front of his office door a stuffed, full-grown Alaskan grizzly.[65] In the name of "healthy forests," Norton and Bush have lifted government rules that require environmental studies before trees are logged or burned. Despite strong public support for a 2001 Roadless Rule, the Bush administration announced a decision to permit snowmobiles in Yellowstone and Grand Teton National Parks and acceded to claims brought by Utah county officials and others who claim that federally-designated, roadless wilderness areas violate ancient cart tracks, dirt trails and other "historic" rights of way.[66]

"Sue and settle," that's what the government is doing, say critics. "The industry sues and then the current administration does a poor job of defending itself or comes to a sweetheart settlement," Kristen Boyles of Earthjustice explains.[67] It's a strategy legal outfits like Mountain States and Pacific Legal have supported for years. As lawsuit negotiations, unlike congressional debates, are closed, the public has no opportunity to comment or object. In the snowmobile case, the Department of the Interior responded to a suit by snowmobile manufacturers and Wise Use outfits. Wise Use may have become less visible as a movement, but it has not gone away. Fifteen years after the '88 conference, Wise Users make the best of the worldwide web to mobilize supposedly "spontaneous" consumer response to government proposals. The public image is of upstanding, if rowdy, citizens—dirt bikers, ranchers, snowmobilers, and the rest; the private language is something else entirely. Off-road.com, which claims to be the second biggest motor sports site on the web (after NASCAR) is underwritten by ads from SUV-makers, Hummer, Chevy, Isuzu, and Dodge. The site lists the Forest Service, Bureau of Land Management, and DoI plans on which the government is seeking public comment. It also features an "Eco-Nazi Event of the Month" notice, to inform Wise Users where environmentalists can be found.[68]

Talk of "Eco-Nazis" would be easier to dismiss if the Wise Use movement, in its day, had not attracted some pretty unsavory types. The California-based "Sahara Club," to name one of the most extreme, seems to have existed for a while solely to threaten and intimidate environmentalists. In 1990, when Earth First! activist Judi Bari was involved in a summer-long campaign to stop old-growth logging by Louisiana-Pacific in the Northwest, a bomb planted beneath her car-seat exploded, shattering her pelvis. Sahara, which had sent Bari a series of death-threats before the bombing, cheered in their newsletter: "BOMB THAT CROTCH! Bari, who had her crotch blown off, will never be able to reproduce again."[69] Bari went to her death (from cancer a few years later) believing that Louisiana-Pacific and the FBI colluded with Wise Use groups (including Sahara Club) to intimidate environmentalists. In 2001, her estate and her co-defendants won a $4.4 million verdict, when a jury concluded that the FBI had indeed falsely framed Bari and Earth First! as terrorists in an effort to shut them down, but had failed to investigate who really bombed her car.

In the post-9/11 environment, not only mountain-men maniacs are equating environmentalism with terrorism. In 2003, the American Legislative Exchange Council (ALEC) drew up the "Animal and Ecological Terrorism Act," which criminalizes virtually all forms of environmental or animal rights advocacy.[70] Gale Norton was the Keynote Speaker at ALEC's 2001 "States and Nation Policy Summit." The group was founded by Paul Weyrich, and the chairmen of Coors Brewery and Koch Industries sit on the board.[71]

Thirty-three years after the first Earth Day, the ultra Right has made gains they only dreamt of in 1970. Years of activism—from lawsuits to death threats—have had their effect. The legislative environment has changed and things that were unthinkable in Watt's day are underway. Gale Norton, one of their own, is in control. Halfway through her first term, Wise User Ron Arnold reflects that Norton's turning out well: "She's marginally better than Clinton was on our issues, and infinitely better than Bush #1."[72]

Norton herself may be no glad-hander, but to her side at the Department of the Interior, she brought a garrulous former hippy, Lynn Scarlett (former editor and CEO of the Reason Foundation in Los Angeles, which publishes the Libertarians' premier magazine, *Reason*). Scarlett is familiar with the subtleties of schmooze. She came to Interior (where she is assistant secretary for policy, management and budget) from the anti-regulatory Foundation for Research on Economics and the Environment (FREE), which is best known for holding expense-paid seminars on market economics for federal judges.

"The '60s preoccupation with political power and group rights led—inevitably, I think—to a politics of victimhood," Scarlett once wrote in an article for the American Enterprise Institute.[73] The movements she was talking about were preoccupied with political power because they wanted some. Women, African Americans, Native Americans, immigrants, gays and lesbians, they fought for "group rights" because, as a group, they had experienced those rights denied. The groups

Norton, and Watt, and Ron Arnold, and Scarlett represent claim that private landowners and public-land leasers, drillers, ranchers, and corporate polluters are "victimized" by the environmental laws that elected legislators have passed. Talk about land developers as victims to Suzan Harjo, however, and prepare to step aside.

"Communication, consultation, cooperation. We've seen none of it," exclaims Harjo, a Native American rights activist. Norton, who said famously that "I hate government telling me what to do, and I assume other people do too,"[74] has become "the Great White Mother when it comes to Indians," Harjo fumes.[75]

In 1994, Elouise Cobell, an Oklahoma Blackfoot, sued the Department of the Interior on behalf of some 300,000 Native Americans nationwide who claim that the department, which administers Indian lands in a trust for individual Indians, has lost billions of dollars of revenue owed to individuals and tribes for the use of their land. (Estimates of what is owed range from $10 billion to ten times that. The DoI used the same firm as the disgraced Enron Corporation, Arthur Andersen, to do the accounts.)

"The whole Indian Trust Fund suit could have been resolved by now," says Keith Harper, one of the lawyers on the Cobell case. "When Norton came in, she could have done the right thing and settled and been a hero," he says. Instead, a month into office, she signed a memorandum undermining everything ordered by the federal judge who had been working on the case with her predecessor, Bruce Babbitt. Not long after that, the judge declared her in contempt of court. "She threw down a gauntlet and made Babbitt's albatross her own," comments Harper.[76]

The same people who were involved in Indian Trust mismanagement under James Watt are back at the DoI: J. Steven Griles and James Carson. (Griles served as a lobbyist for Occidental Petroleum and the Mining Association, in the meantime.) Ross O. Swimmer, who was assistant secretary for Indian affairs in the Watt years, has been put in charge of Indian Trust assets. "Swimmer's idea for fixing Trust problems is turning over major Indian programs to states and private industries," says Harjo. "The goal is more land grab, more money grab," she sighs.

Norton's assistant secretary for land and minerals management is Rebecca Watson, a woman who has spent almost her entire legal career defending the mining and timber industry. Watson works with Defenders of Property Rights (a legal group that exists to promote "takings" laws. Norton sits on the board with Robert Bork and Orrin Hatch.) At the end of 2001, Norton announced that her department was overturning a Clinton-era ruling that rejected a Canadian gold mining company's request to open a major open-pit gold mine in a sacred site belonging to the Quechan Indian nation in the southern California desert. The largely pristine area is adjacent to designated wilderness, critical habitat for the federally-protected desert tortoise, and a portion of the nationally recognized native Trail of Dreams.

"She's for religious rights, except for Indian religions, individual rights, except for ours. Property rights, except for Indian property," says Suzan Harjo. Norton is getting away with things that Watt never could, she says. ''She'll finish the Watt agenda because there are a lot of people helping her.''[77]

CONCLUSION

SISTERS

In 1977, Arnold Schwarzenegger boasted to a porn magazine about taking a "black girl" upstairs for a "gang bang" at his gym. Thirty-some years later, he is still mouthing off to magazines. He had a blast making the third *Terminator* film, the former body-builder told *Entertainment Weekly* in 2003: "How many times do you get away with this—to take a woman, grab her upside down, and bury her face in a toilet bowl? I wanted to have something floating in there." [1] Just weeks after that story appeared, Schwarzenegger announced his intention to run for Governor of California.

In 1977, Republican political strategists would have paled at the prospect of Hollywood's biggest symbol of unreconstructed machismo running on their ticket for Governor in arguably the most progressive state of the union. In 2003, far from shying away from the crass former Mr Olympia, the GOP cozied up. In April, Schwarzenegger met with the President's election guru, Karl Rove, at the White House. (They both deny they talked about politics.) By August, Schwarzenegger was the Republican Party's lead candidate in a Republican-driven effort to replace Governor Gray Davis, a Democrat. Former Secretary of State George P. Shultz joined Schwarzenegger's official campaign team. So did the GOP's last California Governor, Pete Wilson. In mid-summer, the Republican National Committee's communications director, Mindy Tucker, relocated to California to "consult" with the state GOP on the race.

That the GOP had no qualms about backing Arnold the Barbarian for Governor speaks volumes about where gender relations stand under George W. Bush. Macho man is back, and it isn't a camp disco send-up; it's the stuff of photo-opportunities and campaign ads. Consider the President's most famous made-for-TV moment. In May 2003, in a carefully choreographed (and taxpayer-funded) show of bravado, Bush leapt from the cockpit of a fighter jet and strutted across the deck of an aircraft carrier off the coast of San Diego to claim success in the invasion of Iraq. Thanks to a few, well-placed, jumpsuit groin-straps, Bush literally showed his balls to the world and barely a titter was heard. Bush has brought butch-swagger to the world stage, and it's serious; Butch Bush comes complete with flesh and blood dead people on several continents, and the cruelest social policy in a century.

Some blame 9/11. "In the horror that followed we struggled for a way to respond—and we found it in the icon of the neo-macho man," *Village Voice* columnist Richard Goldstein wrote in March 2003.[2] But while the attacks of 9/11 gave Butch Bush a pulpit—or a cockpit—it didn't take a terrorist attack to create Bush's inner Terminator.

Bush has always been part Barbarian. During the presidential campaign, Mindy Tucker and Karen Hughes (then his press secretary and his communications director) spent half their time keeping a lid on revelations that the law-and-order candidate had been arrested in his youth for brawling and drunk-driving and stands accused of illegal drug use as an adult (he will only say he's been drug-free since the age of twenty-eight).[3] The supposedly clean-living, sober church-goer couldn't stop saying ''fuck'' in an interview with *Talk* magazine,[4] and he was picked up on a microphone calling a *New York Times* reporter a ''major league asshole.'' (Like father, like son. The elder Bush thought he was talking confidentially when he said he had ''tried to kick a little ass'' debating Democrat Geraldine Ferraro in 1984.) Asked to apologize, W. would only say that he regretted the comment had been heard by the public.[5]

It was thuggery, in the end, that brought the Florida vote count to a halt. Just days before the deadline, a mob invaded the Miami office building where officials were trying to conduct a recount. The louts kicking local Democrats and pounding on the officials' walls were not disgruntled Floridians, as the Bush campaign media team would have had you believe, but rather Republican congressional aides and lobbyists sent down, expenses-paid, from Washington. After the Miami-Dade vote counters called off the count, citing intimidation, the so-called ''Brooks Brothers Battalion'' partied down at a nearby Hyatt hotel. Their celebratory bash received phone calls from the candidates, Bush and Cheney, who joked about the Miami-Dade riot and the shutdown of the count that followed.[6] (Who headed up Bush's media operation in Florida? Mindy Tucker.)

So when Schwarzenegger responded to his critics with a nod and a wink and a gesture towards Maria Shriver, his Kennedy-

cousin wife (a Democrat), he was merely acting presidential.
Bush stole the White House just that way: with a lot of nods
and winks, and a bevy of Bushwomen.

First Ladies Laura Bush and Lynne Cheney (the wife of the
Vice-President) are the White House's Maria Shriver. Unelected, supposedly not political, they speak to the "personal"
side of their men. Just as Shriver attempted to assure voters
that the nasty stories about Arnold were only movie-fun or
rumor, so the first wives act as the Bush team's character
witnesses. There's one for each Bush constituency, and they're
summed up by their attitudes to literature: Laura Bush said
famously: "there's nothing political about American literature."[7] By contrast, it's Lynne Cheney's belief that one book, *I
Pierre*, by Michel Foucault, turned American culture "away
from reason and reality" and against "Truth" itself.[8] As you
might have guessed, Laura speaks to moderates; Lynne delights
the Right.

It's hard to imagine the *Terminator* presidency without the
culture wars that came before it, and in those wars Lynne
Cheney was a key warrior. The social change movements of the
1960s and '70s were cultural as well as political: Gay Pride,
Earth Day, *Ms.* magazine, Black is Beautiful . . . By the start of
the 1980s, white male domination was decidedly *uncool* (and
socially unpopular). To prepare the ground for Bush's butch-
swagger and basket, a backlash had to turn all that around, and
from her spot as the head of the National Endowment for
the Humanities from 1986 to '93, Cheney helped to do the
turning.

Conservative culture warrior is an odd career outcome for a

woman who started life as a baton twirler and once penned a
steamy lesbian romance, but Lynne Cheney, throughout her
life, has been nothing if not flexible. She has a knack for
molding herself and her opinions to suit the opportunities of
her time. Born in 1941, in Casper, Wyoming, Lynne (née
Vincent) met Richard Bruce Cheney at Natrona County High
School. Both their fathers worked for the government, both
their mothers were liberated Western women: Lynne's was a
deputy sheriff—she had a badge, but no gun; Dick Cheney's
was an infielder on the Syracuse (Neb) Bluebirds, a nationally-
ranked women's softball team in the 1930s.[9]

In the 1950s, Vincent was a bobbysox girl. A straight-A
student, the elected "Mustang Queen," she took up baton-
twirling, she has said, because it was one of the few competitive
sports available to girls, and Lynne was competitive.[10] Lynne
and "Dick" graduated in 1959—the same year as the Rydell
High gang made famous in the movie *Grease*. He wasn't quite
the John Travolta to her Olivia Newton John, but Cheney was
class president and captain of the football team, and Vincent
certainly knew how to light up a stage. Dick would stand by her
side with a coffee can filled with water while she twirled
batons, on fire at both ends. He'd douse them when she was
done.[11]

During the 2000 race, Dick Cheney commented to a
reporter that he and Lynne might never have met. "You'd be
married to someone else now," he said to her. "Right," she
piped up. "And he'd be running for Vice-President of the
United States instead of you."[12] She had a point. After high
school, it was Dick, not Lynne (the academic star), who

received a full scholarship to Yale, but after two failed attempts to make the grade, he dropped out, returned to Wyoming, picked up two drunk-driving convictions in a single year, and took a union job laying power lines for the local company. It was Vincent—who was eager-beavering away at state colleges, earning a BA and an MA in English—who pestered Cheney to return to school. Only after her graduation would she agree to marry. ("Dick *should* have finished college," too, she says, but he "hadn't quite.")[13]

The year was 1964 and marriage was the thing to do—not least because the Vietnam War was on, and marriage secured for Dick Cheney the first of several draft deferments reserved for married men. After the draft expanded to include married men without children, Cheney got another deferment when Lynne gave birth to their first child—nine months and two days after the expansion-order was announced. (Cheney received a total of five student and marriage deferments. He told *The Washington Post* in '89, "I had other priorities in the '60s than military service.")[14]

By 1970, he was on his way to a career in politics, and Lynne, now the mother of two, was finding out how hard it was to be taken seriously in her own right. Like many women, she didn't have to work, but she wanted to. "I just never didn't work," she says. "When we were married, and through moving and everything else, I have always been teaching or writing."[15] She'd written a very serious dissertation on the effect of Immanuel Kant's philosophy on the poetry of Victorian didact Matthew Arnold. She liked to write; she hated to cook. But finding rewarding employment was not so easy. Her first ambition had been to be a movie star; her second, a college professor. "This was before people were enlightened about women, and married women in particular," she told *Fox News*. A prospective employer asked her point-blank: "Are you interested in the job, Dr Cheney, or are you married?" "That was illegal at the time," she comments.[16] (As Cheney acknowledges, people didn't simply become "enlightened," Congress passed laws. It wasn't until 1978 that the US outlawed firing pregnant workers.)

Cheney took up a more convenient career for a politician's wife, that of writer. Her first book, a political thriller titled *Executive Privilege*, came out in 1979. Her second, *Sisters*, tapped directly into the feminist spirit of the age.

The novel that today's Mrs Cheney leaves out of her official biography came out in 1981, from Signet, in a gloriously gothic paperback edition. Breathy cover copy promises "a novel of a strong and beautiful woman who broke all the rules of the American frontier," and *Sisters* delivers on the promise. The star of the book is a condom-carrying Wyoming woman who runs away from convent school to join the theater, where she comes under the influence of a music-hall celebrity who teaches her how to "enjoy" men, but not get "trapped."[17] Protagonist Sophie develops into a strong-willed East Coast intellectual—a magazine publisher, member of the dreaded media elite—who only returns to Cheyenne after her homebody sister turns up dead. At first, suspicion falls on Amy, Sophie's sister's "dearest lover." Amy is exonerated (in fact, the murderer turns out to be the patriarch in the picture). The relationships women have with women in the book offer

attractive—and sexy—refuge from the gruff lives they lead
with men. Watching two women holding each other in a car-
riage, Cheney writes, Sophie "felt curiously moved, curiously
envious of them. She saw that the women in the cart had a
passionate, loving intimacy forever closed to her. How strong it
made them. What comfort it gave."[18]

Lynne Cheney's Sophie thinks sex should be pleasurable for
women, and contraceptives made the difference. "She had
encountered this idea, that no respectable woman would use
preventive devices. It seemed senseless to her." Marriage, on
the other hand, should be optional, she says: "They should seek
companionship and love from one another because they wanted
it, not because they were obliged by the forms and expectations
society imposed upon those who married."[19] Sophie ultimately
agrees to marry her dead sister's husband and raise his children
(although not before enjoying protected sex with him in front
of the living room fireplace).

Lynne Cheney, having had her fun with feminism, then
signed up to join the anti-feminist backlash. Sexual liberation,
unmarried couples, even family planning—by the middle of the
1980s, Sophie's values read like a catalogue of all that the
Reagan GOP was against. A 1986 report written by Gary
Bauer, then undersecretary for education, laid out the state's
interest in the male-headed, heterosexual, married family:
"Attitudes to work are formed in families," declared the
report. Families "prepare skilled and energetic workers who
are the engine for democratic capitalism." Based on Bauer's
report, Executive Order 12606 (signed in 1987) required that
"federal agencies must assess [the] impact on [the] family when

formulating and implementing policies and regulations."[20] In the name of "family values" (the words were just then gaining resonance), the Reagan revolutionaries were out to reverse every trend that encouraged independent, wage-earning moms, unmarried parenting, divorce, protected sex, and non-nuclear arrangements of every kind. *Sisters* was definitely off the reading list.

Meanwhile, Dick was a rising star in the Republican House of Representatives.[21] (He was elected Wyoming's only congressman in '78 after a race in which Lynne did six weeks' of his campaigning, in the wake of his first heart attack.) He voted against busing and the establishment of a federal Department of Education, against reauthorizing the Legal Services Corporation (which offers free legal aid to the poor), against the Panama Canal Treaty (of course), the Equal Rights Amendment, and the imposition of sanctions on apartheid South Africa. Lynne, who now says she is more conservative than her husband, found a niche for herself, too.

When William Bennett left the National Endowment for the Humanities (NEH) to become secretary of education, she put herself forward to chair. The federal agency had long provided a pulpit for the administration's views on the arts and education. Confirmed to the job largely because she was "a published author," at NEH Cheney railed against "political correctness" on campus, especially in Women's Studies and African-American studies, and took up arms against the very field of research she'd credited with "guiding her thinking" in the acknowledgements to *Sisters*. (Cheney writes that she "owes a particular debt" to, among others, Linda Gordon, author of *Woman's*

Body, Woman's Right: the History of Birth Control in America, and Carroll Smith-Rosenberg, the author of "The Female World of Love and Ritual," which appeared in 1975 in the feminist journal *Signs*. Both are campus progressives: a history professor at New York University, Gordon specializes in the history of reproductive rights and welfare; Smith-Rosenberg, at the University of Michigan, focuses on the politics of gender and sexuality.)[22]

Even as she berated women's rights advocates for embracing "victim status" for women, Cheney made her mark by claiming that classicists like herself, and "western values," were being victimized in the academy. Even "truth" itself was under attack, she wrote in a 1995 book, *Telling the Truth*.[23] Censorious feminists and left-wing professors had become what she called an on-campus "thought police." Cheney came out against a PBS television series, *The Africans*, which analyzed the lasting effects of colonialism, calling it "an anti-western diatribe," and she demanded the NEH name be taken off the credits. She persuaded the Senate to vote down new national history standards for the public school curriculum, and in '95, she recommended ending government financing of NEH altogether (she fancied turning arts funding over to the private sector).

Cheney's work was part of a concerted attack. Conservative foundations—Olin, Bradley, Carthage, Scaife—poured cash into the cultural backlash just as they had funded legal groups to battle in courts, and "think-tanks" to influence Congress. The same outfits that backed Dinesh D'Souza's attack on progressive academics, *Illiberal Education*, and the scurrilous *Real Anita Hill* (which David Brock now recants) funded one project after another to push conservative views into mainstream consciousness.[24] Brock, in an article for the *American Spectator* magazine (which was funded by Richard Scaife—the same man who underwrote the Clinton impeachment effort), called Hill a "little bit nutty and a little bit slutty" and his work was heavily promoted by Rush Limbaugh on radio, which sent sales soaring. "I had stumbled onto something big, a symbiotic relationship that would help create a highly profitable, right-wing Big Lie machine that flourished in book publishing, on talk radio and on the Internet through the '90s."[25]

In 1994, the Independent Women's Forum, of which Cheney was a founding member, received $100,000 in start up funds from the Carthage Foundation and $40,000 from the Bradley Foundation to produce a media directory of conservative women. Cheney and her ilk were hardly "censored" or "victimized"—far from it. She was put on a stipend at the American Enterprise Institute (where she wrote *Telling the Truth*, her manifesto against contemporary culture and education), she joined the board of the defense contractor Lockheed Martin, and she was hired as a Sunday co-host on CNN's flagship debate program, *Crossfire*.

The backlash had a serious impact. The discrediting of Anita Hill was followed by the confirmation of Clarence Thomas to the Supreme Court. The attacks on Hillary Clinton guaranteed that her healthcare proposal failed to be taken seriously.[26] An onslaught of propaganda against poor mothers, especially African-American women and immigrants, set the scene for the ending of federal welfare and the stiffening of work requirements under the TANF system.[27] While Cheney went after academics for spreading "untruth" and leftist ideology, pundits and politicians pursued artists who received public grants. In 1990, the National Endowment for the Arts withdrew grants from four artists on the grounds of "obscenity."[28] The expression of gay identity was cast as the "promotion" of homosexuality.[29] Academics who wanted tenure were under pressure to depoliticize their research.

The backlash worked, not because conservatives like Brock or Cheney or D'Souza were correct on their facts—*Telling the Truth* is mostly anecdote—but because the Right's accusations fed a paranoia that was already brewing, stoked by changing attitudes towards race, shifting gender roles, a recession, the AIDS epidemic, and a globalizing economy. On campus, in Congress, in the media, and in the arts, at just the time that legislators were discussing state protection for the vulnerable— welfare—or the best way to prevent sexually transmitted diseases, or to protect the environment, people who had worked for decades in those fields—and even the data they'd collected—were considered suspect.

By the time the attacks of 9/11 occurred, those who pointed to a link between *Terminator* posturing and people ending up dead were under siege. The media declared open season on Susan Sontag for three paragraphs in which she had written that "a few shreds of historical awareness might help us understand what has just happened and what may continue to happen."[30] Those who dared to speak out in the seclusion of their own classrooms against a retaliatory response to the 9/11 attacks (or against any Bush policy of the moment) found themselves written up in a report that listed "incidents" of alleged anti-Americanism on campus and claimed that "colleges and university faculty have been the weak link in America's response to the attacks." The American Council of Trustees and Alumna, which produced the report, was founded by Lynne Cheney.[31]

When First Lady Bush turned to the nation after the attacks of 9/11 and urged Americans to "talk with your children; listen to them. Tell them they are safe," nothing could have been further from the truth. Thanks to a combination of incompetence and aggression, Americans weren't safe—not from terrorist attacks from abroad, or, indeed, from home-grown maniacs mailing anthrax. (Women's healthcare providers knew that already—they'd been stalked by anti-abortion terrorists for years.) But the likelihood of being caught up in a building attacked, or receiving anthrax in the mail, was remote in comparison with the threats to freedom coming from Washington.

Laura Bush has one job: Laura lulls. Bush is a great dad, she told the Republican National Convention in 2000. (He read Dr Seuss's *Hop on Pop* to the twins, and "spends every night with a teacher.")[32] In response to a question about Roe v. Wade on the *Today* program just before the inauguration she said, "No, I don't think it should be overturned."[33] Barbara Bush and Nancy Reagan said the same. The very next day, her husband let it be known that he intended to restore the Reagan-era "global gag" rule on groups that receive US funding abroad for family planning and women's healthcare services, such that they may not even mention abortion, even to take a position on abortion policy.

It's possible that Laura is misrepresenting herself on abortion. There's one sentence in her official biography to the effect that in the early '80s she and W. "participated in a Focus on the Family series about raising children." Focus on the Family is a vehemently anti-abortion, Christian Right group. Alternatively, Laura is cover art, used by the White House to reassure middle-of-the-road voters, while her husband curries favor with hardliners.

In April 2001, Laura Bush, a former librarian, appeared at a public library in Washington to kick off the "Campaign for America's Libraries." A week later, the self-proclaimed "education President" proposed shrinking funding for the Library Service and Technology Act and cancelled funding for Reading is Fundamental as well as the National Commission on Libraries and Information Science. When asked about the contradiction, she said, "We're just like any other married couple. We don't talk that much about what we do."[34]

In November 2001, Laura, who claims to dislike public speaking, addressed the nation about war.[35] A few weeks into the attack on Afghanistan, the President's early talk about an all-American "crusade" to "smoke 'em out and get 'em runnin'" was falling flat. With the apparent escape of the invasion's alleged target—Osama bin Laden, the man the White House accused of plotting the September 11 attacks—the President's "dead or alive" lingo gradually gave way to talk of "liberation" for the people of Afghanistan, specifically, Afghanistan's women. The new message to the world was that the US was not a dangerous superpower seething with revenge; but rather that the US, with its ally, the UK, was global headquarters for women's liberation. The messengers were female.

As US bombers rained cluster bombs on the people of Afghanistan and the bombing of Kabul was at its height, out came the First Ladies of the US and the UK: Laura Bush and Cherie Booth. Bush became what her publicists described as "the first First Lady to deliver an entire presidential radio address" by herself, when she used the weekly broadcast from the White House to denounce the "severe repression against women in Afghanistan." (One letter writer to the *Los Angeles Times* pointed out that First Lady Eleanor Roosevelt was in the habit of addressing the nation directly on radio "by herself," but no other commentator saw fit to mention that.)

"I'm delivering this week's radio address to kick off a worldwide effort to focus on the brutality against the women and children by the al-Qaeda terrorist network and the regime it supports in Afghanistan, the Taliban," she said. "Long before the current war began, the Taliban and its terrorist allies were making the lives of children and women in Afghanistan miserable. Seventy percent of the Afghan people are malnourished. One in every four children won't live past the age of five because healthcare is not available. Women have been denied access to doctors when they're sick.

"All of us have an obligation to speak out," said Laura Bush. "The fight against terrorism is also a fight for the rights and dignity of women."

In London, Cherie Booth (who chose this moment to identify herself uncharacteristically as Mrs Cherie Blair) gathered several Afghan women and a bevy of female Members of

Parliament to say many of the same things as her American counterpart. Completing the sisterhood, Hillary Rodham Clinton, with some of her Senate colleagues, hosted a press conference for Afghan women's rights activists on Capitol Hill. "We, as the liberators, have an interest in what follows the Taliban," Clinton wrote in *Time* magazine.

The First Lady's history lesson on Afghanistan conveniently ignored the key players. During the Soviet invasion of Afghanistan, the CIA, through Pakistan's intelligence service, sent more than $4 billion in lethal weapons and training to seven different Afghan resistance groups, and it was in the fractious war that followed (which claimed 1.5 million lives) that both the Taliban and the factions that make up today's Northern Alliance grew. That period "long before the current war began" included a very recent time in which US energy companies were lobbying Kabul for a Central Asian pipeline to run through Afghan territory (rather than through Russia or Iran). As recently as June 2001, the Bush administration, via the United Nations, sent the Taliban $43 million for "poppy-seed eradication" and welcomed Taliban representatives in Washington.[36] Under the new US-friendly government in Kabul, the pipeline project is back on track.

The First Lady's speech put a feminist glow on some of the most brutal bombing of the 2001 campaign. NBC's Tom Brokaw picked up the First Lady's spin and ran with it, dedicating an entire segment of his news program to what were called the "Women of the War Room," which began: "The war on terrorism and the major role for American women at almost every level, especially the top . . . a striking contrast to

the way women have been treated in Afghanistan.'' Referring
to the women in the White House (Karen Hughes, Con-
doleezza Rice, Pentagon spokeswoman Victoria Clarke and the
Vice-President's chief of staff, Mary Matalin, as well as the
First Lady), reporter Andrea Mitchell waxed eloquent:
''They're not only making the strategy, their gender is part of
the strategy . . . a weapon to attack the Taliban's treatment of
Afghan women.''

''Hope blooms for Afghan women,'' wrote Rhonda Chriss
Lokeman, editor of the opinion page of the *Kansas City Star*.
Lokeman called Laura Bush, ''One part Jackie O to two parts
Rosalyn Carter.'' ''Power to the (female) people,'' wagged the
Washington Times's Suzanne Fields. [37]

''It will do nothing but help them with female voters,'' one
White House advisor told *The New York Times* that December,
''it'' being the attacks on the Afghans. He was right. Bush's poll
numbers, already high, started creeping up, even among
women. On-the-fence voters, even those who hated the
bombing, found in the ousting of the Taliban rulers something
to celebrate. Although women in post-invasion Afghanistan
faced a critical lack of food, unexploded ordinance and the
destruction of roads and water supplies, freedom was measured
by one thing: the veil. News coverage turned the floor-length
covering, the burqa, into the ultimate totem of female
oppression. No story on events in Afghanistan—from *Fox News*
to *Business Week*—was complete without a woman with or
without her burqa.

Reporting on the burqa far out-numbered reports on
women's struggle for fundamental rights—to education,

health, personal safety, political participation—perhaps because
the people the US had chosen as allies had rotten records on
granting any of those. Of the Northern Alliance leaders who
received US support and training, General Rashid Dostum
stands accused of raping, killing and looting around Kabul in
1992. His forces committed atrocities from 1992 to '97 when
he controlled the northern city of Mazar-e-Sharif. As Laura
Bush was speaking, Dostum was leading a brutal assault on that
city, assisted by US bombing raids.[38]

"There are even more documented cases of women raped
by members of the Northern Alliance than there are by the
Taliban," Alex Arriago, director of government relations for
Amnesty International USA, told the press shortly after the
First Lady's address.[39]

Afghanistan's "new" government intends to keep "Sharia
law," the strict code adopted by some Islamists, reported the
French news agency Agence France-Presse in December 2001.
A judge told AFP that public executions and amputations would
continue, with some changes. "For example, the Taliban used
to hang the victim's body in public for four days. We will only
hang the body for a short time, say fifteen minutes."[40] The dire
warnings about the Northern Alliance leaders that came for
years from women's rights warriors such as those in RAWA
(the Revolutionary Association of Women of Afghanistan) have
proven dismally true. Two years after the 9/11 attacks, Sima
Samar, head of Afghanistan's Independent Human Rights
Commission, said Islamic activists were consolidating power.
When western feminists and US negotiators applied pressure,
Samar was made Afghanistan's Vice-President and its first

minister of women's affairs, but Islamists had her ousted for comments she made in Canada to the effect that she didn't believe in the Taliban version of Sharia law. "I was disappointed that nobody said anything," she told the *Wall Street Journal* in September 2003. "This isn't democracy."[41]

When George W. Bush signed the Afghan Women and Children Relief Act of 2001, he surrounded himself with Afghan women and children in traditional clothing, but Bush's Act had no figures attached to it and, two years later, only a tiny amount of the money ever committed to Afghanistan has been distributed. Bush didn't even request full funding in his initial budget request for 2003.[42]

Whatever the bombing did and did not do for Afghan women and girls, it did wonders for Bush in the polls. In early January 2002, the President denied thinking about politics. "I'm going to have to start thinking about it next year," he told the press. But Karl Rove was keeping a close watch. An unnamed "Republican official" told *The Washington Post* that George W. Bush "has not only erased any question about legitimacy, he has also erased the gender gap."

He did come close. In midterm elections in 2002, the Democrats won the "women's vote" by a meager two points. (Laura Bush campaigned for pro-choice moderates like Republican Connie Morella of Maryland, one of the sponsors of the Bush administration's least-favorite pieces of legislation, the Violence Against Women Act.) For the first time in a century, a Republican president saw his party gain seats in an off-year election and, for the first time in two decades, the Republicans and the Democrats had near parity with women. Rove told

Time that the shift among women with young children was a major factor. ''9/11 changed everything,'' said a senior Bush aide.[43]

Not exactly. For thirty years, the most powerful entities in the country have claimed that Americans are vulnerable to attack—from civil rights marchers, school desegregators, poor people who need income support, labor unionists who demand liveable wages, environmentalists, even family farmers, people with AIDS demanding public money for prevention and treatment, women who call for equal rights. *Before* the attacks of 9/11, Bush's staunchest support came from religious, conservative, not-urban, married voters who were unsettled by the changes wrought by the movements of the late 20th century; people to whom he promised protection from the Clinton-loving, tree-hugging, pinko, feminazi homos that the right-wing think-tanks, and Rush Limbaugh and the folks at what Gore Vidal calls ''19th Century Fox TV,'' talked about.

After 9/11, the population of the frightened grew. Thousands of men and women lost loved ones in the attacks on the United States. Thousands more were shaken to the core by what they witnessed and desperately afraid of a repeat. Still more were scared by continuing alerts, a deadly anthrax scare, and talk of ''terrorist cells'' that supposedly lurked like some malignancy, preparing to strike. More still were worried by FBI, round-ups and months-long detentions without trial under the hurriedly enacted USA PATRIOT Act. After 9/11, Bush's target constituency broadened to include anyone who feared what he called ''evil-doers.'' ''We're a nation that can't be cowed by evil-doers,'' the President said on September 16 2001.[44] "You're either for us or you're against us."[45]

"When people are feeling insecure, they'd rather have someone who is strong and wrong rather than somebody who is weak and right," said former President Clinton in an effort to explain the GOP's midterm results.[46]

But the "GOP sweeps" hailed after the 2002 elections were "sweeps" of pretty small substance. Once the excitement cleared, it turned out that the vast majority of people either didn't vote in November 2002, or voted against the Bushmen—and women. In the congressional races where Bush claimed his mandate, only about one third of eligible voters cast a ballot. About 15 percent voted for Democrats, while 1.1 percent voted for others.[47] That "everything is changed" mandate Rove is talking about actually represents only 17 percent of the people. Some people are truly scared of terrorism, for sure, but a whole lot more are fed up.

As election 2004 approaches, the *Terminator* President is in trouble. US job losses stand at three million, poverty is up such that one child in five is destitute.[48] While the President asks Congress for an additional $87 billion to occupy Iraq, child tax credit checks to low-income families have never gone out. In Iraq, more Americans have died since Bush strutted across the carrier USS *Abraham Lincoln* than died in the first weeks of the assault. Gun-related killings in Baghdad have increased twenty-five-fold in the same period.[49] Cosmopolitan Iraqi women who'd never before worn a veil are covering themselves; they've fled their jobs and they're hiding indoors, for fear they'll be raped.[50]

The public is beginning to see through the GOP's selling job. Speaking on public radio in San Francisco in August 2003, Communications Director Mindy Tucker described the Republicans' plan to attract those all-important women voters. "Sometimes," she said, "we complicate policy and processes so much that busy women don't have time to sift through it all and figure out how it really matters to their lives." To help women out, the GOP had launched a website, "Winning Women," she explained, which profiles the successful women who are in the Bush administration. "We are always striving to find women to talk about our policies," she said, "because [women] are more credible to women." Women, continued Tucker, "have a way of being able to boil things down for other women in a way that they can understand."

She had barely finished speaking when the phone lines lit up. Women don't need anything boiled down, said Kelly from San Francisco. The very idea is "offensive," chimed in another caller, Rita. Ken in Sausalito asked about the women who were losing their sons (and daughters) in Bush's illegal Iraq war. "What are the parties going to do to win them over?"[51]

Rejecting the color-coded alert panics of Bush's Office of Homeland Security, groups of women calling themselves "Code Pink" have been giving pink slips to politicians of both parties and to media personalities. (For instance, to Senator Hillary Clinton, for her vote for the Iraq invasion; to Bill O'Reilly, for just about everything he says on Fox.) Code Pink greeted a fundraising George W. in Los Angeles with a forty-foot pink rejection slip in the shape of women's underwear, blasting the words: "You Lied, You're Fired." (Weeks later, the same pink slip appeared outside Arnold Schwarzenegger's office: "You're terminated.") When there's a massive piece of lingerie dangling in the background, it's hard for macho to look serious.

The hypocrisy in the White House is rank. Even as the Vice-President and his wife run on a platform that is blatantly homophobic, their campaign is run by Mary, their openly lesbian daughter.[52] As the President talks up a storm about getting tough on law-breakers, his own family would be in a bad way without other people's compassion. The Bushes' twin daughters, Jenna and Barbara, have been caught drinking underage; their cousin Noelle (Florida Governor Jeb Bush's daughter) was found with cocaine at a rehabilitation center where she was undergoing drug treatment. Noelle's mother was caught by immigration officials trying to sneak $19,000 worth of jewelry into the country without declaring it and paying tax on it.[53] Even Laura Bush has been shown mercy. In 1963, two days after her seventeenth birthday, Laura Bush was involved in a fatal accident when she drove through a stop sign, hit another car, and killed a young man who happened to be a school friend. She refers to it as "a very tragic time in my life." No charges were ever brought.[54]

When it comes to Bush hypocrisy, however, it's political as well as personal. Even as First Lady Bush talks about the rights and dignity of women in Afghanistan, women in the US face attacks on their rights in the workplace, at the doctors' office, and even in the bedroom. Even as the President lectured the nation on his education policy, dubbed "leave no child behind," Secretary of Education Rod Paige formed a commission to "reassess" Title IX, the 1972 law that mandates equal opportunities for women and girls in education, including sports. Bush's budget slashed funding for the Equal Employment Opportunity Commission (EEOC), even as discrimination claims reached a seven-year high.[55] Not only access to abortion, but access to what Lynne Cheney's Sophie called "preventive devices"—contraceptives—is in peril. Bush's first budget denied contraceptive coverage to federal employees who get their health insurance through their job. The White House tried to remove the obligation on insurers who provide prescription coverage to include the five birth-control methods already approved by the Food and Drug Administration (FDA). At the urging of the administration, an overdrawn federal government dedicated $120 million for censorious sexual education programs which talk about abstinence but stay silent about condoms or family planning. (The White House wants that to go up to $135 million, and there's still no proof that education on abstinence does anything to stop teenage sex.) And over at Health and Human Services, they're supporting legislation that would elevate the rights of a fetus over a woman's right to health, and manipulating welfare benefits to "promote" marriage. The Bush AIDS pledge to Africa is held up in a wrangle about whether any US dollars will pay for condoms.

First Lady Laura said, "All of us have an obligation to speak out." This is a good time for speaking.

For twenty years, the people who brought Bush to power have been making the same few arguments against enforcing civil rights, gender equality, environmental protection, and fair treatment of organized labor. Desegregation, affirmative action, welfare, living wages, ecology—they're too expensive, conservatives say; the government shouldn't intervene, and besides, there's a question of privacy.[56] As Gale Norton puts it, "people don't like government telling them what to do."[57]

Since 9/11, every one of those arguments has been contradicted by the Bush administration. The country faces a $500 billion debt; at unknown expense, the federal government is intervening in the affairs of people halfway around the world. Big Brother has come to Laura Bush's beloved libraries. The USA PATRIOT Act allows the FBI to subpoena records from libraries and bookstores, defines "terrorism" to include direct action by protestors, expands the government's power to tap phone calls and emails, and makes it possible to intern several thousand foreign nationals for months on end without trial. On the eve of September 11 2003, George Bush asked Congress to pass three additional "anti-terror" laws, and declared that federal agents needed yet more power to reduce the nation's vulnerability to attack. Attorney General John Ashcroft mocked librarians who complained, calling them "hysterical." (Laura Bush, of course, said zip.)[58]

The party of "pre-emptive" war, bankruptcy and the PATRIOT Act cannot possibly hope to keep the confidence of a coalition pulled together in the name of non-intervention, fiscal conservatism and personal privacy. The Bush administration's response to 9/11 pulls the Right's delicately-crafted coalition of the past twenty years apart at the seams. Loyalists like Phyllis Schlafly are tearing their hair. (Too many prominent Republicans are cozying up to increased federal control and the spending that goes with it, she complained in 2002, in a column headlined, "Homeland security or homeland spying?")[59] After years of being defined by the Right's coalition, it's time for progressive people to rethink. The Bush presidency deserves to have its bluff called. The President chose to muster popular support with phoney talk about liberating women and preventing possible future harm. Instead of going along with Bush's sham, it's time for progressive politicians to fight just as hard for policies that could achieve the real thing.

Butch-swagger has brought us to this point: the early premises of feminism just might lead us out. It is not credible, domestic violence survivors say, to claim that you love someone while you hurt them. It makes no sense to bankrupt a family or a nation to make it safe. Can you have security for states, but insecurity for the people who occupy them, or are occupied—security without community? Means and ends are connected: you can't seize office through racist means and claim to stand for freedom and equality. Justice is indivisible; you can't tout a handful of "Winning Women" when the vast majority are losing out.

"Democratic anything presupposes equal membership in the body politic," wrote poet and essayist June Jordan.[60]

For twenty years, both major parties have fought over a tiny sliver of the population. Halfway through the first decade of the new century, the policy options are wide open and there is a world of voters waiting. The Right has a popularity problem it tried to solve with a handful of Bushwomen. Those who believe in democracy have an alternative: everybody else.

ABBREVIATIONS

ACLU	American Civil Liberties Union
EPA	Environmental Protection Agency
FCC	Federal Communications Commission
GATT	General Agreement on Trade and Tariffs
GOP	Grand Old Party: Republican Party
IWF	Independent Women's Forum
MSLF	Mountain States Legal Foundation
NAACP	National Association for the Advancement of Colored People
NAFTA	North American Free Trade Agreement
NOW	National Organization for Women
NRA	National Rifle Association
NSC	National Security Council
OECD	Organization for Economic Cooperation and Development
OSHA	Occupational Safety and Health Administration
PRI	Pacific Research Institute for Public Policy
RNC	Republican National Convention
SCLC	Southern Christian Leadership Conference

TARAL	Texas Abortion Rights Action League
UFW	United Farm Workers of America
WTO	World Trade Organization

NOTES

INTRODUCTION—WINNING WOMEN

1 Alan Judd, ''Polk native in GOP race for secretary of state; Sen. Katherine Harris has been under fire for election problems,'' *Ledger*, Lakeland, Florida, September 20 1997, p. B1.

2 CNN Early Edition, November 16 2000.

3 Some did try to call for closer attention: ''She's no mere flunky carrying water for higher-ups,'' commented Cynthia Tucker, an experienced watcher of Southern politics, editorial page editor of the *Atlanta Journal-Constitution*. ''Girlfriend has a game plan with her own ambitions at the center,'' wrote Tucker. See Cynthia Tucker, ''Florida's Harris has her sights set on advancement,'' *Atlanta Journal-Constitution*, November 19 2000, p. 12G.

4 Robin Givhan, ''The eyelashes have it,'' *The Washington Post*, November 18 2000, p. C01.

5 Lesley Clark and Martin Merzer, ''Harris's computer files may be lost,'' *Miami Herald*, August 8 2001, p. 1A.

6 Julian Borger, ''How Florida played the race card: 700,000 people with criminal past banned from voting in pivotal state,'' *The Guardian*, London, December 4 2000, p. 3. Also, Greg Palast, *The Best Democracy Money Can Buy*, London: Pluto Press,

2002, chapter 1. And John Nichols, *Jews for Buchanan: Did You Hear the One about the Theft of the American Presidency?*, New York: the New Press, 2001.

7 Jake Tapper claims that "a high-ranking Gore advisor" urged him to investigate a rumor that Katherine Harris and Jeb Bush had or were having an affair. Tapper refused. "I think it's disgusting that Strep Throat [the unnamed advisor] would even pitch the story to me, a story that, as far as I know, Strep Throat invented out of whole cloth," wrote Tapper. There was certainly no shortage of real leads to investigate. Jake Tapper, *Down and Dirty: the Plot to Steal the Presidency*, Boston: Little, Brown and Co., 2001, pp. 221–2.

8 Rachel La Corte, "2000 notoriety gives Harris high profile in Congress," Associated Press, December 26 2002.

9 Erica Marcus, "It was a ball!" *Newsday*, New York, January 22 2001, p. B06.

10 Ibid.

11 CNN exit poll: http://www.cnn.com/ELECTION/2000/epolls

12 Colbert I. King, "Bush caters to the bigotry of Bob Jones," *The Washington Post*, February 28 2000, p. A15.

13 "We have no king but Jesus," transcript of Ashcroft speech at Bob Jones University, *ABC News*, July 12 2001; see abcnews.go.com/sections/politics/DailyNews/ashcroft_bjutranscript010112.html

14 "IDS Insights," Institute for Democracy Studies, vol. 2, issue 1, September 2001, p. 2; http://www.idsonline.org

15 Ceci Connolly, "AIDS panel director leaves amid controversy over activist," *The Washington Post*, February 5 2003, p. A10.

16 John B. Judis and Ruy Teixeira, *The Emerging Democratic Majority*, New York: Scribner, 2002.

17 Alison Mitchell, "The 43rd President: news analysis; conservative at the core," *The New York Times*, January 3 2001, p. A1.

18 David S. Broder, "Not his father's cabinet," *The Washington Post*, January 7 2001, p. B7.

19 Andria Hall, "Bush cabinet beginning to reflect spectrum of Republican Party," *CNN Saturday*, December 23 2000.

20 Barry Hillenbrand, "The true blue Bush cabinet," *Time* magazine, January 15 2001, p. 18.

21 Anne Kornblut, "Shut office signals shift on women," *Boston Globe*, March 28 2001, p. A1.

22 By the end of Bush's first term, *Ms.* magazine reported that out of 448 candidates for executive branch posts requiring Senate confirmation, Bush had appointed 115 women, or roughly 25 percent, compared with 37 percent in Bill Clinton's executive. Marie Tessier, "Window dressing—or policy makers?" *Ms.*, December 2002/January 2003, p. 9.

23 Mary Leonard, "Transfer of power/the female contingent; women's status grows in Senate, legislators hope influence expands with larger presence," *Boston Globe*, January 19 2001, p. A28.

24 Tanya Melich, *The Republican War against Women: an Insider's Report from Behind the Lines*, New York: Bantam Books, updated edition, 1998, p. 170.

25 Susan Faludi, *Backlash: the Undeclared War Against American Women*, New York: Crown Publishers Inc., 1991, p. 258.

26 "Pfotenhauer appointed to DOL committee on workplace issues," http://www.iwf.org/news/0020618b.shtml.
Pfotenhauer also secured a spot on the secretary of energy's advisory board. As director of the Washington office of Koch Industries, one of the largest sponsors of the libertarian CATO Institute, she lobbied hard against emissions-control CAFÉ

standards. See http://www.energy.gov/HQPress/releases02/maypr/pr02079_v.htm

27 Alicia Montgomery, "Down and dirty, the release of the Civil Rights Commission report on the Florida election turns into another partisan catfight." See http://archive/salon.com/politics/feature/2001/06/08/commission.html

28 Peter Carlson, "Uncivil fights: the commissioners have a job to do. But first, they have to agree to meet," *The Washington Post*, October 30 2002, p. C01.

29 Frank Bruni, "GOP tries to counter lack of support among women," *The New York Times*, August 1 2002, p. A14.

30 Mike Allen, "Bush's war message brings political gains: return to 'compassionate conservative' themes yielding benefits, strategists say," *The Washington Post*, January 2 2002, p. A02.

31 Elisabeth Bumiller, "Red faces in White House over '02 analysis," *The New York Times*, June 14 2002, p. A28.

32 Interview with Anna Greenberg, January 22 2003.

33 Carla Marinucci, "Memo casts recall as windfall for Bush grassroots appeal to 'women against Davis'," *San Francisco Chronicle*, August 6 2003, p. A1.

34 John Wildermuth and Carla Marinucci, "Candidate's past bubbles up again, racy 1983 video starring Schwarzenegger may be re-released," *San Francisco Chronicle*, September 6 2003, p. A10.

35 William Greider, *Who Will Tell the People: the Betrayal of American Democracy*, New York: Simon & Schuster, 1992, p. 263.

36 Susan Faludi, *Backlash*, p. 274.

37 Derrick Z. Jackson, "Bill Clinton as 'Superfly;' his record on incarcerations proves he's no black hero," *Boston Globe*, February 22 2001, p. 23.

38 Bruce Fein, "Counterterrorism inquisition?", *Washington Times*, June 15 2000, p. A21.

39 Jim Garamone, "Joint vision 2020 emphasizes full-spectrum dominance," American Forces Press Service, June 2 2000; http://www.defenselink.mil/news/Jun2000/ n06022000_20006025.html

40 Edwin Chen, "The presidential transition . . ." *Los Angeles Times*, December 18 2000, p. A1.

41 MSNBC, *Donahue*, January 17 2003.

42 Mike Allen and Dana Milbank, "Bush won't resist leadership change: President's agenda feared in jeopardy," *The Washington Post*, December 17 2002, p. A01.

43 Defense Department briefing, November 19 2001.

44 Radio address by Laura Bush to the nation, November 17 2001; see http://www.whitehouse.gov/news/releases/2001/11/ 20011117.html

45 Remarks by National Security Advisor Condoleezza Rice at the 28th Annual Convention of the National Association of Black Journalists; see http://www.whitehouse.gov/news/releases/ 2003/08/20030807–1.html

46 See http://riverbendblog.blogspot.com/2003_08_01_ riverbendblog_archive.html

47 "Remarks at the Announcement of Appointments to White House Posts," *New York Times*, December 18 2000, p. A23.

48 "The 43rd President: Rice on power and democracy," *The New York Times*, December 18 2000, p. A22 (from an article by Rice in *Foreign Affairs*, January/February 2000).

SWEETNESS AND LIGHT—
CONDOLEEZZA RICE

1 I owe this observation to Fiona Morgan, "No way to treat a lady," *Salon.com*, December 18 2000; see http://archive.salon.com/politics/feature/2000/12/18/rice

2 Elaine Sciolino, "The 43rd President: woman in the news: compulsion to achieve—Condoleezza Rice," *The New York Times*, December 18 2000, p. A1.

3 Interview with Rice, June 17 2003.

4 Interview with Skinner, June 23 2003.

5 From a letter by Dr King to President John F. Kennedy, quoted in Taylor Branch, *Parting the Waters: America in the King Years, 1954–63*, New York: Simon & Schuster, 1988, p. 684.

6 Angela Davis, *With My Mind on Freedom*, New York: Bantam Books, 1975, p. 95.

7 *Four Little Girls*, Spike Lee, 1997, produced by 40 Acres and a Mule Filmworks and HBO.

8 Branch, op. cit. (see note 5), p. 883.

9 Condoleezza Rice, "Almost like a train coming," *Time* magazine, May 29 2000, p. 55.

10 Dale Russakoff, "Lessons of might and right: while others marched for civil rights, Condoleezza Rice's family taught her to make her own freedom. It's a philosophy she's brought to the Bush White House," *The Washington Post*, September 9 2001, p. W23.

11 Thomas was born into destitution, but he was pulled out of it by his grandfather at the age of six. Thereafter, Thomas attended parochial schools and was never known to want for anything. (Thomas's sister was not so lucky; she was left behind with Mom.) Thomas benefited from affirmative action and welfare,

but he grew up to scorn both and to edit them out of the official version of his life. As his grandfather's best friend told reporters Jane Mayer and Jill Abramson, ''[Clarence Thomas] likes to talk so much about pulling yourself up by your bootstraps. But how are you going to do that if you've got no boots? He forgets to say that first someone had to give him boots—and that person was his grandfather.'' Like Rice's, Clarence Thomas's grandfather switched religion to be able to send his grandsons to (Catholic) school. See Jane Mayer and Jill Abramson, *Strange Justice: the Selling of Clarence Thomas*, New York: Houghton Mifflin, 1994, chapter 2.

12 In 1942, when George Bush Sr was an eighteen-year-old naval pilot in training, FDR's government ordered that Prescott's Union Banking Corporation be seized under the Trading with the Enemy Act. The stocks of three Nazi executives, Bush and three associates were vested. Susie Davidson, ''The Bush family— Third Reich connection: fact or fiction?'' *The Jewish Advocate*, April 19 2001, vol. 192, no. 15, p. 11.

13 Gail Sheehy, ''The accidental candidate,'' *Vanity Fair*, October 2000, quoted in Mark Crispin Miller, *The Bush Dyslexicon*, New York: W.W. Norton & Company, 2002, p. 227.

14 Jim Hirsch, ''Dean Rice expresses concern over state of university minorities,'' *Denver Clarion*, January 18 1971.

15 Ibid.

16 Ibid.

17 Interview with Chip Berlet, June 12 2003.

18 Interview with Connie Rice, June 17 2003.

19 Rice herself doesn't shy away from the term ''house slave''—see Nicholas Lemann, ''Without a doubt,'' *The New Yorker*, October 14 2002, p. 164.

20 Davis, op. cit. (see note 6), p. 92.

21 Interview with Angela Davis, June 16 2003.

22 Russakoff, op. cit. (see note 10), and "John W. Rice," *Palo Alto Weekly*, May 6 1998.

23 Lemann, op. cit (see note 19).

24 Interview with Kiron Skinner, June 23 2003.

25 "People in the news," CNN, February 22 2003.

26 Interview with Gilbert, June 18 2003.

27 Interview with John Prados, June 17 2003. Prados is author of *Keepers of the Keys: a History of the National Security Council from Truman to Bush*, New York: William Morrow & Company, 1991. He suggests that Rice's familiarity with Czech affairs was impressive. Joseph Kalvoda, who reviewed Rice's book, *The Soviet Union and the Czechoslovak Army 1948–83*, found the research impressively bad. Kalvoda claims Rice "frequently does not sift facts from propaganda and valid information from disinformation or misinformation." To be fair Kalvoda thought Rice was a man, which casts his own research in a dubious light. "Condoleezza Rice, *The Soviet Union and the Czechoslovak Army, 1948–1983: Uncertain Allegiance*," *America Historical Review*, Vol. 90, No. 5 (December 1985), p. 1236.

28 "The President's prodigy," *Vogue*, October 2001.

29 Ibid., quoted in Antonia Felix, *Condi, the Condoleezza Rice Story*, New York: New Market Press, 2002, p. 116.

30 Interview with Anders Aslund, June 9 2003.

31 Paul Van Slambrouek, "California think-tank acts as Bush brain trust," *Christian Science Monitor*, July 2 1999.

32 Alan Gilbert, *Must Global Politics Constrain Democracy?*, New Jersey: Princeton University Press, 1999.

33 Kiron Skinner, "Reagan's Plan," *National Interest*, summer 1999.

34 Caspar Weinberger also worked at Bechtel, as Vice-President and general counsel of the Bechtel Group, before going to

Washington in 1980. Pratap Chatterjee, "Bechtel's friends in high places," Corpwatch, April 24 2003; www.corpwatch.org

35 Teicher's NSC files are in the Ronald Reagan presidential archives in Simi Valley, CA. The affidavit can be found online at www.realhistoryarchives.com

36 "Crude vision: how oil interests obscured US government focus on chemical weapons use by Saddam Hussein," Washington, DC: Institute for Policy Studies, March 2003. Also, "Bechtel: profiting from destruction," Corpwatch, Global Exchange, Public Citizen, June 5 2003. www.corpwatch.org/issues/PRT.jsp?articleid=6975

37 Romesh Ratnesar, "Condi Rice can't lose," *Time* magazine, September 27 1999, p. 51.

38 Chuck Conconi, "Personalities," *The Washington Post*, February 6 1990, p. C3.

39 William Safire, "Victory in the Baltics," *The New York Times*, November 21 2002.

40 Michael Dobbs, "US had key role in Iraq build-up," *The Washington Post*, December 30 2002, p. A01, and "Crude vision" (see note 34) at http://www.ips.dc.org/crudevision/crude_vision.pdf

41 Condoleezza Rice, "You couldn't find better credentials," *Los Angeles Times*, September 16 1991, p. B5.

42 "Exchange with reporters aboard Air Force One," Public Papers of the President, June 8 1990.

43 Dan Morgan, David B. Ottaway, "Vast Kazakh field stirs US–Russian rivalry," *The Washington Post*, October 6 1998, p. A01.

44 James Gerstenzang, Edmund Sanders, "Bush staff well invested in energy," *Los Angeles Times*, June 2 2001, p. A11.

45 Felix, op. cit. (see note 28), p. 164.

46 Greg Rohloff, "Cheney sees smooth road for merger, Caspian

Sea region now hot spot for oil companies,'' *Amarillo Globe-News*, May 9 1998; see http://www.amarillonet.com/stories/051098/bus_chaney.shtml (*sic*)

47 It's worth noting, too, that deal-making in Kazakhstan is a funny business indeed. In March 2003, an American counselor to the Kazakh President was arrested and accused of funnelling $78 million in oil commissions into his boss's secret Swiss bank account and that of another top official, in the biggest-ever prosecution under the Foreign Corrupt Practices Act. According to the US indictment, international companies paid bonuses to secure access to the Tengiz field and the Caspian Pipeline Consortium. The companies that negotiated such deals include Mobil, Chevron, and BP. In June 2003, Mobil pleaded guilty. In September 2003, ChevronTexaco was being questioned by the Justice Department as the investigation broadened. (See http://search.ft.com/s03/search/article.html?id=030911000322.)
James Baker III, who spearheaded George W.'s victory in the Florida election dispute, heads a law firm, Baker Botts, which represents a consortium of oil companies involved in Caspian Sea oil drilling. The *Financial Times* reported that, in 1996, the Kazakh President offered Baker $1 billion if the pipeline deal went through, according to someone who was present. Baker refused. See Joshua Chaffin, ''The Kazakh connection,'' *Financial Times*, June 25 2003, also Christopher Pala, ''Oil scandal hits Kazakhstan,'' *The Washington Times*, May 16 2003; see http://washingtontimes.com/world/20030516–102246–2439r.htm

48 In 1983, Morgan Chase lent Saddam Hussein $500 million, which may have helped pay for the Bechtel chemical plant. ''Carving up the new Iraq,'' *Sunday Herald*, Glasgow, April 13 2003; see http://www.sundayherald.com/print33079

49 Paul Wolfowitz, who worked for Shultz at the State Department

under Reagan, honored Shultz at an award dinner at the Hudson Institute in 2002. "Shultz's 'Good Housekeeping Seal of Approval' means a lot to a lot of people," said Wolfowitz, recalling that it was Shultz who pulled together Ronald Reagan's policy team in 1979, and gathered George W.'s brains trust, too. "George Shultz was a major driver in some of the most remarkable developments of his time," said Wolfowitz. See http://www.hudson.org/publications/doolittle_transcript.doc

50 Special to *The New York Times*: "From 'Not college material,' to Stanford's # 2 job," *The New York Times*, July 23 1993, p. B7.

51 US Department of Energy, "Country analysis brief," http://www.eia.doe.gov/emeu/cabs/kazak.html

52 "News and Views: Stanford's faculty diversification effort is now picking up steam," *The Journal of Blacks in Higher Education*, October 31 1998, p. 29. The percentage of black students declined from 6.1 percent in 1980 to 5.2 percent in 1996, a 14.8 percent decrease.

53 Interview with Estelle Freedman, June 12 2003.

54 Ibid.

55 Interview with Sharon Holland, June 16 2003.

56 Karen De Sa, "J.W. Rice, father of incoming security adviser dies at 77," *San Jose Mercury News*, December 28 2000, p. 1B.

57 Horton, on a weekend pass, brutally raped a woman and stabbed her husband. Bush's campaign ad accused the Democratic contender of "letting murderers out on vacation to terrorize innocent people." See Tanya Melich, *The Republican War against Women: an Insider's Report from Behind the Lines*, New York: Bantam Books, 1998, p. 263.

58 The case dragged on and pretty much ground to a halt under the leadership of Elaine Chao.

59 Crispin Miller, op. cit. (see note 13), pp. 195–9.

60 See CivilRights.org, Research Reports and Curricula, http://www.civilrights.org/publications/reports

61 See http://www.corporate-ir.net/ireye/ir_site.zhtml?ticker=cvx&script=1901

62 Human Rights Watch report, 1999, "The price of oil: corporate responsibility and human rights violations in Nigeria's oil producing communities," www.hrw.org/africa/nigeria.php

63 *The Laura Flanders Show*, KWAB-AM in Boulder, Colorado, July 2000.

64 Stephen Lunn, "US beefs up S. Korea arms," *The Australian*, July 2 2003, p. 12.

65 Interview with Brisibe, June 12 2003.

66 See http://www.buzzflash.com/contributors/03/07/25_condi.html

67 "Face the Nation," CBS, October 20 2002.

68 "This Week with George Stephanopoulos," ABC, March 9 2003.

69 Nicholas Lemann, "How it came to war," *The New Yorker*, March 31 2003, p. 36.

70 Jim Puzzanghera, "GOP buzzing about Rice as a candidate for the California Governor," *San Jose Mercury News*, June 19 2003. The poll, by Ray McNally, was taken in April 2003.

71 Robin Wright, "Confrontation with Baghdad," *Los Angeles Times*, September 9 2002, p. 1.

72 Randall Miikkelsen, "White House points at CIA over Iraq uranium charge," Reuters, July 11 2003, 9.33am.

73 Neil MacKay, "Official: US oil at heart of crisis," *Sunday Herald*, October 6 2002, p.1.

74 See http://www.globalresearch.ca/articles/MAR201B.html

75 Stephen J. Glain and Robert Schlesinger, "Halliburton unit expands war-repair role," *Boston Globe*, July 10 2003.

76 Karen De Sa, op. cit. (see note 56).

77 "Speakers denounce war before sparse audience," *Denver Clarion*, May 5 1971.

COVER GIRL—KAREN HUGHES

1 Paul Burka, "Karen Hughes: as George W. Bush's spokesperson, she meets the press and faces the nation," *Texas Monthly*, September 1999.

2 Judy Keen, "Communications chief now counselor to Bush," *USA Today*, December 18 2000, p. 6A.

3 *Facts on File World News Digest*, December 24 1977. For more, see Susan Faludi, *Backlash: the Undeclared War against American Women*, New York: Crown Publishers Inc., 1991, chapter 13, and Kay Mills, *A Place in the News*, New York: Columbia University Press, 1990, chapter 10.

4 Faludi, op. cit. (see note 3), p. 371.

5 Megan Rosenfeld and Bill Curry, "Behind the big movement— 5-hour lines, dissidents, unburned underwear," *The Washington Post*, November 21 1977, p. A6.

6 Interview with Bill Sanderson, February 13 2003.

7 Tanya Melich, *The Republican War against Women: an Insider's Report from Behind the Lines*, New York: Bantam Books, updated edition, 1998, p. 119.

8 Ibid.

9 Thomas J. McIntyre with John C. Obert, *The Fear Brokers: Peddling the Hate Politics of the New Right*, Boston: Beacon Press, 1979, quoted on p. 120.

10 Dave Montgomery, "Life in D.C. drives Hughes back to Austin," *Fort Worth Star Telegram*, April 24 2002, p. 25.

11 *Life in the Canal Zone*, Smithsonian Institution Libraries; see *Make the Dirt Fly* at http://www.sil.si.edu/Exhibitions/Make-the-Dirt-Fly/zonelife.html

12   See   http://goldenfrog/org/goldenfrog/articles/Governors-house.htm

13   Interview with Huber, February 20, 2003.

14   Walter H. Huber, letter, "In defense of Karen Hughes," *The Dallas Morning News*, December 10 2000, p. 3J.

15   See http://www.soawatch.org.new/article.php?id=243

16   McIntyre and Obert, op. cit. (see note 9), p. 133.

17   Thomas M. DeFrank, "The Canal Zone is Paradise Lost: Panama evicting last Americans," *Daily News*, New York, November 19 1999.

18   George W. Bush, *A Charge to Keep*, New York: William Morrow, 1999, p. 3.

19   Dan Balz, "Team Bush: the Governor's 'Iron Triangle' points the way to Washington," *The Washington Post*, July 23 1999, p. C01.

20   Melich, op. cit. (see note 7), p. 201. "In August 1983, the Reagan Justice Department filed a brief in a pending Supreme Court case brought by Grove City College in Pennsylvania against the government. The college argued it was exempt from Title IX of the 1972 Education [Amendments] Act, which banned sex discrimination by educational institutions that received federal financing, because *it* didn't accept direct government aid; only its students were the recipients of federal grants and loans. The Justice Department argued that the ban applied only to specific educational programs or departments that received federal money, not to the college as a whole ... What the Justice Department was doing was narrowing the scope of civil rights law." Melich, p. 190.

21   Interview with Mark McKinnon, February 21 2003.

22   Molly Ivins and Lou Dubose, *SHRUB: the Short but Happy Political Life of George W. Bush*, New York: Vintage, 2000, p. 46.

23   Sam Attlesey, "Turnout called key in close race for Governor—

focus is on women, minorities,'' *The Dallas Morning News*, September 5 1994, p. 1A.

24 Interview with McKinnon (see note 21).

25 Interview with Lou Dubose, *Working Assets Radio with Laura Flanders*, April 29 2003; see http://archive.webactive.com/workingassets/wa20030429.html. President Bush would like to see federal law fall in line with Texas's, says Dubose.

26 Burka, op. cit. (see note 1).

27 Geraldine Baum and Elizabeth Mehren, ''She has the President's ear as a loyalist and alter ego,'' *Los Angeles Times*, April 1 2000, p. 1.

28 Interview with Bill Cryer, February 12 2003.

29 Melinda Henneberger, ''Driving W,'' *The New York Times*, May 14 2000, section 6; p. 52.

30 Sam Attlesey, ''GOP wasting taxpayers' money in seeking files, Richards aide says,'' *The Dallas Morning News*, October 6 1993, p. 16B.

31 Dave McNeely, ''The spread of spin doctors,'' *The Dallas Morning News*, October 27 1993, p. 21A.

32 Burka, op. cit. (see note 1).

33 Alan Bernstein, ''Campaign briefs,'' *Houston Chronicle*, October 28 1992, p. A18.

34 ''Bush distances himself from remarks a campaign official made about gays,'' Associated Press, August 27 1994.

35 Interview with Chuck MacDonald, February 12 2003.

36 Richards received 83 percent of the Hispanic vote, 97 percent of the African-American vote, and led Williams by 20 percent among women. Attlesey, ''Turnout called key'' (see note 23).

37 Jake Tapper, ''Prodigal son,'' *Salon.com*, April 9 1999. See http://www.salon.com/news/feature/1999/04/09/bush

38 Bush retained the support of conservative white males with slash-

attacks on Richards's position against a concealed weapons law, among other things. Exit polls showed that women still preferred Richards over Bush, 53 percent to 47 percent, but that was nowhere near the 20 percentage-point advantage she had enjoyed over Williams in 1990. Sam Attlesey, "Analysts, exit polls credit Bush tactics, conservative positive campaign drew public," *The Dallas Morning News*, November 9 1994, p. 1A.

39 R.G. Ratcliffe, "Shoring up support: Governor hopeful Bush ducks abortion flap," *Houston Chronicle*, November 7 1993, p. 5.

40 Interview with Cryer (see note 28).

41 Maureen Dowd, "3 Sisters (sorry, Chekhov)," syndicated column, January 16 2001.

42 Interview with MacDonald (see note 35).

43 Michelle Cottle, "The enforcer," *The New Republic*, November 29 1999.

44 Interview with MacDonald (see note 35).

45 Louis Dubose, Julie Holler, and Nate Blakeslee, "Dubya and the press: in the Texas media, the Governor walks on water. But, elsewhere, he's beginning to get caught in the backwash," *The Texas Observer*, September 17 1999; see http://www.texasobserver.org/showArticle.asp?ArticleID=264

46 *The American Heritage Dictionary*, Boston: Houghton Mifflin, third edition, 1992.

47 Bill Minutaglio, "Welfare warrior," *The Dallas Morning News*, January 11 1997, p. 1G.

48 Interview with Phyllis Dunham, February 19 2003.

49 Pamela Colloff, "Remember the Christian Alamo," *Texas Monthly*, December 2001; see http://www.texasmonthly.com/mag/issues/2001–12–01/feature2.php

50 Interview with Kay McLaughlin of TARAL, February 12 2003.

51 Christopher Lee, "Official on paid leave for remarks," *The*

Dallas Morning News, October 20 2000, p. 1A.

52 *Texas Trail: Firsthand in Bush Land*, directed by Judith LeBlanc for *Changing America*, New York City, 2000, and interview with Maxey, November 3 2003.

53 "Bush cancels visit to West Bank settlement," *The Hotline*, December 1 1998.

54 Dubose, Hollar, and Blakeslee, op. cit. (see note 45).

55 Cottle, op. cit. (see note 43).

56 Mark Crispin Miller points out that George W. speaks most fluently when he's talking about war, or executions, or things he's really sure of. It's when he knows he's fabricating that he gets in the most trouble; rarely has his "dyslexicon" been more vividly on display than when he talked to CBS *News* (February 25 2000) about his Bob Jones "denunciation": "I did denounce it. I de—I denounced it. I denounced interracial dating. I denounced anti-Catholic bigotry . . . no, I—I—I spoke out against inter-racial dating. I mean, I support the inter—the policy of interracial dating." Miller, *The Bush Dyslexicon*, New York: W.W. Norton & Co., 2002, p. 189.

57 Interview with Richard Wolffe, February 18 2003.

58 Bill Minutaglio, *First Son George W. Bush and the Bush Family Dynasty*, New York: Three Rivers Press, 2001, p. 18.

59 Interview with Cryer (see note 28).

60 Anne Marie Kilday, a former *Dallas Morning News* reporter, told Melinda Henneberger of *The New York Times* about being called at home by Rove during the Richards race. "Republicans had been shopping a story about supposed malfeasance by a female state official Kilday covered. According to Kilday, Rove said he was looking over the telephone records of this official, who is a lesbian, and said he found it interesting that there had been a number of calls to Kilday from the official "at your residence.""

Kilday recalled, "He said, 'You've just got to be so careful about your reputation and what people might think.' " Rove denied having made the call. Henneberger, op. cit. (see note 28). For another hint of the stories that swirl around Rove, see *Fortunate Son* by the much-pilloried Jim Hatfield. Hatfield later told filmmakers Suki Hawley and Michael Galinsky about having received death threats from a Rove aide. Soon after, he committed suicide. J.M. Hatfield, *Fortunate Son*, New York: Soft Skull Press, third edition, 2002, p. xii.

61   Interview with Wolffe (see note 57).

62   Ibid.

63   David Frum, *The Right Man*, New York: Random House, 2003, p. 41.

64   *Texas Trail* (see note 52).

65   Interview with Wolffe (see note 57).

66   Elisabeth Bumiller, "An influential Bush advisor, Karen Hughes, will resign," *The New York Times*, April 24 2002, p. 24.

67   Robin Toner, "The nation: women's place—at the table, but not for dinner," *The New York Times*, April 28 2002, late edition—final, section 4, p. 3.

68   *Journal for Biblical Manhood and Womanhood*, vol. 3, no. 4, winter 1998.

69   James Carney, "A few small repairs," *Time* magazine, July 9 2001.

70   Martha Brant, with Tamara Lipper and T. Trent Gegax, "West wing story: Karen we hardly knew ye," *Newsweek*, April 23 2002.

71   Or so he claimed to an audience of cadets at the US Air Force Academy in 1996. Quoted in Sheldon Rampton and John Stauber, *Weapons of Mass Deception: the Uses of Propaganda in Bush's War on Iraq*, New York: Penguin Books, 2003, p. 5.

72 Franklin Foer, "Flacks, Americana: John Rendon's shallow PR war on terrorism," *The New Republic*, May 20 2002, p. 24. For more on Rendon, see Rampton and Stauber, op. cit. (see note 72).

73 *The Late Show with David Letterman*, CBS, September 17 2001, as transcribed by FAIR. See http://www.fair.org/extra/0111/patriotism-and-censorship.html

74 Matthew Miller, "A win-win job plan for Bush's adviser Hughes," *Sacramento Bee*, April 25 2002, p. B9.

75 Barton Gellman and Walter Pincus, "Depiction of threat outgrew supporting evidence," *The Washington Post*, August 10 2003, final edition, p. A01.

76 Jena Heath, "Karen Hughes is still in the game," Cox News Service, September 20 2002.

77 Ibid.

FLAVR SAVR—ANN VENEMAN

1 Rachel Carson, *Silent Spring*, New York: Houghton Mifflin, 1994 edition.

2 Interview with Dolores Huerta, January 5 2003.

3 Gladwyn Hill, *The New York Times*, November 30 1969; see http://earthday.envirolink.org/history.html

4 George Skelton, "A Peach of an Appointment," *Los Angeles Times*, December 25 2000, p. A1.

5 In the mid-1970s, the Federal Trade Commission had received enough complaints to launch an investigation. Among the practices investigated, the Gallo salesmen admitted tampering with their competitors' merchandise. Salesmen reportedly "carried oil that they would apply to competitors' bottles so that dust would cling. And when Gallo salesmen arranged comparative

tastings in retail stores, they sometimes unscrewed bottle caps of competitors' brands and squeezed in heads of dead mice, mice feces and cigarette butts ..." In 1978, the Gallos signed a consent order with the FTC, banning many of the alleged practices, although not admitting guilt. Ellen Hawkes, "Family secrets," *Los Angeles Times* magazine, February 28 1993, p. 16.

6 According to veteran California labor reporter Dick Meister, although Bird's opposition to the death penalty was the anti-Bird campaign's main theme, wealthy growers and other business interests who bankrolled the effort were concerned mainly with the court's pro-labor stance in regard to farm workers and public employees. Bird and two other left-leaning justices were removed by a two-to-one vote in 1986. Bird retreated into anonymity.

7 See http://www.governor.ca.gov/govsite/govsgallery/h/biography/governor 35.html

8 Cranston assisted in the passage of a tax bill that was dubbed the "Gallo Wine Amendment." (It extended tax breaks to the Gallo heirs.) Mark Arax, "US judicial nominee's ties to Gallo family questioned," *Los Angeles Times*, April 20 1997, p. A1.

9 Brenda Jahns Southwick and Rebecca Dee Sheehan, "Farmer's daughter heads US Department of Agriculture," *Sacramento Lawyer*, October/November 2001; see http://www.sacbar.og/saclawyer/oct_nov2001/veneman.html

10 Testimony, Ann Veneman, Secretary of California Department of Food and Agriculture, Senate finance committee, international trade subcommittee, April 21 1998.

11 Charles Abbott, United Press International, April 12 1989.

12 Laurie Goering, "End farm subsidies, 3rd world demands," *Chicago Tribune*, August 28 2002, p. 3; see http://www.tradeobservatory.org/news/index.cfm?ID=3727

13   Mark Ritchie et al, "United States dumping on world agricultural markets," Institute for Agriculture and Trade Policy;
see http://www.iatp.org. According to the Institute, in 1998,
"US based multinational corporations sold US wheat abroad at
an average price of $34 per metric ton below the cost of pro-
duction. US wheat exports totalled 28,332,000 metric tons in
'98, which means the companies sold the wheat at a discount
worth a total of $963,288,000 (almost $1 billion.)"

14   Goering, op. cit. (see note 12).

15   Kathie Smith, "Stars come out for Veneman gala," *Modesto Bee*,
August 15 1991, p. B1.

16   Quoted in Marion Nestle, *Safe Food, Bacteria, Biotechnology, and
Bioterrorism*, Berkeley: University of California Press, 2003, p.
147.

17   Alex Barnum, "Biotech tomatoes closer to market," *San Francisco Chronicle*, October 17 1992, p. B1.

18   Richard Lawrence, "NAFTA to give boost to US farm exports,"
Journal of Commerce, August 14 1992.

19   "Down on the farm: NAFTA's seven-years war on farmers and
ranchers in the US, Canada and Mexico," *Public Citizen*, June
2001; see http://www.citizen.org/publications. Also Michael
Doyle, "Clinton just can't win with Ag. despite tangible
accomplishments, Valley vote eludes him," *Modesto Bee*, August
31 1995, p. A1.

20   Scripps-McClatchy Western Service, "Trade barriers high on
agenda 'fast track': unions oppose President's plan, cite
employment and ecological concerns," *Ventura County Star*,
California, September 2 1997, p. D01.

21   Richard Estrada, "Exports fuelling Ag. growth—California serves
as world's supermarket," *Modesto Bee*, August 23 1998, p. D1.

22   Quoted in Ritchie et al, op. cit. (see note 13).

23 The total number of farms in the US, which had stood at 6.5 million when the system was started in the 1930s, dropped to 2.05 million by 1997. Cited in Ben Lilliston and Niel Ritchie, "Freedom to fail," *Multinational Monitor*, July/August 2000, vol. 21, nos. 7 and 8.

24 "Corporate hogs at the public trough," Smithfield Foods, NC-CAFO's report, 1999; see Sierra Club at http://www.sierraclub.org/factoryfarms/report99/smithfield.asp. And see David Celcelski and Mary Lee Kerr, "Hog Wild," *Southern Exposure*, fall 1992, pp. 9–15.

25 Dan Morain, "Wildon uproots tradition with new Agriculture chief," *Los Angeles Times*, May 31 1995, p. A3.

26 Ibid. Wilson received $23,000 from Dole and at least $90,000 from Sun-Diamond for his campaign for Governor.

27 Richard Estrada, "Veneman gets oath of note—Wilson personally swears in Ag. chief," *Modesto Bee*, June 2 1995.

28 Morain, op. cit. (see note 25).

29 Interview with Carole Whiteside, May 16 2003.

30 Ibid.

31 Carl Ingram, "Support grows for Agriculture Secretary," *Los Angeles Times*, May 27 1996, p. A3.

32 Hallye Jordan, "Proposed organic standards raise a ruckus— farmers, consumers blast USDA recommendations," *San Jose Mercury News*, May 1 1998, p. 1A. The quotation comes from Linda J. Fisher, now deputy director of the Environmental Protection Agency under Christine Todd Whitman.

33 Interview with Bob Scowcroft, executive director of the Organic Farming Research Foundation, May 11 2003.

34 George Raine, "Global food under scrutiny: a bill to boost safety raises agriculture industry hackles," *San Francisco Examiner*, April 12 1998, p. C1.

35 "Answers needed on a deadly toxin; How risky is use of Methyl Bromide on produce? State growers seek another phaseout delay," *Los Angeles Times*, January 8 1996, p. B4.

36 For more, see Eric Schlosser, *Reefer Madness*, New York: Houghton Mifflin, 2003, pp. 77–108.

37 David Bacon, "A company union battles the UFW in Watsonville," August 7 1998, at http://dbacon.igc.org/FarmWork/01 coast.html

38 Senate Agriculture, Nutrition and Forestry Committee, confirmation hearing for Agriculture Secretary-Designate Ann Veneman, *FDCH Political Transcripts*, January 18 2001.

39 Anthan George, "Iowans give wary OK to Agriculture nominee," *Des Moines Register*, December 21 2000, p. 1A.

40 Senate Agriculture, Nutrition and Forestry Committee, op. cit. (see note 38).

41 Interview with Tom Buis, April 28 2003. The normally outspoken union backed Veneman, nonetheless, for fear of someone worse.

42 News conference with Secretary of Agriculture Ann Veneman and US Trade Representative Robert Zoellick, Federal News Service, July 22 2002.

43 Interview with Rhonda Perry, April 29 2003.

44 Interview with Kathy Ozer, May 2 2003.

45 Farmers are not allowed to save genetically modified (GM) seed from one harvest to another, and evidence is mounting that GM crops yield less, and require more, not fewer chemicals. See Marc Lappe, Ph.D, and Britt Bailey, *Against the Grain: Biotechnology and the Corporate Takeover of Your Food*, Monroe Maine: Common Courage Press, 1998, p. 53; and "Research shows roundup ready soybeans yield less," Institute of Agriculture at the University of Nebraska; http://ianrnews.unl.edu/static/0005161.shtml

46 Robert Weissman, "Defending contractor irresponsibility," *Multinational Monitor*, May 1 2001, vol. 22, no. 5, p. 18.

47 Testimony, Ann Veneman, Secretary of California Department of Food and Agriculture, Senate finance committee, international trade subcommittee, April 21 1998.

48 European Commission document, quoted in Marion Nestle, *Safe Food, Bacteria, Biotechnology, and Bioterrorism*, Berkeley: University of California Press, 2003, p. 23.

49 Kate Campbell, "Ann Veneman poised for major challenges in Washington D.C.," *California Farm Bureau Federation, Ag Alert*, December 29 2000; see http://www.cfbf.com/agalert/1996–00/2000/aa-1227a.htm.

50 Rey served as vice-president of forest resources for the American Forest and Paper Association, the country's leading advocate for logging in national forests. As undersecretary for national resources and the environment, Rey is responsible for the management of 156 national forests, 19 national grasslands and 15 landuse projects on 191 million acres in 44 states. See http://www.earthjustice.org/policy/profiles

51 Philip Brasher, "Harkin vows Filibuster or Dorr" *Des Moines Register*, June 19 2003, p. 1D.

52 See http://www.beeline.com.au/media/press/TS-001.US%20WOOLF.pdf

53 Testimony Gary R. Grant, a founder of Black Farmers and Agriculturalists, the Agriculture Department Civil Rights Program, September 25 2002. Federal Document Clearing House Congressional Testimony. The case is Pigford v. Veneman.

54 Rick Lazio, "Some Trade Barriers Won't Fall," *The New York Times*, Op. Ed. August 9 2003, p. A11.

55 Jennifer 8. Lee, "Neighbors of vast hog farms say foul air endangers their health," *The New York Times*, May 11 2003,

section 1, p. 1. One scientist wasn't allowed to present his findings at public or private meetings after the news of an appearance he was to make at an Iowa Board of Health was passed from an environmental group to a TV station, to a member of the Iowa Pork Producers' Association, and from there to someone in the National Pork Producers' Council in the USDA building.

56 Data from the Environmental Working Group, quoted in Elizabeth Becker, ''As House prepares farm bill, questions of who needs help, and how much,'' *The New York Times*, September 9 2001, p. 28.

57 Rick Lazio, ''Some trade barriers won't fall,'' *The New York Times*, op. ed., August 9 2003, p. A11.

58 John Nichols, ''The Three Mile Island of biotech?'', *The Nation*, December 30 2002.

59 In May 2003, a stock ratings company, Innovest, sounded an alarm about the risks inherent in GM seed. ''We approached the report from a very strict fiscal perspective, namely: is Monsanto going to make money on genetic engineering?'' said an Innovest senior analyst. ''We don't think they will.'' William Baue, ''Innovest report identifies business risk of genetic engineering for Monsanto investors,'' *SocialFunds.com*, May 1 2003; see http://www.socialfunds.com/news/article.cgi/article1108.html

60 Farmers Guardian, January 11 2002, p. 16.

61 ''US calls food aid refusal a crime against humanity,'' Reuters, September 12 2002.

62 Center for Responsive Politics, see http://www.opensecrets.org

63 ''Liberalizing agriculture: why the US should look to New Zealand and Australia,'' Heritage Foundation *Backgrounder*, February 19 2003; see http://www.heritage.org/research/Agriculture/bg1624.cfm

64 Lazio, op. cit. (see note 57).

65 Jeffrey St Clair, "Rat in the grain, Dan Amstutz and the looting of Iraq's fields," *Counter Punch*, May 16–31 2003.

66 Heather Stewart, "Fury at Agriculture post for US business-man," *The Guardian*, April 28 2003; see http://www.guardian.co.uk/international/story/0,3604,94472,00.html

67 "Taco Bell recalls shells that used bioengineered corn," *Los Angeles Times*, September 23 2000, p. 1.

68 George Raine, "Global food under scrutiny," *San Francisco Examiner*, April 12 1998, p. C1.

69 Sandra Chereb, "Food chief backs agency in beef recall at Sparks session," the Associated Press State and Local Wire, July 26 2002.

70 Carson, op. cit, (see note 1), p. 297.

71 Ibid, p. 293.

FIRST DAUGHTER FOR THE FIRST SON—ELAINE CHAO

1 "Hearing of the Senate health, education, labor, and pensions committee," Federal News Service, January 24 2001.

2 Frank Wu, "Unlocking the cabinet: all you need to know about Elaine Chao and Norman Mineta," *A. Magazine*, May 31 2001, p. 29.

3 Christine Nifong, "Drawing on women's skills," *Christian Science Monitor*, May 8 1997, p. 12.

4 "An American success story, Elaine Chao," originally published in *Heritage Today*, Heritage Foundation, fall 1999. See http://members.truepath.com/AAFC/ASAM1.htm

5   Geraldine Baum, "An insider moves out, up," *Los Angeles Times*, January 19 1992, p. E1.

6   "Hearing of the Senate health, education, labor, and pensions committee" (see note 1).

7   Interview with Victor Chen, April 11 2003.

8   Mae M. Cheng, "Immigrant's success story," *Newsday*, New York, January 14 2001, p. A06.

9   Clark T. Randt, "A message from Clark T. Randt," *The China Business Review*, 2003, see http://www.chinabusinessreview.com/0303/randt.html

10 Lee Siew Hua, "Stories my father told me," *The Straits Times*, Singapore, August 12 2001, p. 31.

11 Caitlin Liu, "Earning it: life on the bottom rung: top executives remember; a double dose of work," *The New York Times*, September 8 1996, section 3, p. 9.

12 Helen Zia, *Asian American Dreams*, New York: Farrar Strauss Giroux, 2000, p. 48.

13 See http://www.reagan.utexas.edu/resource/findaid/chao.htm

14 "Elaine Chao praised as successful US deputy marine administrator," Central News Agency, Taiwan, November 25 1986.

15 Zia, op. cit. (see note 12), p. 51.

16 Marie Belson, "Chao is proud of her heritage," *Washington Times*, October 6 1989, p. B6.

17 George H.W. Bush, "Remarks on signing the Asian/Pacific American Heritage Week Proclamation," *Public Papers of the Presidents*, May 5 1988; see http://www.archives.gov/federal_rgister/publications/public_papers.html

18 David Briscoe, "Elaine Chao: top-ranking Asian American, youngest deputy secretary," Associated Press, August 2 1989.

19 The spill, still one of the largest ever in the United States, spewed eleven million gallons of oil (the equivalent of 125

Olympic-sized swimming pools) into the Prince William Sound, directly affecting over 1,000 miles of spectacular shoreline rich in fish species and wildlife. In a settlement approved in 1991, Exxon was fined $150 million, the largest fine ever imposed for an environmental crime, but forgiven all but $25 million in recognition of the company's cooperation in the clean-up. Environmentalists are still furious that of the criminal fine, and the $900 million civil settlement, Exxon's insurance companies covered the vast majority. In addition, Exxon was made eligible for as much as $2 billion in *Valdez* spill-related tax deductions. "In essence," activists say, "ordinary Americans have paid for the *Valdez* disaster far more than Exxon has." How much Chao had to do with the case is unclear, but as one of the most experienced shipping professionals in her department, it is a question that deserves an answer. For more, see http://www.oilspill.state.ak.us/facts/qanda.html and http://www.jomiller.com/exxonvaldez/investigative.html

20 Martha Hamilton, "Canal closing underscores US concern; waterway shuts down for first time in its 75-year history," *The Washington Post*, December 21 1989, p. A31.

21 The government claimed the invasion was one of those surgical strikes during which nobody was injured; but reporters were not allowed to move around freely in Panama City. Having conducted her own investigation when she visited Panama the following year, war correspondent Martha Gellhorn put the figure killed at around 8,000. See Martha Gellhorn, "The invasion of Panama," in Ian Jack, ed., *The Granta Book of Reportage*, Berkeley: Publishers Group West, 1999, pp. 267–87.

22 Baum, op. cit. (see note 5), p. E2; and Amy Kaslow, "Volunteers to break new ground," *Christian Science Monitor*, May 13 1992, p. 8.

23 Michael Specter, "Plunging life expectancy puzzles Russia," *The New York Times*, August 2 1995, p. A1.

24 Baum, op. cit. (see note 5), p. E2.

25 Christina Nifong, "Former United Way chief talks about workplace and volunteerism," *Christian Science Monitor*, May 8 1997, p. 12.

26 Annie Groer, "The reliable source," *The Washington Post*, February 4 1998, p. D3.

27 Hua, op. cit. (see note 10).

28 David Mudd, "Mitch and the machine: the GOP's resurgence and a million-dollar war chest have Sen. Mitch McConnell gearing up to be a kingmaker in Kentucky and big wheel in Washington," *Louisville Chamber of Commerce, Inc.*, April 1995, vol. 46, no. 4, section 1, p. 26.

29 Eleanor Clift, "Capitol letter: Republican regulator," *Newsweek* online exclusive, July 5 2002.

30 John B. Judis, "Sullied heritage: the decline of principled conservative hostility to China," *The New Republic*, April 23 2001, p. 19.

31 *Courier Mail*, editorial, May 20 2001, p. 03D.

32 Evans, Novak, Hunt and Shields, CNN, September 1 2001.

33 Tracy Thompson, "United Way chief rejects personal gift," *The Washington Post*, June 18 1996, p. D03.

34 Interview with Kevin Ronnie, April 11 2003.

35 D. Mark Wilson, "How to close down the Department of Labor," Heritage Foundation Backgrounder, October 19 1995.

36 Penny Colman, *A Woman Unafraid: the Achievements of Frances Perkins*, New York: Atheum, 1993, p. 25.

37 Wilson, op. cit. (see note 35).

38 The Wards Cove story is a painful one. In a landmark 1989 ruling, the court, in a slim five-to-four majority, threw out the

lawsuit of Filipino workers whose working conditions, the dissenting justices declared, bore "an unsettling resemblance to aspects of the plantation economy." Having persuaded the Congress that the courts could no longer be relied upon to enforce existing civil rights law, the case then became a bargaining chip on the Senate floor, and the 1991 Civil Rights Act passed, with the key votes of Alaska's two senators, with an amendment that exempted Wards Cove Packing Company from compliance. See Zia, op. cit. (see note 12), p. 51.

39 Richard J. Herrnstein and Charles Murray, *The Bell Curve: Intelligence and Class Structure in American Life*, New York: the Free Press, 1994.

40 Wage and salary workers paid hourly rates with earnings at or below the prevailing federal minimum wage by selected characteristics, ftp://ftp.bls.gov/pub/special.requests/lf/aat44.txt

41 US Census: women's earnings as a percentage of men's earnings, by race and Hispanic origin, 1960 to the present. See http://www.census.gov/hhes/income/histinc/p40.html

42 Household Data; table 39. median usual weekly earnings of full-time wage and salary workers by detailed occupation and sex. See ftp://ftp.bls.gov/pub/special.requests/lf/aat39.txt

43 In 1987, CBS's *60 Minutes* presented a glowing report on the achievements of Asian Americans in universities. "Why are Asian Americans doing so exceptionally well in school?" Mike Wallace asked, adding, "They must be doing something right, let's bottle it." See Ronald Takaki, *A Different Mirror: a History of Multicultural America*, Boston: Little, Brown and Co., 1993, p. 416. When polled in their own languages, Asian Americans in California actually showed up large majorities in favor of affirmative action. Asian Americans opposed proposition 209, the anti-affirmative action proposition. For more, see Zia, op. cit.

(see note 12).

44 Frank Wu, "*Washington Journal*: the conversation continues," *Asian Week*, January 14 1998, p. 10.

45 Laura Flanders, *Real Majority, Media Minority: the Cost of Sidelining Women in Reporting*, Monroe, Maine: Common Courage Press, 1997, p. 155. For more on IWF's funding, see http://www.mediatransparency.org

46 In 2003, the IWF teamed up with Chavez's Center for Equal Opportunity and Ward Connerly's American Civil Rights Institute to file an amicus brief against the University of Michigan in the landmark affirmative-action cases of Grutter v. Bollinger and Gratz v. Bollinger, then being considered by the Supreme Court. IWF update, see http://www.iwf.org/news/030401.shtml

47 Richard Sisk, "Immigration tale mixed up in the telling," *Daily News*, New York, January 12 2001. In 2001, Chao spoke "movingly" about her arrival as an immigrant, implying that she first set foot on US shores in New York, but in a 1992 interview with the *Los Angeles Times*, Chao said her "first port of call" was Los Angeles.

48 Baum, op. cit. (see note 5), p. E2.

49 Sonia Shah, "The celebrated immigrant," *Zmag.org*, April 1 2001.

50 Elaine Chao, keynote speech at the opening lunch of the 29th annual meeting of ALEC, orlando, Florida, 2002. See http://www.alec.org/viewpage.cfm?pgname=1.274

51 Jeff Young, "Spotlight on mine safety: a report from public radio: who is influencing mine regulators," West Virginia Public Radio transcript, February 21 2003; see http://www.courier-journal.com/cjextra/columns/hawpe/0316forum1.html

52 Interview with Jeff Young, April 8 2003.

53 Interview with Davitt McAteer, April 8 2003.

54 Debra Erdley and Richard Gazarik, "Feds resist calls for hearing," *Tribune Review*, Pittsburgh, August 11 2002; see http://www.pittsburghlive.com/x/tribune-review/news/s_85678.html

55 Young, op. cit. (see note 51).

56 David Hawpe, "Talk of war in Iraq is being used to cover a multitude of sins at home," *Courier-Journal*, September 25 2002, p. 12A.

57 Vicki Haddock, "Who will fight the war?" *San Francisco Chronicle*, March 2 2003.

58 Interview with Ellen Bravo, April 7 2003.

59 Text of Chao's speech to the Republican National Convention 2000, from the website of the *Courier-Journal*, Louisville; see http://www.courier-journal.com/localnews/2000/0008/01000801chaotext.html

60 Interview with Dan-Thanh Nguyen, April 11 2003.

DON'T CRY FOR CHRISTIE— CHRISTINE TODD WHITMAN

1 See, among others, "Building a Government: Bush begins to construct broad team," *Dallas Morning News*, editorial, December 27 2000; Martin Sieff, "Two faces of the cabinet," United Press International, December 29 2000; Dana Milbank, "Ford administration players return for an encore," *The Washington Post*, December 29 2000, p. A16.

2 "Moderate voice, Whitman brings GOP's liberal wing to EPA," *ABCNews.com*, December 22 2000; see http://abcnews.go.com/sections/politics/DailyNews/profile_whitman.html

3 Editorials in the *Chicago Tribune, San Francisco Chronicle, New York Times*, May 22 2003.

4 Richard Tomkins, "Whitman resigns from EPA," United Press International, May 21 2003.

5 Susan Ferraro, "EPA chief says water, air are safe," *Daily News*, New York, September 14 2001, p. 23.

6 EPA press release, "EPA, OSHA update asbestos data, continue to reassure public about contamination fears," September 16 2001; see http://www.epa.gov/wtc/stories/headline_091601.htm

7 EPA press release, "Whitman details ongoing agency efforts to monitor disaster sites, contribute to cleanup efforts," September 18 2001; see http://www.epa.gov/wtc/stories/headline_091801.htm

8 Interview with Robert Martin, March 12 2003.

9 Interview with Hugh Kaufman, March 11 2003.

10 Interview with Cate Jenkins on *Working Assets Radio with Laura Flanders*, September 11 2003; http://www.webactive.com/page/427

11 Laurie Garrett, "EPA misled public on 9/11 pollution, White House ordered false assurances on air quality, report says," *Newsday*, New York, August 23 2003, p. A03.

12 Interview with Jenkins (see note 10).

13 Eleanor Clift and Julie Scelfo, "Exclusive: we were not told to lie about 9/11 and health," *Newsweek*, September 8 2003, p. 8.

14 Interview with Martin (see note 8).

15 EPA Daily Monitoring Report, quoted in Juan Gonzalez, *Fallout: the Environmental Consequences of the World Trade Center Collapse*, New York: the New Press, 2002, appendix B, p. 138.

16 Andrew Schneider, "Public was never told that dust from ruins is caustic, scientists found residue as corrosive as drain cleaner," *St Louis Post-Dispatch*, Missouri, February 10 2002, p. A1.

17 EPA Daily Monitoring Report, op. cit. (see note 15).

18 Kirk Johnson, "Federal study shows high number of Ground Zero workers had health problems last year," *The New York Times*, January 28 2003, p. B6.

19 William Neuman, "Toxic fallout slashed infants' birth weight," *New York Post*, August 6 2003. "The Mt. Sinai research found that 8.2 percent of the WTC babies had smaller than expected birth weight, compared to 3.8 percent for a control group of infants born to women who were not exposed directly to the Trade Center dust, ash and smoke."

20 Mark Hertsgaard, "Conflict of interest for Christine Todd Whitman?" *Salon.com*, January 14 2002; see http://www.salon.com/politics/feature/2002/01/14/whitman

21 Interview with Tom Devine, March 12 2003. When it comes to such conflicts, the bar is typically set pretty low. Whitman's predecessor at the EPA, Carol Browner, recused herself when her sister worked for a company involved in an EPA settlement, and again, when her husband worked for an environmental group that had expressed a position in a case. Whitman, by contrast, told Congress upon her confirmation that she would shed assets that might provoke a conflict, but she hasn't.

22 Interview with Kaufman (see note 9).

23 Lisa Belkin, "Keeping to the center line," *The New York Times* magazine, May 5 1996.

24 Ibid.

25 "The environment: a cleaner, safer, healthier America," the Luntz Research Companies—Straight Talk, see http://www.ewg.org/briefings/luntzmemo/pdf/LuntzResearch_environment.pdf

26 Lynne Duke, "On the inside looking out: EPA chief Christie Whitman's agenda: adjust self to changing environment, and vice

versa," *The Washington Post*, March 23 2001, p. C01.

27 Ibid.

28 Alison Vekshin, "Governor to sell stake in oil wells in 3 months," *Record*, Bergen County, New Jersey, January 24 2001, p. A1. Whitman reported holdings worth between $50,001 and $100,000 and shares in several other oil operations, too.

29 Belkin, op. cit. (see note 23).

30 Jerry Gray, "Whitman pursues family business," *The New York Times*, June 9 1993, p. B4.

31 Patricia Beard, *Growing up Republican: Christie Whitman, the Politics of Character*, New York: HarperCollins, 1996, p. 22. Beard is features editor at *Town and Country* magazine.

32 Ibid., p. 26.

33 Ibid., p. 51.

34 The only thing her biographer Beard says Whitman forbade her from writing about were her report cards: "I don't care if you look at them, but I'd prefer if you wouldn't mention my grades. My kids are still in school and I don't want to set a bad example," said Whitman. Ibid., p. 6.

35 Bill Bradley and Frank Carlucci also worked at the Office of Economic Opportunity.

36 Nicholas Lemann, "The quiet man," *The New Yorker*, May 7 2001, p. 56.

37 Beard, op. cit. (see note 31), p. 131.

38 Ibid., p. 159.

39 Ibid.

40 Chris Mondics, "Whitman attacked on land transfer," *Philadelphia Inquirer*, September 21 1993, p. S1.

41 Interview with Bill Wolfe, March 11 2003.

42 Mary Amoroso et al, "On again: briefing by Nixon," *Record*, Bergen County, New Jersey, September 8 1991; and Eugene

Kiely, "Whitman to be among mourners at Nixon's funeral," *Record*, April 26 1994, p. A21.

43 Beard, op. cit. (see note 31), p. 167.

44 Interview with Elizabeth Volz, March 10 2003.

45 Sherry Wallace, "Women in New Jersey celebrate their progress," *The Times of Trenton*, December 17 1993, p. A4.

46 Interview with Volz (see note 44).

47 Ruth Padawer, "The woman in question," *The New York Times*, August 8 1993, p. L01.

48 James Ahearn, "Governor's impolitic response," *Record*, Bergen County, New Jersey, October 8 1997, p. L09.

49 The law prohibited a girl younger than eighteen from obtaining an abortion unless her parents were notified, with exceptions in the case of parental physical, sexual or emotional distress. David Kicieniewski, "Whitman quietly signs bill limiting teenage abortions," *The New York Times*, July 29 1999, p. B5.

50 Interview with Sherryl Gordon, March 11 2003.

51 Ibid.

52 About 109,500 jobs were created in 1994 and 1995, reported the *Record*, but temporary workers, who make up less than 2 percent of the state's workforce, accounted for about 12 percent of those jobs. Dunstan McNichol and Kelly Richmond, "Open for business: market rising," *Record*, Bergen County, New Jersey, July 15 1996, p. A01.

53 McNichol and Richmond, op. cit. (see note 52).

54 Survey done by a Washington DC-based group. Public Employees for Environmental Responsibility. Representative questions and answers from the 1997 survey of 700 employees of the New Jersey Department of Environmental Protection are available at PEER's website: http://www.peer.org/publications/srvy_nj.html. Also see Bruno Tedeschi, "DEP employees

say agency failing: many cite lack of resources,'' Record, Bergen County, September 30 1997, p. A3.

55 Interview with Wolfe (see note 41).

56 McNichol and Richmond, op. cit. (see note 52).

57 Interview with Wolfe (see note 41).

58 Interview with Amy Goldsmith, March 10 2003.

59 Interview with the Rev. Reginald Jackson, March 11 2003.

60 Beard, op. cit. (see note 31), p. 191.

61 Ibid.

62 Interview with Jackson (see note 59).

63 Interview with William Buckman, March 10 2003.

64 Paul H. Johnson, ''New Jersey settles racial profiling suits, 12 who claim harassment will share $775,000,'' Record, Bergen County, New Jersey, p. A03.

65 Interview with Laila Maher, March 12 2003.

66 In fact, profiling was official federal policy, too. In November 2000, The New York Times revealed that since 1986 the Drug Enforcement Administration's ''Operation Pipeline'' taught state and local police to make highway stops on the basis of race. See Gary Webb, ''Driving while black,'' Esquire, April 1999.

67 Mike Allen, ''Bush settles on more cabinet choices; Fla official slated for HUD, campaign chief for commerce,'' The Washington Post, December 20 2000, p. A01.

68 See http://www.public-i-org posted March 31 2003.

69 Jennifer Gonnerman, ''Dirty dancing,'' On the Issues, winter 1997, pp. 26–8.

70 Lisa Belkin, ''Keeping to the center lane,'' The New York Times magazine, May 5 1996, p. 50.

71 Laurence Arnold, ''Whitman: GOP is for women,'' Record, Bergen County, New Jersey, May 1 1998, p. A02.

72 Katharine Q. Seelye, ''Rule could let mine debris fill in valleys

and streams," *The New York Times*, April 26 2002, p. A14.

73 G. Robert Hillman, "Environmentalists turn up heat on Bush, dig in for new clashes: White House dismisses renewed efforts as 'stale, old political attacks,'" *Dallas Morning News*, December 9 2002, p. 1A.

74 Eleanor Clift, "Q&A: I didn't expect an easy ride," *Newsweek*, May 23 2003.

75 Interview with Eric Schaeffer, March 11 2003.

76 Environmental Protection Agency press release, "EPA announces unprecedented first 'Draft Report on the Environment,'" June 23 2003.

77 Andrew C. Revkin with Katharine Q. Seelye, "Report by EPA leaves out data on climate change," *The New York Times*, June 19 2003.

78 Environmental Protection Agency, *Draft Report on the Environment 2003*, 1–11; see http://www.epa.gov/indicators/roe/html/roeAirGlo.htm

79 G. Robert Hillman, "EPA Administrator Whitman resigns," *Dallas Morning News*, May 23 2003.

80 Interview with Mike Casey, August 14 2003.

81 John Heilprin, "Criminal agents diverted to drive EPA boss;" see http://www.washingtonpost.com/wp-dyn/articles/A4237-2003Apr26.html

82 Robert Trigaux, "Senior discount takes on an ominous new meaning," *St Petersburg Times*, Florida, May 19 2003, p. 1E.

83 Cindy Skrzycki, "Under fire, EPA drops the 'senior death discount,'" *The Washington Post*, May 13 2003, p. E01.

84 Seth Borenstein, "Exiting EPA chief Whitman was a self-styled team player; unconfrontational, she was often caught between the White House and environmental activists," *Philadelphia Inquirer*, May 25 2003, p. C02.

85 Brent Israelsen, "Governor given shovel by Nevada road pro-
    testors," *Salt Lake Tribune*, August 26 2000, p. B3.
86 Katharine Q. Seelye, "Bush nominates Utah Governor to lead
    Environmental Agency," *The New York Times*, August 12 2003,
    p. A1.

MARLBORO WOMAN—GALE ANN NORTON

1   Interview with Ruth Bennett, July 18 2003.
2   Interview with Ron Arnold, July 22 2003.
3   "Hearing of the Senate Energy and Natural Resources Com-
    mittee," Federal News Service, January 18 2001.
4   Michael Harrington, *The Other America: Poverty in the United States*,
    New York: Macmillan, 1962; Rachel Carson, *Silent Spring*,
    Boston: Houghton Mifflin, 1962; Ralph Nader, *Unsafe at Any
    Speed*, New York: Grossman Publishing, 1965.
5   Stewart Udall, quoted in David Helvarg, *The War against the
    Greens*, San Francisco: Sierra Club Books, 1997, p. 57.
6   Ibid., p. 60.
7   Bill Briggs, "Rising Star," *Denver Post* magazine, February 12
    1994, p. 12.
8   Interview with Marci Albright, July 23 2003.
9   Michelle Dally Johnson, "Against the wind, contrary to popular
    opinion, Gale Norton's quest for the Senate will be anything but
    a breeze," *Westword*, Denver, July 7 1995, p. 26.
10 Patrick May, "Critics to confront Norton on property-rights
    passion; Interior nominee faces Senate hearings today," *San Jose
    Mercury News*, January 18 2001, p. 1A.
11 Interview with Albright (see note 8).

12 Alan Crawford, *Thunder on the Right*, New York: Pantheon Press, 1980, p. 98.

13 Briggs, op. cit. (see note 7).

14 Richard Morin, "Free radical, libertarian—and contrarian—Ed Crane has run the Cato Institute for 25 years. His way," *The Washington Post*, May 9 2002, p. C1.

15 Crawford, op. cit. (see note 12), p. 99.

16 Interview with Bennett (see note 1).

17 Briggs, op. cit. (see note 7).

18 William Perry Pendley, press release, "Joseph Coors, MSLF's founder and first chairman, has died," March 17 2003; see http://www.mountainstateslegal.org

19 In 1975, the Indian Self-Determination and Education Assistance Act was passed, and in 1978 the American Indian Religious Freedom Act.

20 Paul Weyrich told *The Washington Post* that Coors contributed money from his employees. "How did Coors raise the money?" asked the *Post*. "He just goes around the office and collects it," Weyrich answered. Crawford, op. cit. (see note 12), p. 15.

21 Thomas J. McIntyre with John C. Obert, *The Fear Brokers: Peddling the Hate Politics of the New Right*, Boston: Beacon Press, 1979, p. 68.

22 Helvarg, op. cit. (see note 5), p. 64. The West, in fact, was secured for settlers by the American military and developed by a series of government land programs and the railroads.

23 McIntyre with Obert, op. cit. (see note 21), p. 82.

24 Ibid., p. 67.

25 Ibid., p. 70.

26 William Booth, "For Norton, a party mission: nominee fights GOP environmental image," *The Washington Post*, January 8 2001, p. A1; and Traci Watson, "Norton is longtime friend of

property rights; critics slam Bush's pick for Interior,'' *USA Today*, January 12 2001, p. 7A.

27 The advantage of the pro-business, nonprofit-making bodies was that they did the same work as private lawyers for a fraction of the fee, subsidized by taxpayers. The work of these pro-business nonprofits ''stretches the concepts of charity and public interest practice beyond meaningful definition,'' wrote Tulane Law School Professor Oliver Houck. Quoted in Leslie Goodman-Malamuth, ''Professor blasts tax breaks for right-wing legal groups,'' *Legal Times*, November 19 1984, p. 3.

28 ''Epstein argues that minimum wage laws are 'undoubted partial takings, with all the earmarks of class legislation which requires their complete constitutional invalidation.' ... Thus, while regulatory takings has come to be deployed in the war against environmental regulations and by extension the environmental movement, it threatens to undo the gains of other great movements for progressive social change of the last century and a half: the labor movement, the civil rights movement, the women's movement, the anti-poverty movement, and others. Indeed, this is part of the strategy of takings advocates who hope to use anti-environmental campaigns to popularize 'property rights' rhetoric and build support for takings legislation, as well as a redefinition of takings by the courts.'' See Tarsos Ramos, ''Regulatory takings and private property rights,'' http:www.publiceye.org/eyes/privpop.html. ''While arguing that the poor and disabled should be denied government aid, Epstein maintains that business corporations deserve full compensation for the costs of complying with a whole range of government regulations.'' Heritage Foundation, *Policy Review*, summer 1986, no. 37, p. 78.

29 Thomas Frank, ''Campaign trail a test for Norton,'' *Denver Post*, August 4 1996, p. A23.

30 See http://www.perc.org and http://www.nationalcenter.org/GreenPages897.html

31 David Helvarg, "Unwise use: Gale Norton's new environmentalism," *The Progressive*, June 2003.

32 Briggs, op. cit. (see note 7).

33 Helvarg, op. cit. (see note 5), p. 72.

34 Ibid., pp 69–70.

35 Ibid., p. 71.

36 Booth, op. cit. (see note 26).

37 Memorandum from Gale Norton to Mark Levin, August 19 1986, quoted in National Resources Defense Council et al, "Gale Ann Norton, an environmental profile," January 2001; see http://www.nrdc.org/legislation/norton/findings.asp

38 Interview with Arnold (see note 2).

39 Paul de Armond, *Wise Use in Northern Puget Sound*, Bellingham, Washington state: Whatcom Environmental Council, 1997; see http://nwcitizen.com/publicgoog/reports/wuinps/preface.htm and Helvarg, *The War against the Greens* (see note 5), p. 77.

40 They claimed to be playing catch-up to the Left's civil rights litigators and the environmentalist movement's legal operation, but the Federalists had resources the Left never did. An article in the *Washington Monthly* identified the society as "quite simply the best-organized, best-funded, and most effective legal network operating in this country . . . There is nothing like the Federalist Society on the Left." See Jerry M. Landay, "The conservative cabal that's transforming American law," *Washington Monthly*, March 2000, quoted in People for the American Way, "The Federalist Society from obscurity to power," August 2001; http://www.pfaw.org

41 Gale Ann Norton, "Takings analysis of regulations," *Harvard Journal of Law and Public Policy*, vol. 13, no. 1, p. 84.

42 Briggs, op. cit. (see note 7).

43 Ibid.

44 Ibid.

45 From an email exchange with a Coloradoan Libertarian who knew Norton during her dark campaign days, and who prefers to remain anonymous, July 21 2003.

46 For an extensive listing of cases, see Natural Resources Defense Council, op. cit. (note 37).

47 Mark Obmascik, "Norton's record on pollution mixed: she took on US but not business," *Denver Post*, January 7 2001, p. A1.

48 Scott C. Yates, "The Marlboro Woman," *Westword*, Denver, May 1 1997.

49 Ibid.

50 John Sanko, "Amendment 2 defeat costs $1 million," *Rocky Mountain News*, January 3 1997, p. 4A. The state paid $950,000 to the lawyers who opposed the Amendment, and spent $400,000 on their own appeals.

51 Ward Harkavy, "Say it with a smile: Paul Cameron's mission to stop homosexuality is hard to swallow," *Westword*, Denver, October 3 1996.

52 Interview with Pat Steadman, July 14 2003.

53 Dally Johnson, op. cit. (see note 9).

54 John Sanko and Katie Kerwin, "Gale Norton: private, polished moderate. Supporters say she's shy and fiercely focused: others wonder if she has the drive to win," *Rocky Mountain News*, August 4 1996, p. 31A.

55 See http://i2i.org/SuptDocs/Stevinson/vail96.htm/Norton

56 Ibid.

57 Interview with Carman, July 22 2003.

58 Interview with Helvarg, July 7 2003.

59 Interview with Arnold, July 22 2003.

60 Mark Sherman, "Tax-exempts: the hidden force," *Atlanta Journal and Constitution*, June 29 1998, p. 4A.

61 Mr Luntz's remedy is not to change the policy, but to "dress it up with warm, fuzzy words." Editorial, "Environmental word games," *The New York Times*, March 15 2003, p. A16. The full memo is at http://www.ewg.org/briefings/luntzmemo/pdf/ Luntz.Research_environment.pdf

62 Emily Gest and Corky Siemaszko, "Panned on paint: lobbies for firm in lead-poisoning suits," *Daily News*, New York, January 12 2001, p. 5.

63 "Secretary Norton falsified Arctic Refuge data," Public Employees for Environmental Responsibility, October 19 2001; see http://www.peer.org/190.html

64 "Norton said the Fish and Wildlife Service correctly reported that concentrated caribou calving did occur in the area designated for drilling in 11 of the past 18 years, [but] her letter 'transposed it, saying that in 11 of the 18 years, that the calving appeared outside of the area.'" See "Nation in brief," *The Washington Post*, October 20 2001, p. A28.

65 Michael Schnayerson, "Sale of the wild," *Vanity Fair*, September 2003, p. 335.

66 Theo Stein, "Udall blasts Utah—Interior roads deal Colorado lawmaker hopes to block," *Denver Post*, July 14 2003, p. B03.

67 Staff, "White House busy gutting environmental rules while closing public out of say," *Asheville Citizen-Times*, April 28 2003, p. 6A.

68 In July 2003, the Eco-Nazi Event of the Month was "an eco-nazi get together in Utah. September 12–14 in the San Rafael Swell, celebrating 20 years of being a thorn in the side of motorized recreation. If you would like to rub shoulders with some of the most annoying eco-nazis around contact ..." See http://

www.off-road.com

69 Judi Bari, *Timber Wars*, Monroe, Maine: Common Courage, 1994, p. 224.

70 Karen Charmar, "Environmentalists = Terrorists: the New Math." Versions of the proposed law were introduced in Texas in February and in New York in March 2003. "The Texas bill defines an 'animal rights or terrorist organization' as 'two or more persons organized for the purpose of supporting any politically motivated activity intended to obstruct or deter any person from participating in an activity involving animals or . . . natural resources.' The bill adds that ' "political motivation" means an intent to influence a government entity or the public to take a specific political action.' Language in the New York bill is similarly broad." See http://tompaine.com/feature2.cfm/ID/7748

71 See http://www.alec.org

72 Interview with Arnold (see note 2).

73 Lynn Scarlett, "Power to the politics," at http://www.theamericanenterprise.org/taemj97o.htm

74 Frank, op. cit. (see note 29).

75 Interview with Suzan Harjo, July 17 2003.

76 Interview with Keith Harper, July 15 2003.

77 Interview with Courtney Ann Coyle, lawyer for the Quechan people July 22 2003; National Resources Defense Council, "Rewriting the rules: the Bush administration's unseen assault on the environment," January 2002.

CONCLUSION—SISTERS

1 Jeff Jensen, "The Running Man: he's back—but for how long? With Terminator 3, action hero-turned possible political candidate Arnold Schwarzenegger tries to win the popular vote," *Entertainment Weekly*, July 11 2003, p. 42.

2 Richard Goldstein, "Neo-macho man," *The Nation*, March 24 2003, p. 16.

3 "As Governor of Texas, Bush oversaw 152 executions and toughened penalties for drug users as well as pushers, signing laws that sent juveniles as young as 14 to prison for especially serious crimes, including some drug crimes." Paul Duggan, "Despite Bush stance, Texas drug laws changed little," *The Washington Post*, September 20 1999, p. A03, and Stuart Taylor Jr, "Why the story matters," *Newsweek*, August 30 2000, p. 29.

4 Jake Tapper, "Prodigal Son," *Salon.com*, News, April 9 1999; see http://www.salon.com/news/feature/1999/04/09/bush

5 Thomas M. DeFrank with Barbara Ross, "Open mike catches W. cussword," *Daily News*, New York, September 5 2000, p. 7. In 1988, CBS technicians caught Bush's father boasting, after an interview with Dan Rather, "The bastard didn't lay a glove on me."

6 For more, see, John Nichols, *Jews for Buchanan: Did You Hear the One about the Theft of the American Presidency?* New York: the New Press, 2001, pp. 150–59.

7 Elisabeth Bumiller, "Quietly, the First Lady builds a literary room of her own," *The New York Times*, October 7 2002, p. A1.

8 Lynne V. Cheney, *Telling the Truth: Why Our Culture and Our Country Have Stopped Making Sense—and What We Can Do About It*, New York: Torchstone, 1995, "From truth to transformation," chapter 3.

9   Susan Page, "Lynne Cheney defies easy characterization," *USA Today*, January 19 2001, p. 8A. Women in the under-populated western states received the right to vote before women won that right nationally in 1920. As such, women out West have long had freedoms denied to women in other parts.

10 Live with TAE, Dick and Lynne Cheney, *The American Enterprise, Online*, http://www.taemag.com/issues/articleid.15584/article_detail.asp

11 James Carney, "7 clues to understanding Dick Cheney," *Time* magazine, December 30 2002, p. 98.

12 Joanna Powell, "The new second lady: Lynne Cheney," *Good Housekeeping*, February 1 2001, p. 85.

13 "Fox on the record with Greta Van Sustern," *Fox News*, November 28 2002.

14 Robert Burns, "Cheney said to be persuasive," Associated Press, July 24 2000.

15 Manuel Schiffres, "Congressional wives carve their own careers," *U.S. News & World Report*, September 14 1981, p. 55.

16 "Fox on the Record with Greta Van Sustern" (see note 13).

17 Lynne Cheney, *Sisters*, New York: Signet, 1981, p. 46.

18 Ibid., p. 162.

19 Ibid., p. 213.

20 See http://www.dennisfox.net/papers/reagan-family.html

21 In late 1988, he became GOP whip, the number two position in the House.

22 Interestingly, in her acknowledgements, Cheney omits the subtitle of Gordon's book. *Woman's Body, Woman's Right: the History of Birth Control in America*, New York: Grossman, 1976, was runner-up for the National Book Award in 1976.

23 Cheney, *Telling the Truth* (see note 8).

24 Dinesh D'Souza, *Illiberal Education: the Politics of Race and Sex on*

Campus, New York: the Free Press, 1990; and David Brock, *The Real Anita Hill: the Untold Story*, New York: the Free Press, 1993.

25 David Brock, *Blinded by the Right: the Conscience of an Ex-Conservative*, New York: Crown Books Inc., 2002, pp. 100–1. He thought twice about it, but decided to go ahead: "I had fallen in with radicals of the Gingrich–Limbaugh stripe. After all, how far was the 'nutty/slutty line' from news rants about the 'grotesque' and 'sick' Democrats, or [Rush] Limbaugh's slurs on blacks and women?"

26 The *American Spectator* still won't forgive Hillary for taking a policy role in the Clinton administration. The August/September 2003 issue put Clinton on the cover. The article, by Mark W. David, was headlined, "The once and future President." If there were fewer women in the public eye, the *Spectator* would have to invent some. The same issue also featured an attack on "Sister [Susan] Sontag." Algis Valiunas, "Sister Sontag," *American Spectator*, August 9 2003, p. 56.

27 Jonathan Alter, writing in *Newsweek*, compared poor women to "drunk drivers" and claimed "the public is game for a little humiliation." Jonathan Alter and Pat Wingert, "The return of shame," *Newsweek*, February 6 1995, p. 21. For more, see Laura Flanders, *Real Majority, Media Minority: the Cost of Sidelining Women in Reporting*, Maine: Common Courage Press, 1997.

28 The members of the NEA Four were Holly Hughes, Karen Finley, John Fleck and Tim Miller.

29 In 1990, David Gergen, whom Bill Clinton hired as a consultant in 1993, criticized the work of Tim Miller—one of the NEA Four—solely because he used his work "to encourage education, understanding and eventual acceptance" of the gay community. This, in Gergen's words, amounted to "wanton destruction of a nation's values," and "decadence and blasphemy." David

Gergen, "Who should pay for porn?" *US News & World Report*, July 30 1990, p. 80.

30 Susan Sontag, "The Talk of the Town," *The New Yorker*, September 24 2001, p. 32.

31 Following Cheney's lead, Bill Bennett, who sits on ACTA's board, compiled a list of those who'd criticized the Bush administration anywhere, and published full-page ads in the country's newspapers, threatening to "take to task those who blame American first and who do not understand—or who are unwilling to defend—our fundamental principles." Jim Lobe, "Politics—US: hawks deploy for public opinion war," Inter Press Service, March 12 2002.

32 Antonia Felix, *Laura: America's First Lady, First Mother*, Avon, MA: Adams Media Corporation, 2002, p. 114.

33 Sharon Jayson, "Roe v. Wade should not be overturned, Laura Bush says," Cox News Service, January 19 2001.

34 Jena Heath, "First Lady Laura Bush: unfazed, unchanged, unflappable," *Atlanta Journal-Constitution*, July 10 2001, p. 1E.

35 Felix, op. cit. (see note 32), p. 76.

36 Bill Wallace, "Opium trade keeps Taliban in business, experts charge," *San Francisco Chronicle*, October 4 2001, p. A1. Also, "The accidental operative," *Village Voice*, June 19 2001, p. 28: "Early this year, the Taliban's ambassador at large, Hashami, a young man speaking perfect English, met with CIA operations people and State Department reps, [Taliban representative, Laila] Helms says. At this final meeting, she says, Hashami proposed that the Taliban hold bin Laden in one location long enough for the US to locate and destroy him. The US refused, says Helms, who claims she was the go-between in this deal between the supreme leader and the feds ... As of May 2001, "the US had committed $124 million in aid to Afghanistan, according to the

State Department.''

37 Rhonda Chriss Lokeman, ''Hope blooms for Afghan women,'' *Kansas City Star*, December 9 2001, p. B9; and Suzanne Fields, ''The last rites of chivalry,'' *Washington Times*, December 3 2001, p. A19.

38 Sally Buzbee, ''Northern Alliance rebels: not exactly poster boys for fighting terror,'' Associated Press, October 25 2001.

39 James Gerstenzang, Lisa Getter, ''Response to terror: Laura Bush addresses state of Afghan women; speech: First Lady decries 'deliberate human cruelty,' '' *Los Angeles Times*, November 18 2001, p. 3.

40 ''Afghanistan to apply Sharia law with discretion: minister,'' Agence France-Presse, December 27 2001.

41 Local Islamists compared Samar to Salman Rushdie, whose novel *The Satanic Verses* prompted Iranian clerics to sentence him to death in absentia for blasphemy. Philip Shishkin, ''Afghanistan's Islamic reaction: the Taliban are gone, but fundamentalists try to reassert power,'' *Wall Street Journal*, September 17 2003, p. A11.

42 Jeffrey Allen, ''Women's groups give Bush an 'F' on Iraq, Afghanistan,'' *OneWorld.net*, http://www.commondreams.org/headlines03/0827-01.htm

43 Karen Tumulty and Viveca Novak, et al, ''Goodbye soccer mom, hello security mom,'' *Time* magazine, June 2 2003, p. 26.

44 Deborah Orin, ''Dread decision: down the plane,'' *New York Post*, September 17 2001, p. 9.

45 Michael Kramer, ''Waging war on two fronts,'' *Daily News*, New York, September 16 2001, p. 16.

46 Adam Nagourney, ''Clinton says party failed midterm test over security issue,'' *The New York Times*, December 4 2002, p. A1.

47 Jim Hightower, *Thieves in High Places; They've Stolen our Country and it's Time to Take it Back*, New York, Viking, 2003, p. 105.

48 Lynette Clemetson, "Census shows ranks of poor rose in 2002 by 1.3 million," *The New York Times*, September 3 2003, p. A 16. In 2001, the poverty line stood at $17,960—for a family of four.

49 Jeffrey Fleishman, "Baghdad's packed morgue marks a city's descent into lawlessness," *Los Angeles Times*, September 16 2003, p. A1. "Before the war began the morgue investigated an average of 20 deaths a month caused by firearms. In June, that number rose to 389 and in August, it reached 518. Moreover, the overall number of suspicious deaths jumped from about 250 a month last year to 872 in August."

50 Lauren Sandler, "Veiled and worried in Baghdad," *The New York Times*, September 16 2003, p. A25; also "Baghdad burning," http://riverbendblog.blogspot.com

51 *Working Assets Radio with Laura Flanders*; see http:/www.webactive.com

52 See http://www.georgewbush.com/News/Read.aspx?ID=1926

53 Marcia Gelbart, "Gov. Jeb Bush: Florida Republican is younger, taller, and more partisan than George W.," *The Hill*, July 30 2000. Quoted in Michael Moore, *Stupid White Men*, New York: Regan Books, 2001, p. 3. According to Justice Department statistics, 6.6 million people were on probation, in jail or prison or on parole in 2001. That number represents 3.1 percent of all US residents, or one in every thirty-two adults. Patricia Lefevere, "Locked up: activists mark 30 years of struggle to reform criminal justice system in face of prison expansion," *National Catholic Reporter*, May 2 2003, p. 10.

54 Felix, op. cit. (see note 32), p. 28.

55 Richard Goldstein, "Bush's war on women, stealth misogyny," *Village Voice*, March 5–11 2003; http://www.villagevoice.com/issues/0310/goldstein.php

56 H. R. 3162, October 24 2001; http://www.epic.org/privacy/

terrorism/hr3162.html

57   Thomas Frank, "Campaign trail a test for Norton," August 4 1996, *Denver Post*, p. A23.

58   Eric Lichtblau, "Ashcroft mocks librarians and others who oppose parts of counterterrorism law, *The New York Times*, September 16 2003, p. A23.

59   Phyllis Schlafly, "Homeland security or homeland spying?" Copley News Service, July 23 2002.

60   June Jordan, *Some of Us Did Not Die*, New York: Basic Books, 2002, p. 115.

INDEX

LAURA FLANDERS is the host of "Your Call," a Monday–Friday program heard on public radio, 91.7 FM KALW in San Francisco, and on the Internet. She writes regularly for Tompaine.com, Znet, *The Nation*, and appears often on TV. She was founding director of the Women's Desk at the media watch group FAIR, and is the author of *Real Majority, Media Minority: The Cost of Sidelining Women in Reporting*.